PRACTITIONER ENQUIRY

Practitioner Enquiry: Professional Development with Impact for Teachers, Schools and Systems offers an accessible, step-by-step guide to practitioner enquiry, describing what practitioner enquiry is, what its adoption in schools entails, and what research and experience says about its benefits and possible pitfalls. Written by an experienced Headteacher who has worked with many schools to support their own engagement with practitioner enquiry, and who has been using the approach himself for over eight years, the chapters examine all aspects of its theory, practice and engagement.

The book includes a variety of case studies to explore the effect of practitioner enquiry across a range of settings, and to show how you can bring about deep, sustainable and embedded change that has positive impacts for all learners. Chapters cover:

- how you can create the conditions for succeeding with practitioner enquiry
- the process of enquiring into your practice
- the role of school leaders and teachers in successful enquiry processes
- the benefits you may expect from such enquiry
- case studies from a number of different contexts, showing enquiry in action
- examples of research posters produced by teachers involved in enquiry.

Practitioner Enquiry serves as a much-needed injection of up-to-date research into the field, combining theory and practice in an engaging and comprehensive style. It will be key reading for teachers and school leaders in both primary and secondary sectors.

George Gilchrist is a former Headteacher, whose last role was as leader of two primary schools in Scotland. He is a Fellow of the Scottish College for Educational Leadership, and a member of the Scottish Educational Research Association and the International Congress for School Effectiveness and Improvement. George has written extensively for professional texts and blogs. He has spoken regularly on leadership and learning and has his own blog which focuses on these areas. He can be found on Twitter @GilchristGeorge.

PRACTITIONER ENQUIRY

Professional Development with Impact for Teachers, Schools and Systems

George Gilchrist

Routledge
Taylor & Francis Group

LONDON AND NEW YORK

First published 2018
by Routledge
2 Park Square, Milton Park, Abingdon, Oxon OX14 4RN

and by Routledge
711 Third Avenue, New York, NY 10017

Routledge is an imprint of the Taylor & Francis Group, an informa business

British Library Cataloguing in Publication Data
A catalogue record for this book is available from the British Library

Library of Congress Cataloging in Publication Data
A catalog record for this book has been requested

ISBN: 978-1-138-29302-1 (hbk)
ISBN: 978-1-138-29303-8 (pbk)
ISBN: 978-1-315-23227-0 (ebk)

Typeset in Interstate
by HWA Text and Data Management, London
Printed and bound by CPI Group (UK) Ltd, Croydon, CR0 4YY

CONTENTS

Acknowledgements   vi
Introduction   1

1 Why practitioner enquiry?   7

2 Creating the conditions for practitioner enquiry to be successfully adopted   19

3 Carrying out an enquiry: the process   28

4 The role of school leaders/principals in practitioner enquiry   42

5 The role of the teacher in practitioner enquiry   55

6 What are the benefits from the adoption of practitioner enquiry?   66

7 Case study of a whole-school approach to practitioner enquiry   83

8 Practitioner enquiry across contexts: case studies furthering professional
   and school development   96

9 Pedagogical changes   116

10 Some final thoughts and considerations   130

Appendix: research posters   137
Index   168

ACKNOWLEDGEMENTS

This book is the culmination of eight years, and more, of working with some fabulous educators. Every single person I have had the pleasure to work with or lead has impacted on my thinking and my practice. Education is filled with lots of wonderful committed people who are working every day to make a difference for learners and their families. I salute you all and I thank you for your work and for helping me, directly and indirectly, on my own journey of professional and personal growth. I never cease to be amazed by the willingness within the profession to help and support others, and I certainly have been a beneficiary of this.

However, I would like to thank a number of people, schools and leadership teams for their support in helping me produce this book, by sharing their stories or just helping me develop my own.

I would like to thank all the staff of both Ancrum and Parkside primary schools, who I had the pleasure of working with, and lead, for almost ten years. They were nothing but amazing and supportive, and I learnt so much from them. Thank you for letting me share so much of your stories and insights shared with me and others.

Thank you to Dr Gillian Robinson of Edinburgh University who provided so much support to myself and staff in both schools as we embarked on our journey with practitioner enquiry. Your knowledge, wisdom and encouragement, and your ability to completely understand how schools work, were crucial in our engagement with enquiry. Thank you for always listening to all of us and helping us to shape real professional development processes that made a difference for everyone. A great 'critical friend' to us all.

Thank you to all the schools and leadership teams who have allowed me to visit and share their development journeys. I learnt so much from all of you and I hope I was also able to help and support some of you at the same time. I have spoken to and worked with school leaders across Scotland but would particularly like to mention the following schools and their leadership teams for their input.

Melrose Primary School
North Berwick High School
Ayton Primary School
Reston Primary School

Greenlaw Primary School
Swinton Primary School
Howdenburn Primary School

Lots of other schools, and teachers, also shared their journeys with me, and I appreciated hearing every single story and experience. Thank you to all the teachers and school leaders I have had the pleasure of working with on this collaboration.

Thank you also to SCEL, and CEO Gillian Hamilton, for supporting me on my own development journey, and giving me the opportunity to engage with so many knowledgeable colleagues, academics and researchers from across the educational world, many of whom have supported me with the production of this book.

This book is the result of years of collaboration, thinking and sharing with colleagues and I would like to thank you all. You know who you are, but there are far too many to name individually here.

Special thanks to Susan and my family for your ongoing support and encouragement. Hope I didn't drive you too mad at times!

George

Introduction

Much has been written, over many years, about professional development for teachers, as well as more general school development. Traditionally, professional development (PD) and continuous professional development (CPD) have been recognised as important by teachers and schools, but tended to be focused on attending courses, which may or may not be linked to school developments and improvement. Teachers were asked to demonstrate that they had engaged in professional development, usually by the production of a certificate awarded on completion of a course or series of courses. They were rarely asked to demonstrate the impact of these courses for their learners, or even their schools. However, our attitude towards professional development activity, as a process, has moved on, and now teachers are more likely to be asked to demonstrate how their thinking and practice have developed as a result of professional development activities, but also to show how this has led to positive outcomes for learners, and their schools. In Scotland the GTCS (General Teaching Council Scotland) professional standards[1] for teaching staff reflect this fundamental change in emphasis towards professional development. This is reflected not only in the standards themselves, but also in the reflective question practitioners are asked to consider when using the standards to self-assess and reflect on their practice.

> As a result of my professional learning, how has my practice developed in order to improve outcomes for all learners? How do I know? What evidence of impact do I have? What does this tell me about my practice?
>
> (GTCS, Reflective Questions: online self-evaluation, 2015)[2]

The requirement to *enquire into your practice* as part of your ongoing and career-long professional development features in each of the professional standards: *Standard for Registration*, *Standard for Career Long Professional Learning* and *Standard for Leadership and Management*.[3] A similar development of attitudes and approaches towards professional development and its impact has occurred across a number of different education systems. If we look at Australia, for instance, they too have developed a suite of professional standards to underpin the professional work of their schools and teachers. On the Australian Institute for Teaching and School Leadership (AITSL) website they have identified three key questions for teachers to consider when evaluating themselves against their own professional standards:

1   What prompted you to undertake research and what processes did you follow to investigate your research question/s?
2   How has research you have undertaken about student learning contributed to your professional knowledge and practice?
3   How have you improved student outcomes through research you have undertaken?
                    (Australian Institute for Teaching and School Leadership, 2013)[4]

These three questions very much chime with what we see happening in Scotland and elsewhere, where teachers are being asked to demonstrate improved outcomes for learners as a result of their professional development activities. The other key element is that they need to demonstrate that they have engaged with research and have enquired into their practice and the impact they are having on the learning taking place in their classrooms. Professional development is now viewed as a continuous ongoing process of professional growth, initiated by the individual, rather than a series of disparate 'things' done to, or by, individuals. In addition, more and more professional development is being recognised as needing to be context specific, both for individuals and for schools.

The development of the standards both in Scotland and Australia were influenced very much by the work of Helen Timperley. In a background-paper she prepared for AITSL in 2011 to help inform the development of a framework for professional development in Australia, she reiterated a lot of the key messages regarding how we should consider professional development. In her paper she identified four 'principles for quality effective professional learning' (pp. 14-19).[5] These were:

1   professional learning is core school business;
2   improving outcomes for students forms the reason to engage in professional learning opportunities and the basis for evaluating its effectiveness;
3   professional learning opportunities build deep pedagogical content and assessment knowledge focused on what is needed to improve outcomes for students; and
4   professional learning environments are consistent with how people learn.

She added the comment that:

There is little evidence that focusing on teacher or leader beliefs, attitudes, dispositions, styles, knowledge, skills or practices independently of changes for students has much impact on student outcomes. (p. 11)

Which reflects some of her key messages around professional development.

Timperley goes on to argue that, through the adoption and application of the four key principles above, the 'adaptive expertise' that we should look to develop in all teachers and leaders is facilitated and promoted (p. 22).

The particular challenge for leaders is to develop schools with high adaptive capacity so that on-going professional learning becomes a planned part of the development of every professional in every school. (p. 22)

What Timperley, and the others including Michael Fullan, Andy Hargreaves, Alma Harris, have long advocated is that professional development and learning should not just be about attending courses – though that can still have an important role. We should now be viewing professional development very much more as something that is focused on each teacher and the development of their knowledge, understanding and practice, with the aim of bringing about improvement in outcomes for all learners. At the same time, we will as a result bring about improvement and development for our education systems as a whole. Furthermore, this is generally best seen as a collaborative process situated within the school or institution in which teachers work.

A second key element identified by them all is that such changes in thinking and practice need to be grounded in, and *informed by*, focused research and evidence. No longer should it be acceptable that teachers try things on a whim or because it's the latest fad or trend, something which schools and teachers have been seduced by for many years. What they do should be based on evidence and research, and they should be prepared, and able, to cite this in order to explain the basis for the actions they take.

Having read many pieces of research, and engaged with the work of all of the above researchers, combined with my own dissatisfaction around professional development, I, and teachers in the schools I worked, concluded that we needed to change our approach to professional development, and that there must be a better way to help ourselves and our learners to improve. This realisation led to the path that was to take us towards the use of practitioner enquiry as the vehicle to reach our individual and collective aims.

I have described our adoption of practitioner enquiry as the most significant and impactful professional development I have ever been engaged with, both as a teacher and as a school leader. I am hoping this book will explain why I feel so strongly about the benefits for all of adopting such an approach. But, I also want it to show teachers and school leaders what such adoption can look like on a day-to-day basis in a school, and for a classroom teacher. You can read lots of research on practitioner enquiry and other enquiry-based approaches, but I have always asked an important question about any proposed development or change, and that is: 'what will this look, and feel, like on a day-to-day basis for any teacher or a school leader?' We all need to consider how we answer this question, in light of ever demanding agendas in schools and across systems. How do we engage with such a process, but keep it real in the daily working life of a teacher or a school leader?

It is all well and good talking the talk, but how do we go about walking the walk?

The following chapters detail what I, and others, have learned by putting practitioner enquiry into practice. The schools I led have just completed their eighth year of using practitioner enquiry, so I feel particularly well-qualified and experienced to share our learning, and insights gained, in order to help you on your own continuous journey of professional development.

With this in mind, I wish you to understand that this is not an academic tome. Yes, I use and cite various pieces of research and researchers, but my aim is for this book to be accessible for teachers and school leaders. This book represents a meta-enquiry about practitioner enquiry. I have used the same principles and aspects in the writing of this as I have used in practitioner enquiry. Therefore, I have written it in a way which I hope you find accessible and easy to read and understand, and thus engage with. I hope it stimulates your own thinking and to consider your own practice, in order to support you on your own journey of development.

There should be content that is useful for individual teachers, schools and systems, and from which I hope everyone can benefit and use to consider and question their own practice and thinking. I am not aiming to 'share good practice' but am wanting to share principles and insights that I believe can help and support others. Whether you are just thinking about the possibility of adopting practitioner enquiry, you are ready to go, or you have begun your journey, I hope you find this book useful and illuminating.

An initial word of caution, you will not be able to simply replicate what we have done in two schools, then look to drop this into another school, or schools, and expect the same results. Context is crucial and everyone's context is different. What you will be able to do is to take the principles that sit behind the work we have engaged in, and then adjust and fit these to your particular context, and stage of development. Our experiences will help demonstrate some of the actions you can take and illustrate some of the challenges, insights and successes you can expect as you engage with the principles and process of practitioner enquiry.

This is not an easy approach. Like everything worth doing and which is going to have an impact, it can be quite complex and contains a range of intellectual, pedagogical and organisational challenges for all. However, isn't that how we all learn, by stepping out of our comfort zones and risking making mistakes? We all understand that to improve and develop anything, we need to change what we do. We cannot keep doing what we have always done and expect different results. We either, change, develop and improve, built upon the good things we are doing already, or we stay where we are, then stagnate.

We owe it to all our learners to not let this happen. We need to have that *growth-mindset* advocated by Carol Dweck,[6] and really believe we can and will get better at what we do, through the application of effort, knowledge, data and evidence to bring about improvements. To paraphrase Dylan Wiliam: 'We all need to improve, not because we are not good enough, but because we can be even better.'

To me, and many others, practitioner enquiry offers us the best strategy for us to try and continually get better, so that learning experiences for all our learners are similarly improving. You will come to see why I believe practitioner enquiry offers positive impacts for all in our education systems.

First, there are huge *benefits for all our learners*. Professional development, and school development have to provide benefit for all our learners. This is ultimately how we need to measure all development. You will see in this book how there are big gains for our learners, as teachers become better able to meet individual learning needs as they better understand these. My own experiences, and those of others who have used the approach, have consistently demonstrated improved outcomes for learners at all stages of development. Not only is this due to improved understandings and practice by teachers, but also as a result of learners coming to better understand themselves as learners and how they can improve.

Second, there are massive *benefits for teachers*. Not only do they have the opportunity to deepen their thinking and understandings, they can use this to improve their practice so that they have greater positive impacts on learning happening in their classrooms, and elsewhere. They will improve their professional development and see how they can take control of this, and locate it within their particular context and circumstances. Teachers re-professionalise themselves, developing and growing their 'voice', and their ability to influence. Teacher agency and teacher leadership are developed as dispositions, not as ways of just spreading tasks that others don't want to do.

Third, there are *benefits for schools*. If learning and teaching are improving, then schools have to be improving as well. All schools are seeking to develop and grow their practice in order to produce positive impacts for learners and learning. Practitioner enquiry offers a way of this happening continually across schools. This is a way that schools can embed and sustain continuous development across all departments and teaching staff, and can connect these in a significant way to local and national priorities. Such improvements are situated in the local context and where the school is in terms of development. It is driven by the teachers and school leadership knowing their school and themselves well, then identifying steps to improve as a continuous process. Practitioner enquiry develops the learning culture in a school, which will support school leadership in driving forward meaningful change.

Finally, there are *benefits for the system* itself. For a number of years now researchers and academics have spoken of the need to develop 'system leadership' in education. This entails all teachers and school leaders acting and behaving in ways which recognise their responsibilities for all learners in a system, not just the ones in front of them. It requires teachers and school leaders to support and work collaboratively with colleagues in other schools and localities, so that all can grow and benefit from each other. All of this focused on improving outcomes for all learners. Practitioner enquiry helps the development of dispositions and attitudes that support system leadership, with the ultimate aim of developing the self-improving system. Through practitioner enquiry, teachers ultimately can become self-improving, the basic requirement of any self-improving system.

In this book, I use research and various case studies to illustrate how all of the above may come about. I think this is an exciting time for education, when was it not? I think we have an opportunity to reshape and reframe not only professional development, but also ourselves as professional educators and agents for change in the system. I urge everyone to stop being so busy all the time, with little or no identifiable sustainable benefit for our learners, and consider approaches that really can make a difference for all.

Not only is it time for different actions, it's time for different thinking

Throughout the book and my consideration of practitioner enquiry, I also take the opportunity to explore some of my thinking around school leadership and teaching. I think it is also important that I share these thoughts as I feel it's important you understand something more of me, my values and my principles as a school leader. Hopefully, these insights will help you understand more of what I say about practitioner enquiry and why it fits so well into my leadership philosophy and practice, then to consider your own as a teacher or school leader.

Notes

1   The General Teaching Council for Scotland, 2012. 'Professional standards'. [Online] Available at: www.gtcs.org.uk/professional-standards

2   The General Teaching Council for Scotland, 'Professional standards'. Available at: www.gtcs.org.uk/professional-standards/reflective-questions

3   The Standards for Registration: Mandatory requirements for Registration with the General Teaching Council for Scotland. GTCS 2012, Edinburgh. The Standard for Career-Long professional Learning: supporting the development of teacher professional development. GTCS 2012, Edinburgh. The Standards for Leadership and Management: supporting leadership and management development. GTCS 2012, Edinburgh.

3   AITSL, 2010. 'Australian professional standards for teachers'. [Online] Available at: www.aitsl.edu.au/tools-resources/resources/professional-learning

4   Timperley, H., 2011. 'A background paper to inform the development of a national professional development framework for teachers and school leaders'. [Online] Available at: enable.eq.edu.au/support-and-resources/professional-readings

5   Dweck, C. S., 2000. *Mindset: Self-theories: Their Role in Motivation, Personality and Development*. New York: Routledge.

1 Why practitioner enquiry?

Introduction

The first message I would like to give is that we should view practitioner enquiry as a verb, rather than a noun. It is not another of the many 'things' we are asked, or choose, to do in school. In its purest form, it is a way of being, a disposition, a way of thinking, reflected in a series of actions that are embedded as an approach in our professional practice and identity. This is not a fad or a trend, based on little or no evidence or research, but is an approach grounded in reputable research and evidence as to its efficacy and impact.

Education has been rife with 'things', fads, trends, the search for panaceas, 'silver bullets', and overall busyness for many a year. Practitioner enquiry is none of these and if that is what you are looking for, you probably should stop reading now. This is no quick or easy fix. But, it is an approach that can have benefits for all in the system, and especially our learners. It is an approach that, when done well, embeds change in pedagogy and thinking for teachers and leads to individual and school changes that are sustainable, embedded and relentless in nature. In my view, it also goes a long way to re-professionalising teachers and to help us move away from models that view them as mere deliverers, and teaching as a technical activity.

As a school leader, I want, and systems need, professional teachers who have high levels of adaptive expertise and agency, and who see themselves as active participants in school and system leadership. Continuing to do what we have always done won't deliver this, but I believe that practitioner enquiry can offer us practice, and a mindset, that promotes continuous growth and development for both individuals and systems.

Whilst my direct experience in using and seeing such an approach in action is centred very much within the Scottish system, this is most definitely an approach that easily crosses international and system boundaries. How could it not when it is grounded in learning and teaching practices, and teacher dispositions? This is not about systems and structures, this is concerned with pedagogy and ways of being a professional educator in the twenty-first century.

We will explore not only the origins of practitioner enquiry but also its use and advocacy across different systems. There are individual teachers and schools across the globe who have been using this approach for many years now, but perhaps it is in Scotland that we see the first attempt to embed the practice within a whole education system, where all educators are expected and encouraged, by professional standards and national policy, to be *'enquiring professionals'* in their daily practice. There is still a long way to go with this, however, and it is my hope that this book will help move this process on a little, both in Scotland and elsewhere. But, we are where we are, and the first principle in the adoption of this approach is that you have to start from where you are, not where someone else thinks you are, or where they think you should be. This reflects a personal and professional view of mine, that we need to get real in education, and keep things real, if we are ever going to change in a meaningful way, rather than just being busy but producing very little, or very slow, improvement for all our learners.

The General Teaching Council Scotland (GTCS), which is the body with responsibility for teacher registration and standards in Scotland, is a strong defender of, and advocate for, the adoption of practitioner enquiry approaches to professional development. On their website, the Council defines practitioner enquiry thus:

> Practitioner enquiry, as defined by Menter et al (2011), is a 'finding out' or an investigation with a rationale and approach that can be explained or defended. The findings can then be shared so it becomes more than reflection or personal enquiry.[1]

It adds that 'For the experienced teacher, regular engagement in practitioner enquiry supports professional growth by challenging or *"disrupting thinking"* and *"ingrained habits of mind"*'. It then goes on to situate the developing of enquiry dispositions within all its professional standards, so that wherever you are in your particular professional journey, there is an expectation that you will continue to enquire into your practice and your impact on learning.

It is not alone in this view either. If we look to the AITSL professional standards for teachers in Australia[2] we find the following. Highly accomplished teachers should 'engage with colleagues to evaluate the effectiveness of teacher professional learning activities to address student learning needs'. They go on to say that leaders in Australian schools should ensure that they 'advocate, participate in and lead strategies to support high-quality professional learning opportunities for colleagues that focus on improved student learning'. Whilst not mentioning practitioner enquiry directly, what they describe throughout embraces the principles and practices of enquiry. The standards produced in Australia are heavily influenced by the work of Helen Timperley and so it is no surprise that they would advocate such an approach to professional learning for their teachers and school leaders.

In England, the Department for Education published a set of Teachers' Standards in 2011,[3] which laid out the professional expectations for all their teachers and in Standard 8 (TS8) they ask that teachers: 'take responsibility for improving teaching through appropriate professional development, responding to advice and feedback from colleagues'. Whilst not talking about enquiry directly, they are expecting teachers to engage in high-level professional development in order to improve their teaching and outcomes for learners. Looking at all the standards, I can see how the adoption of practitioner enquiry can help teachers in England deliver on aspects of all of these. It will become more apparent of how this would be achieved when we get into the detail of what is entailed in using practitioner enquiry for professional development.

The UK government, through the Department for Education, has also established national standards of excellence for headteachers, published in 2015.[4] These standards for school leaders identify four *'Domains'* for *'Excellence as Standard'* expected of school leaders, and again I could argue that school leaders in England would be addressing all of these domains should they adopt a practitioner enquiry approach. However, it is Domain Four, which deals with the self-improving school system, and system leadership roles, that I think practitioner enquiry would really come to the fore. The two aspects I would particularly pick out are numbers 3 and 4:

3   Challenge educational orthodoxies in the best interests of achieving excellence, harnessing the findings of well evidenced research to frame self-regulating and self-improving schools.
4   Shape the current and future quality of the teaching profession through high quality training and sustained professional development for all staff.[5]

As we progress into this investigation of practitioner enquiry, I am sure it will become obvious how this approach would enable school leaders in English schools meet, and exceed, the standards expected of them by their government and inspection regimes. In Scotland, by the way, we talk much more about 'education' for teachers rather than 'training', which I think is important if we are to move from the view of teaching as a technical one, rather than a professional one.

In Canada 'inquiry' (you should note that enquiry and inquiry are interchangeable and mean the same thing in this context) is central to many of their professional standards. In the Province of Ontario, the Ontario College of Teachers have produced a Professional Learning Framework for teachers.[6] This college fulfils a similar role to the GTCS, overseeing teacher registration and developing standards. Inquiry is one of the key overarching features of their professional standards. They state that for them 'Communities of practice and inquiry enhance professional learning' and schools and districts are encouraged to develop such structures. They advocate the adoption of such self-directed professional learning as an ongoing disposition of professional educators. In their framework a whole section is devoted to how teachers can become inquiring professionals and why they should maintain this disposition throughout their careers. Again, as the Ontario education system has been heavily influenced by the work and input of Michael Fullan and Andy Hargreaves, this recommended approach comes as no surprise. The fact that their Professional Learning Framework was published only in June 2016 reflects how current this thinking is.

What enquiry provides is a way for all to work and develop, so as to bring about deep-seated and embedded improvements in our understanding, thinking and practice as part of a continuous and ongoing process, which will provide benefits for all in the system, as well as the system itself. Practitioner enquiry, when embraced and thoroughly understood, provides benefits for our learners, teachers, school leaders, districts and the system as a whole. Having been engaged in using this approach for over eight years now in the two schools I led, I have seen first-hand all of these benefits and that is why I too became such an advocate.

We will explore the nuts and bolts of carrying out an enquiry during later chapters so you will see what it looks like, and understand the possible impacts, as well as the process itself better.

However, I do not just want or expect you to take my word for the power of practitioner enquiry, that after all would provide you with just one case study, in one particular context, and would have pretty low levels of validity. As you can see from the systems mentioned above, others too are convinced about its efficacy, but I think it is important that we consider some of the research and the evidence that exists, and which is being continually produced, that points to such efficacy of using practitioner enquiry as an approach for individual professional development, as well as for school and system development purposes.

The research base

In 1975 Lawrence Stenhouse published *An Introduction to Curriculum Research and Development*[7] which introduced us to the 'Process Model' of curriculum development and, most importantly, marked the beginning of the 'Teacher as Researcher' movement. In this work Stenhouse set out his vision for teachers becoming researchers in their own classrooms, and how he hoped the results of all such individual studies might then be synthesised to help inform policy and practice generally, with benefits for all. He saw how teacher *'action research'* might lead to improvements at all levels in education systems. There would be benefits for individual teachers, in terms of developing their knowledge, understanding and their practice. This would lead to concordant benefits for schools, and the system as a whole. He cautioned about how such an approach would be 'generational' and would take time to inform and produce the benefits he predicted. This was to be no 'quick fix'.

Stenhouse envisaged that, for this to succeed, teachers' conceptualisation of themselves as professionals, and their approaches to their classrooms and practice would have to change first and foremost. He spoke of teachers having to recognise that no longer could they view their classrooms 'as an island', with them in sole control and charge, largely isolated from everyone else. Collaboration with their colleagues and the development of a common language was essential. They needed to view their classrooms more scientifically than previously. In this way, he postulated, they would be able to share the results of their 'action researches' and then professional researchers could look to identify common trends and themes, through the accumulation of case studies from a range of different contexts.

I am sure that Stenhouse's full original vision remains still to be fulfilled. Action research has been embraced by many as an approach, and one can see how this links into and informs the development of practitioner enquiry approaches. However, many thousands of individual pieces of classroom research projects have taken place, but there has been, and still remains, little attempt to bring these all together and synthesise their results for the improvement of all. What has happened is that thousands of teachers have enquired into aspects of the curriculum and learning in their classrooms, and have moved their practice on as a result. If that has happened, it also means that hundreds of thousands of learners have benefitted from improved learning experiences, and hopefully experienced improved learning outcomes, as a consequence. It is noteworthy that Stenhouse has had, and continues to have, such positive impacts on teachers and schools, but his work, and that of action research teachers, can remain difficult to detect across our education systems and the development of policy and practice within them. I don't believe this is a fault of Stenhouse or his research, nor of all the teachers who followed his lead. No, this is more to do with the systems and structures in which we operate, and the hierarchies and conservatism that still persist in many, if not most, education systems. Another factor is that there were questions about the validity and reliability of a lot of the 'research' undertaken. These questions were particularly asked by full-time professional researchers. As with many good theories, they often mutate into something else by the time they percolate through various filters before they reach classrooms. This is also an issue for practitioner enquiry as we will discuss later.

What we can certainly credit Stenhouse, and others who were to follow his lead, with is the promotion of teacher agency, individualism and professionalism, combined with a more scientific approach to professional development. His work celebrated and encouraged teachers to become more professional and to become thinkers and researchers into their own practice and their impacts on learners. No longer were teachers to be accepting of 'top-down' practices, where they were waiting to be told what to do from above. Now they were to be encouraged, and expected, to question and to look closely and scientifically at their own practice and impact on learning. They were to be encouraged to collaborate with colleagues to research elements of their practice, then to share their insights and findings with colleagues, so that all could benefit.

It should be noted that Stenhouse's call to teachers to become researchers of their own practice was not without controversy. He faced some opposition from academic researchers, who believed that he was undermining their work and its complexity. He also faced opposition from traditionalists within the teaching professions and schools who tended to think academic research was too divorced from the day-to-day work of school and teachers, who needed to concentrate on teaching the curriculum as decided by others. A view that is still prevalent amongst many teachers to this day. A common complaint was, and perhaps still is, that teachers and schools were too busy to undertake any meaningful research and that this was the role of others, who would then tell teachers what to do. However, following Stenhouse, other researchers and academics began to look closely at teacher professional development, leadership development and school development through a different lens than had, perhaps, been common before, with his influence still being detected across many systems to the present day.

It was the work of Stenhouse that provided the basis for the development of teaching as an enquiring profession and for teachers to re-engage with research as part of their ongoing professional development. Much of what he advocated and identified as high-quality professional practice is reflected in many of the principles of practitioner enquiry. We can see and hear echoes of his work in much of the later work of Michael Fullan, Andy Hargreaves, Marilyn Cochran-Smith, Alma Harris, Helen Timperley, Dylan Wiliam, John Hattie and others. All of these have spoken for many years now of the power of teacher collaboration, teacher agency, the breaking down of silos, being research and data-informed, developing reflective practice, distributed leadership and teacher leadership in schools and across systems. All of these academics and researchers have high levels of credibility within the profession, and this is a key factor when engaging critically with research as a teacher or school leader. How we engage critically with research, as very busy teachers and school leaders, is a key component with practitioner enquiry. If we just accept everything and anything we read, we are reverting to type in seeing ourselves as mere deliverers again. Practitioner enquiry promotes, and expects, more than this.

It is in the work of Marilyn Cochran-Smith around teacher education and research that we really see the development of strong advocacy for something called 'practitioner enquiry'. She has been a professor at the Lynch School of Education at Boston College in the USA for a number of years now. She has written and researched extensively on teacher education, teacher research and has put inquiry at the centre of all her work. She and Susan Lytle were the founding editors of Teachers College Press which has published many books and research around practitioner inquiry. Cochran-Smith and Lytle co-authored the book *Inquiry as Stance: Research for The Next Generation* in 2009,[8] and this is the book that has had the biggest impact on my own approach to teacher and leadership development. However, Cochran-Smith had authored a number of other books on the same theme in the lead up to this particular one, and has written others since. Her influence is felt across teacher training and professional development in many countries, and with many other academics and researchers in these areas.

Building on the principles of Stenhouse, and others, Cochran-Smith argues the case for teachers becoming inquirers into their own practice, and as knowledge creators whose findings should be given a lot more credibility than has been traditionally given by academia.

> Inquiry as stance is neither a top-down nor a bottom-up theory of action, but an organic and democratic one that positions practitioners' knowledge, practitioners, and their interactions with students and other stakeholders at the center of educational transformation.
>
> (pp. 123–124)

In *Inquiry as Stance*, Cochran-Smith and Lytle argue the case for more teacher autonomy and agency and against those who would see teachers as mere deliverers or technicians. They desire to value and re-professionalise the teachers by placing them as active participants in their own practical and pedagogical development. They argue that we need to aim to develop dispositions in teachers that promote them as continually inquiring into aspects of their understanding, pedagogy and practice, and considering how these are impacting on the learning of their students. They provide a theoretical framework about how you might go about this, but also include case studies by teachers who have been adopting such approaches in their practice. I would recommend this as an essential read if you are wanting to go further into the theory and research around practitioner enquiry.

At the same time as Cochran-Smith was writing and researching about teacher development through inquiry, Linda Darling-Hammond was doing something very similar as professor of education at Stanford.[9] She too has been very interested in teacher development and particularly how this might look within rapidly changing systems and structures. In her book *Preparing Teachers for a Changing World: What Teachers Should Learn and Be Able to Do* co-authored with John Blansford, she put forward the description of the ultimate teacher identity as one where each teacher has adaptive expertise. In this model teachers were to be encouraged to become thinking, reflective practitioners who were able to adapt their practice in response to learner engagement, and within rapidly changing systems and structures.

The model of teachers as having *adaptive expertise* is very closely linked to Cochran-Smith's vision of teachers having inquiry as stance. In both, the teacher is the active and adaptive professional, constantly reflecting and enquiring into their practice throughout their career. The teacher is supported to develop dispositions that allow them to constantly develop their practice, and Cochran-Smith gave them a process that supports them in this, as well as how they might develop and share knowledge and insights about that practice.

As a school leader, that model of teachers as thinking reflective practitioners, who have inquiry as a disposition or stance, and who have adaptive expertise, is it seems to me a most attractive one. Just as system leadership seeks to develop self-developing and self-improving systems, I see the development of the qualities described above can only help and support teachers to become self-developing and improving individuals and professionals.

Some different iterations of enquiry

This book is, of course, concerned with practitioner enquiry, but it is worth considering other iterations of enquiry models that also exist. Most of these have similarities with practitioner enquiry, and may well be viewed as stepping stones to practitioner enquiry, but they are all different in various degrees. They all have their supporters and advocates, and I would not seek to decry any of them. Any one of them might be an appropriate starting point for you or your school, it all depends on knowing exactly where you are and what you are trying to achieve, hence the power and usefulness of good self-evaluation and awareness practices to any school. More on this later.

The following are some of the school development methodologies that you may come across that can be similar to, or have their roots in, practitioner enquiry. They are not practitioner enquiry, they are all different, but there are commonalities and benefits to be found amongst them all.

Action research

As we have already noted, action research, as an approach to professional development in education, emerged from the work of Lawrence Stenhouse in the mid-1970s. One writer on this approach, Richard Sagor, describes action research as follows:

> a disciplined process of inquiry conducted by and for those taking the action. The primary reason for engaging in action research is to assist the 'actor' in improving and/or refining his or her actions.[10]

Valsa Koshy looked at action research in his book, *Action Research for Improving Practice* (2005).[11] Koshy looked at the approach in some depth and he considered and evaluated various definitions given by other researchers for action research. As a consequence of his examination and consideration of these he came up with his own definition of action research, which was as follows:

> I consider action research as a constructive enquiry, during which the researcher constructs his or her knowledge of specific issues through planning, acting, evaluating, refining and learning from the experience. It is a continuous learning process in which the researcher learns and also shares the newly generated knowledge with those who may benefit from it. (p. 9)

From these definitions, and other very similar ones, it is easy to see and understand when some people regard practitioner enquiry as 'just action research'. Whilst there are definite, and easily identifiable similarities between the two approaches, I still believe they are different. For myself, action research is very much a process to look closely at different aspects of a teacher, or individual's, role. Often action research participants will categorise their activity as a project, and when one finishes another is then looked for. I think practitioner enquiry is more about developing career-long dispositions within teachers, and the reframing of what it means to be a professional educator. Crucially, practitioner enquiry should be seen as a legitimate knowledge creator and a means of contributing to our knowledge base in education. It is not about having to prove anything, but is about continuous reflection and enquiry, as a process and disposition, into a teacher's practice and their impact on the learning of the pupils they teach. Many of the steps to carrying out a piece of action research can also be found in the practitioner enquiry process.

Lesson study

Lesson study is a professional development approach to teaching that originated in Japan in the early twentieth century. It is essentially a collaborative enquiry approach which involves teachers working together to enquire into how they can improve their teaching. A focus is identified and research lessons are set up, so that teachers can observe pupil learning during the lesson, and then speak to them about this afterwards. Such research lessons are often set up by triads of teachers working together and testing out the efficacy of different pedagogical approaches. As with all strategies, some see major faults with this approach, but there are thousands of teachers and schools, and many systems, who vouch for the benefits gained. What lesson study does undoubtedly promote is teachers collaborating and thinking deeply about their practice and their impact on learning for their students. Many tell how this approach has revolutionised and changed their thinking and their practice, as well as their approach to professional development and how this can impact them as educators.

I believe many of the benefits identified for lesson study are common to those achieved by practitioner enquiry. In that when teachers are given time and support to think, plan and enquire collaboratively benefits accrue. Their power lies in the focus on the local context and learning and teaching, conjoined with collaborative working and support. I can see how, for many schools and teachers, this approach will be a great step forward from where they were previously, and how school leaders could use lesson study to help develop collaborative learning cultures and promote professional dialogue.

For myself, I believe, practitioner enquiry goes beyond the lesson study approach, in that its central focus is on learning and each individual practitioner developing those qualities and dispositions they need to be continually improving professionals. Lesson study could be a point on such a journey for many schools and teachers, but then it needs to be taken further and developed so that teacher individual and professional identity changes, and so that learning experiences for all learners keep improving. For more information on lesson study the book *Lesson Study: Professional Learning for Our Time*[12] edited by Pete Dudley would be a good starting point.

Teacher learning communities or professional learning communities

Teacher learning communities (TLCs), also called professional learning communities (PLCs) can be another step in the direction towards the adoption of practitioner enquiry approaches.

Some prerequisite conditions for successful adoption of practitioner enquiry is a supportive culture, based on mutual trust and respect, collaborative practices focused on learning and teaching and the power of professional dialogue. These can all be developed through TLCs, if they are not already in place. If you have school culture where collaboration is not normal, with teachers still operating in their 'silos' as Fullan calls them, or where there are low levels of trust and high levels of mistrust, and where staff are reluctant to talk about their practice or learning or teaching, then all of this has to be changed before you can expect the greatest success through practitioner enquiry.

Basically, TLCs are composed of groups of teachers coming together to collaborate and explore a range of issues, usually common to them all. They could have identified the issues for their focus themselves, or these may have been identified by others, who have then asked them to work on these. TLCs may be composed of individuals from the same school or setting, or of those with similar roles and expertise from across different settings. Their real strength, in my view, lies in the power of professional dialogue, collaboration and the sharing of practice and insights. They can be a great vehicle to stimulate thinking and discussion amongst staff at all levels, especially where this might not have been happening before.

Many schools and researchers have identified the power of TLCs in developing a collaborative learning culture in schools and systems. When they are well-organised, focused and populated by committed individuals, including senior leaders, they can produce large positive impacts for teachers, schools and learners. Of course, the opposite is also true, and this is what we need to guard against if they are to have the biggest impacts. When they lose focus, are poorly organised and are not properly supported or understood by senior managers, don't be surprised if they drift and ultimately fail to deliver. Like a lot of 'things', they were very fashionable in education for a while, until everyone moved onto the next 'thing' to do. Therein lies the danger of so many good strategies and approaches, as long as they are seen as another 'thing' to do, or as an add on, then they will soon disappear or drop off the agenda. Any change has to be deep, embedded and sustainable. The best approaches all take time, and how often are we not given that time, or we don't give it to ourselves, so that deep gains can happen?

For more reading on the power and benefits of well-run and organised TLCs, I would refer you to the National Council of Teachers of (NCTE) website at www.ncte.org 'Teacher Learning Communities'[13] which provides useful information on what makes them work and what doesn't as well as lots of academic articles around TLCs. Alma Harris and colleagues[14] have written much on this also and they have lots to say on how to make such TLCs be most effective and have the greatest impact.

Collaborative professional enquiry

As the name suggests, this approach is perhaps the one that is the most similar to practitioner enquiry. In collaborative enquiry teachers, or others, will collaborate together to investigate an issue that they have identified together. Obviously, the power of this lies in the mutual support, collaboration and the immediate sharing of issues and insights gained. There are benefits not only for the individuals working collaboratively together, but also for the school in which they are located and their learners.

The process involved is exactly the same as that of practitioner enquiry, but instead of the focus being individualised to a particular teacher, it is one which is common to the pair or group. Again, the focus will be on a learning issue identified, the collection of data for a small sample of learners around this, professional reading and dialogue around the issue, the identification of new strategies or approaches to be tried, implementation of these, then the recollection of data to look at the impact of the interventions. This is then followed by a sharing of the insights gained about what worked, what didn't and, most importantly, what the impacts were for learners. More detail about this process is given later in the book.

I have long thought that collaborative professional enquiry might be something that emerges out of the adoption of practitioner enquiry. Certainly in the schools I led, as we got further and further into embedding practitioner enquiry, there were more and more examples of teachers getting together and focusing on common issues. The difference was though, that they still individualised their enquiry and they were sufficiently experienced and adept so as to be able to nuance these to deal with their specific concerns. What emerged was not pure collaborative professional enquiry, but did contain similar elements.

There is no doubt that collaborative working was developed and enhanced across both schools by our engagement with practitioner enquiry. I now believe that collaborative professional enquiry is just another stepping stone that schools and teachers may need to cross on their journey towards practitioner enquiry, then becoming teachers with enquiry as stance. I have long cautioned that practitioner enquiry is not an easy option to undertake and I can see the that approaching this collaboratively at the outset, in order to provide mutual support and share insights and issues, could be a necessary step on the journey for many schools, teachers and their leaders.

In Scotland, Mark Priestley and colleagues of Stirling University have worked for a number of years on a collaborative professional enquiry approach to professional development, school development and curricular development. They have worked with schools and teachers to develop a model of such practice and you can read about this in more detail in their paper, 'Curriculum Development Through Critical Collaborative Professional Enquiry' which was published in the *Journal of Professional Capital and Community* in 2016.[15]

Appreciative enquiry

Another enquiry iteration, and one which seems to be the most recent to appear is appreciative enquiry. This emerged out of the USA in the late 1980s and started life as a tool for developing organisations, emerging from Case Western Reserve University and their department of organisational behaviour. This particular construct identified organisational creation and development as being powered by collaborative working, relationships and conversations. This also took the approach that such organisations should start from their points of strength and seek to grow and develop from these. The philosophy of this method is that you take the best of what you do already, recognise this collectively, then from this imagine and talk about how this could be further developed and built on.

This was an approach that sought to move away from deficit models of development, where organisations focused on what they were not good at and how they might improve on these, to one which was very much focused on building on strengths. Appreciative enquiry would argue that when people in organisations truly recognise their strengths, they can use these as a springboard for rapid development and growth. Such enquiry starts with identification of what the organisation, in this case schools, does really well, and what might it look like if we were able to do these things even better? Another key question is around where do we want to get to? And what steps do we need to take to get there? You perhaps could describe this as a dialogical approach to enquiry and school development, as it is based very much around powerful, focused conversations and understandings about what you are trying to achieve.

There is no doubt that many of the characteristics of practitioner enquiry are also found within the appreciative enquiry approach. The importance of developing the right supportive cultures, the power of relationships, collaboration, the developing of dispositions, enquiring into what is going well in order to help you identify areas of concern, working collaboratively, using research and data, and so on, are all found within this methodology. There is a systematic process identified, which is continuous and ongoing, and which should allow schools to identify and quantify impacts for the school and its learners.

* * *

There is much to commend any approaches which promote an enquiring mindset to professional development. The strategies and facets of each certainly take us forward in terms of providing teachers and schools with more meaningful professional development processes than many have engaged with previously. Teachers need to re-professionalise themselves and see their personal and professional development as lying in their own hands, not someone else's. We have to get away from a view of teaching which sees teachers as mere deliverers and move more towards seeing teachers as adaptive experts empowered with high degrees of agency. We need self-improving teachers, just as much as we need self-improving systems, and any approach that moves us along that continuum is to be welcomed. We all need to start from where we are, some are further on this developmental road than others, but that is okay and needs to be recognised. This is a career-long journey of development and professional growth, both for teachers and schools. It is my view that having teachers and school leaders with 'inquiry as stance' as Marilyn Cochran-Smith describes it, is where we need to get to, and then we really will see the deep and sustained improvement and development of schools and systems that we all seek.

There is a sound research base which lies behind practitioner enquiry. It is built upon the work of many credible educational researchers and practitioners. It involves a reframing and reconceptualisation of professional development as a career-long process and disposition. There are stages teachers and schools may go through to get to a position of full adoption of such enquiry, but all of these can offer benefits and gains for all in the system. It is important that school leaders understand and know exactly where their schools are in terms of development, so that they can locate themselves at a point that will help them move forward and grow their practice, to bring about benefits for all in the system.

Notes

1 The General Teaching Council for Scotland, 2012. 'Professional standards'. [Online] Available at: gtcs.org.uk/professional-update/research-and-practitioner-enquiry

2 AITSL, 2010. 'Australian professional standards for teachers'. [Online] Available at: www.aitsl.edu.au/teach/standards

3 Department for Education, 2011. 'Teachers standards'. [Online] Available at: www.gov.uk/government/publications/teachers-standards

4 Department for Education, 2015. 'National standards of excellence for headteachers'. [Online] Available at: www.gov.uk/government/publications/national-standards-of-excellence-for-headteachers

5 Department for Education, 2015, *National Standards of Excellence for Headteachers*. London: Department for Education, p. 7.

6 Ontario College of Teachers, 2016. 'Professional learning framework for the teaching profession'. [Online] Available at: www.oct.ca/public/professional-standards/professional-learning-framework

7 Stenhouse, L., 1975. *An Introduction to Curriculum Research and Development*. London: Heinemann.

8 Cochran-Smith, M. and Lytle, S., 2009. *Inquiry As Stance*. New York: Teachers College Press.

9 Darling-Hammond, L. and Bransford, J., 2006. *Preparing Teachers for a Changing World: What Teachers Should Learn and Be Able To Do*. San Francisco, CA: Josey-Bass.

10 Sagor, R., 2000. *Guiding School Improvement with Action Research*. Alexandria, VA: ASCD, p. 3.

11 Koshy, V., 2005. *Action Research for Improving Practice: A Practical Guide*. London: Paul Chapman Publishing

12 Dudley, P., 2015. *Lesson Study: Professional Learning for Our Time*. London: Routledge.

13 National Council of Teachers of English, 2010. 'Teachers learning communities'. [Online] Available at: www.ncte.org/library/NCTEFiles/Resources/Journals/CC/0202-nov2010/CC0202Policy.pdf

14 Harris, A., Jones, M. and Huffman, J. B., 2017. *Teachers Leading Educational Reform*. London: Routledge.

15 Drew, V., Priestley, M. and Michael, M. K., 2016. 'Curriculum development through critical collaborative professional enquiry', *Journal of Professional Capital and Community*, 1, pp. 92–106.

2 Creating the conditions for practitioner enquiry to be successfully adopted

Introduction

For practitioner enquiry to succeed and have the greatest positive impacts for learners, teachers and schools, not only has the process to be thoroughly understood and implemented, thought has to be given to the conditions required for enquiry to have the greatest chance of such success. Some of these conditions are to do with structures – internal and external – and organisation, but most of them are connected to mindsets, dispositions and cultures that are required to be in place. I would say that it is not essential for all of these conditions to be in place, but if they are then there is a much greater chance for the successful adoption of practitioner enquiry into your practice. Each individual, and each school, will be at a different starting point, this needs to be recognised, and it should be accepted that the speed of each journey and the level of engagement, will be different for all. However, if you are a school leader, I would say that most of these conditions need to be considered and in place, if you are looking to adopt practitioner enquiry successfully for whole-school development and improvement.

I have seen schools where they have attempted to use practitioner enquiry in order to develop such conditions and dispositions. These have had mixed results. You can use practitioner enquiry to drive forward improvements you are seeking, but that is not its main purpose or intention. In Chapter 1 I explored other iterations and steps you can use on your journey to full implementation of practitioner enquiry. All of these offer the opportunity to develop cultures and structures which lead to school and teacher improvement. My suggestion is that, if you are looking to develop and improve school cultures and practices, you consider some of them, rather than leaping straight into practitioner enquiry. Schools which have used practitioner enquiry to drive forward culture and practice, as they develop the conditions necessary for such enquiry to succeed, have moved themselves forward, but have not achieved all the gains possible, which I explore in Chapter 6.

As with all of my advice, you have to assess where you are and what you are trying to achieve, before you make the decision that works for you and your context.

In 2004, McLaughlin, Black-Hawkins and McIntyre conducted an extensive literature review regarding enquiry and research for teachers. They looked particularly at practitioner enquiry, considering the arguments for practitioner enquiry, the purposes of carrying out such enquiry, the conditions for practitioner enquiry to take place and some of the debates around the use of practitioner enquiry.[1] I would refer you to that piece of work if you wish to explore this further. What I will say is that everything that is reported in this literature review, and the research cited, matches my own experiences and insights gained from enquiry. So, whilst I am giving a lot of information, views and insights based on my own experiences, and that of my own schools, over an eight-year period, a lot of these are reflected in the results of other more systematic pieces of research carried out to specifically look at practitioner enquiry.

I looked at research and read about practitioner enquiry at the start of our own journey, but I have looked at much more in preparation for this book, and I am reassured by much that I have found. I am reassured that we engaged properly, meaningfully, systematically and pro-actively with the process, and as a result the benefits we accrued and insights gained are valid and are supported by much of the literature and research produced around this area. I think it is fair to also say that a lot of our own experiences and insights extend some of those findings and may add a little to the research base around enquiry.

What follows is grounded in our own experiences of engaging with practitioner enquiry in two very busy schools. This process was stimulating and challenging for all involved, but the results, as shown in Chapters 3 and 7, were career-changing for most of our teachers and myself, and equally positive for all of our learners. The process is not a simple one, it can be complex, it needs to be systematic, and there are conditions that can support, or hinder, your own engagement. The following should help you consider your own readiness, and the preparatory steps you may need to take to prepare, in order to start your own enquiry process. Most of the messages in this chapter are aimed at school and system leaders, but many of them need to be considered and understood by individual teachers too. I will return to consider school leader's role further in the next chapter.

The conditions to consider

The first thing I would say is: 'know where you are'.

As each individual and each school needs to start from where they are, not where someone else says, or thinks, they are or they should be, then it is crucial you know exactly where that is. This is why *self-evaluation* processes and honest, critical *self-awareness* are crucial, because it is from these that you will have the data and information that tells you where you are, and gives you confidence in that assessment. Both individuals and schools need to be completely honest in their self-evaluations and assessments, recognising your strengths, as well as areas for development. What skills and knowledge do you have that are going to support you, and which do you need to develop further? How is collaboration in your setting? How reflective are you and your colleagues? How open are you to change? How do you know? These are all good questions to ask in order to ascertain where you are currently. Speak to others who you trust, who know you professionally or know the school, and gather their thoughts on where you are. Use any external evidence and reviews to support your assessment. Speak to your learners about what you do well and what you can do better. Speak to parents and gather their perceptions, so that you have the fullest picture and information of where you are, and how you are doing.

Now, most schools and settings are carrying out such activity continuously and will have a lot of this information available and current. Individuals may have information from peer feedback, observations, or from professional development and review processes. This is not about creating more work for yourself, but it is about *knowing yourself* and where you are in your development, and being absolutely systematic, honest and clear about this. If you are in the position of not having enough information to make an honest assessment, you will need to think about this, and the school may have to consider collectively. Where self-evaluation processes are embedded into everything you do, knowing where you are, becomes easier to identify. This is your starting point on your journey and when you are clear about where this is, you are more able to use this as a *'baseline'* for future self-evaluation. This is crucial in order for you to be able to illustrate the progress you are making as you go, and over time.

Having robust information at the start of your journey, enables you to identify with confidence the progress you have made, and is a key component of any enquiry.

You also need to be clear about why you wish to engage with practitioner enquiry, and what you are looking to gain from that engagement. *'For what purpose?'* is a question we should be asking about practitioner enquiry. This is also a good question to ask all the time about planned changes to practice, or when considering any activity you engage with. By considering the answer carefully, you establish the rationale for any course of action, as well as who the beneficiaries will be. Hopefully, for all that you do, these will ultimately always be the learners.

In Chapter 6 I identify the reasons why we started our own journey with practitioner enquiry. Dissatisfaction with professional development, as well as teachers feeling overwhelmed by all the 'things' they had to do, being our two main drivers. I think the outset of any enquiry process is a good place to revisit, and have conversations around, what you are about and what it is you think your practice and your school should be focused on and driven by. This is best done as a collective and collaborative discussion, involving the whole school community, so that everyone is clear about what you are trying to achieve, and what that *collective vision* for the school is.

We found that revisiting and restating our individual and collective values at this point, was another very useful part of the process. This was done in partnership with learners, parents and others, and helped everyone understand what our two schools were about and what our collective vision for the future was. Being clear about your aims and values helps individuals and school leaders identify what is acceptable and what's not, and what you will do and what you won't, especially when put under pressure for more change, or different agendas from outside the school. My professional values have always helped me draw lines in the sand about what is acceptable, and what is not. How long such conversations take depends on the setting and the context, but out of this dialogue should emerge a strong vision statement about what it is you are seeking to achieve, and the values that underpin this. It is important that teachers are clear about all of this, as they are the main participants in any enquiry.

If you know where you are, and what you are looking to achieve, it becomes a lot easier to identify the initial steps and actions you need to take to set you on that journey. In Chapter 6, I have set out the different stages of carrying out an enquiry, but this counts for little if you are unclear of where you are starting from, and why you are taking the actions identified. Make sure you create a little headspace and time to explore these issues for your setting.

Once you are clear about your vision for what you are trying to achieve, and why, this becomes a point of reference for further ongoing self-evaluation processes. You are now able to measure your actions against the vision statement, and your values, to see if they match what you set out at the outset. If there is a mismatch, this becomes a call for further action. I have always believed that when your actions do not match your professed values, then those spoken values are not your true values. *Values* are what you live your life and your professional practice by, people judge you by your actions, not what you say. If you say one thing, but then do another, these are not real values and people will judge you accordingly, adjusting their perceptions of what they think those values might be. I have always been clear about *'talking the talk, then walking the walk'*. I believe we need more practitioners and leaders who are sufficiently professionally courageous to do the same thing. I believe we have been too compliant for too long in many education systems. As a result, we have been complicit in introducing practices that have no positive impacts, if not negative ones, for learners. In my experience, when you become an enquiring professional such behaviours are less likely to continue.

It is another of my beliefs that everything we wish to achieve in schools and systems, stands or falls on the *cultures and ethos* which are found in those settings. For practitioner enquiry to take hold and have impact, it needs to be situated in a supportive culture, built on *high levels of trust*. Practitioner enquiry is demanding and can lay bare and question individual and school practice. There will be times when collectively and individually you come to recognise that certain practices are not acceptable or appropriate and need to be changed. This will not happen in a culture that people don't trust or feel safe in. If teachers feel they can't trust school leadership to support them, recognise that they will make mistakes, will need to admit what they don't know or don't understand, or feeling they will be judged negatively as a result, then those open and frank dialogues are not going to happen. They need to happen, before any individual or school can move on. They can happen within the head of an individual, or as part of a collaborative professional dialogue. The culture will decide if individuals feel safe enough to have that honest dialogue.

There needs to be high levels of trust between teachers and school leaders, but also between teachers themselves. They will have to *collaborate*, share closely, and be open to this. They will require a culture and ethos that promotes and supports this. There has to be a high level of professional dialogue and openness within a culture where this is understood and embraced by all. There needs to be a deep *learning culture* where all are committed to improving their own learning in order to improve that of their learners, and where learning informs focused *professional dialogue* and discourse. As part of the enquiry process there needs to be a culture that allows and supports critical debate amongst teachers during all aspects of that process.

A lot of these characteristics of the culture and ethos required will develop further and deepen as engagement with practitioner enquiry develops over time. However, a lot does have to be in place before you can embark. It may well be that school leaders and teachers have to change mindsets along with practices and cultures over a period of time, to get to a place where practitioner enquiry has the best chance of success. If teachers are not working collaboratively, are not reflective, if there are low levels of trust between teachers, and between teachers and leadership, if there are strict hierarchies still in place, then all of these need to be addressed before enquiry is embarked on. It may be that individuals and schools will require outside help and support with such issues, and addressing them could take some time. However, it would be my contention that this will be time well spent, and that school leadership, in particular, need to understand that this may be a necessary step on the journey towards enquiry.

I remember our local authority wanting all schools to set up teacher learning communities (TLCs) for professional development activities. Whilst I understood the power of these to promote professional collaboration and ownership amongst teachers, I felt that, as we had been engaged with practitioner enquiry for a few years, there was nothing to be gained by us setting up such formal structures to promote collaboration and dialogue. We already had collaborative cultures focused on learning, and teachers were working with and supporting each other in their development. This was accepted as just a part of how we all worked. When I spoke to staff about TLCs the common response was along the lines of 'that's what we do anyway.' Another key aspect that we were concerned with, in the model being put forward, was that these TLCs would be completely led by teachers, with headteachers and DHTs being told they were not to be part of them. How can you lead and support school development of learning and teaching if you are not part of the process?

We decided to continue down our own path. What we did acknowledge was the formation of such TLCs could help some schools and their leaders bring staff together to talk about learning and teaching, and with a common purpose, and that they may need to do this before they could engage with practitioner enquiry. Indeed, a number of schools who used TLCs for a few years later contacted us to say that they now felt they were ready to look at practitioner enquiry, as they and their staff were in a different and more conducive position for such engagement. Remember, this is not a one-size-fits-all approach, and each individual, or school, has to take their own journey. But we can all learn principles and gain insights for other journeys, and we can support each other, in our different contexts and the systems, in that way.

Get the culture and ethos right in each school, and each classroom, and you give yourself the best opportunity to engage successfully with practitioner enquiry.

Leadership, at all levels, is another vital factor to consider for the successful implementation of enquiry. School leaders are perhaps still one of *the* most important determinants of the success or otherwise of any change in their establishments. Where schools are led by principals who deeply understand learning and practitioner enquiry, how to support this, who have created positive cultures and high levels of trust, they are more likely to succeed with the approach. Where schools are still led by 'control-freaks' who want to micro-manage everything, and maintain strict hierarchies, with low levels of trust, the impact of teachers engaging in practitioner enquiry will be hugely diminished. Leaders, like systems and structures, can support and enhance change, or they can militate against it. They are key influencers in the creation of culture and ethos, and set the tone for much that happens in any particular setting.

I have already in Chapter 1 referred to Helen Timperley's work around professional development.[2] She is very clear that not only do school leaders need to actively support professional development of their teachers, they need to be active participants in the process. This is echoed by Michael Fullan, Andy Hargreaves,[3] Alma Harris[4] and many other researchers. This is an equally crucial factor with the leadership of practitioner enquiry. What is required are school leaders who not only wish to understand and support the process, but who want to be actively involved and seek to apply the principles to their own practice. When they do this, they are more likely to develop a deep understanding of the process and the complexity. This puts them in a better position to recognise the issues teachers may be grappling with as they try to grow their practice, whilst still delivering on the day job, i.e. teaching a class.

When a school leader is committed to the process and the changes required, they are able to adjust school priorities in their development planning to reflect this. They need to understand why, and how, they will be required to support teachers engaged in enquiry. Yes, they have a *challenge* role as well, but the *support* role should have primacy, especially at the start of such engagement. They can support day-to-day, through conversations and actions, but they can also support by protecting teachers from outside agendas by gatekeeping these for their teaching staff. We need leaders with professional courage and values that ensure they take the right actions to support staff, and to explain why they are doing this in a professional and informed way.

As well as supporting and protecting teachers from outside pressures and demands, we also require leaders to deal with internal and individual pressures. This requires leaders who really know their staff in terms of their professional development, and the personal factors that impinge on their working lives. They need to understand some of their home life, family and health issues to better be able to target the required support when necessary. This may involve reducing expectations for periods of time because of differing circumstances. Principals need to recognise the rhythm, and shifting demands, of the school year, and all the regular activities that have increasing impacts on workloads and thinking of teachers. These include things like parents' evenings, report writing, Christmas time performances, concerts and parties, inspections and reviews, exam periods, residential visits, or any other events that may be high consumers of teacher time, and high producers of teacher stress. The school leader with highly attuned emotional awareness, emotional intelligence, who understands the power of relationships, recognises the impact of all this and that there are times during a school year, or an individual's life, that adjustments need to be made. This is what the leadership of people is about.

The leader has to take all of this into account, but still ensure the school and teachers are delivering for all learners. This means they need a vision and values to underpin an implementation plan in order to ensure the direction of travel is forward, and that change is deep, sustainable and embedded. The best plans are flexible, working documents that develop and grow as the improvement process is happening. They should not be set in stone and inflexible, or they become unworkable and undeliverable very quickly. The leader needs to be reassessing collaboratively the development as they are gathering data and evidence to support future actions, as well as to provide evidence on the effectiveness of the actions undertaken. One of the earliest insights I gained as a school leader implementing practitioner enquiry, was to have the courage to say 'stop, we are going too fast.' Teachers had become so engrossed in the enquiry process, they had forgotten about some of the other practices that are key to good learning and teaching. This had happened because we had gone too quickly, as a result we had all taken our eyes of other crucial areas of practice. As a leader, I learnt that you have to be an active participant in the process, monitor what is going on, and make decisions about stopping, or even going back a step or two, to enable you to get where you are ultimately trying to get to. I learnt all that during our first year of engagement. I applied those same principles to every year of our journey. Remember, this is a process being done by you, not to you!

An ideal situation would also require teachers who have dispositions or inclinations towards *teacher leadership*. School principals have formal leadership roles, which are very important, but having a teaching staff who have agency and see how they can lead in personal and school development can be a massive bonus. Practitioner enquiry is not a 'spoon-fed' type of professional development. As its title implies, it has to be led by the practitioner, and as such it requires reflective and adaptive practitioners with high levels of agency. Of course, such dispositions can depend on the formal school leadership and cultures in place, but where you have teachers with the inclination and confidence to identify what they need to do, as well as the reasons why, then act on this, you already have mindsets and practice that will support enquiry. Such dispositions will be enhanced and should develop further during any enquiry process.

Having the right kind of open-minded and supportive leadership goes a long way to ensuring the success of the implementation of practitioner enquiry. Where leaders are new to enquiry, and are just developing their understanding themselves, they will benefit greatly from the support and input of a '*critical friend*'. Preferably this will be someone with a thorough understanding of the process of carrying out practitioner enquiry, and the theory behind this. We were fortunate to be able to call on Dr Gillian Robinson from Edinburgh University to support with our initial engagement. Much of the research around this, suggests that having a high level of support from a local university and its staff can be very beneficial as you take your first steps. In the first couple of years, we were very dependent on Gillian's input and support, including myself as a school leader, But, as we became more confident, and better understood the process, Gillian's involvement lessened as we were better able to support ourselves. After three years into the process, we were able to offer ourselves as 'critical friends' to support other teachers or schools who were undertaking enquiries. By this time, I was using Gillian more as a sounding board from time to time, to ensure we were still on track, and to explore any issues that had cropped up. I understand not every school is going to have access to someone from a university, though such partnerships are becoming a lot more common in Scotland. You may need to explore other avenues for such support. There are more practitioners and school leaders out there who understand practitioner enquiry, and it may be that you will need to get together with another interested colleague as you begin your journeys together in order to mutually support each other. I think the use of online forums and social media platforms, like Twitter, have much to offer here in terms of accessing high-level support. A few of the case studies I detail further on in the book went ahead lacking any physical support, but used online resources for information and support purposes. I have found social media very useful in my own journey, but I think this remains a relatively untapped professional development resource. Hopefully, you will also find this book helpful during your own journey. A good starting point for school leaders interested in introducing practitioner enquiry is to read and then discuss various chapters to stimulate debate and explore the issues particular to your own establishments.

School *policy and structures* should be adjusted to support practitioner enquiry. This will be dependent on each setting's context and circumstances, but it would be expected that key policies and structures should reflect your engagement with practitioner enquiry. Certainly, any professional development and learning and teaching policies, should encourage, support and reflect the approach being taken. I was never a great fan of lots of written policies in school, but the few we had, which were specific to the schools, were about learning and teaching, assessment and professional development. All of these reflected, and were amended, according to where we were on our journey with enquiry. We cleared out our School Improvement Plan (SIP) when we first started with practitioner enquiry, in order to create, and protect, the time and the space teachers would need for enquiry. This meant that we created professional development time for teachers to carry out aspects of each enquiry, but also for them to have time together for collaboration and professional dialogue around these. We also used management time to help support teachers with their enquiry, and to give them more time to collect data. These are important elements of the process, so the time has to be created for this to happen. Practitioner enquiry is likely to fail if it is just added onto everything else teachers are trying to grapple with. If it is seen as worthwhile and valuable, then time and other resources have to be dedicated to it, so that practitioners have the best opportunity to succeed in their endeavours. By doing this, you are also demonstrating your commitment and support for the work.

It will help even more if *local* and *national policies* also support and promote your endeavours. We are lucky in Scotland in that developing enquiring dispositions is enshrined in our professional standards[5] and is supported by key national policy documents like *Teaching Scotland's Future*.[6] We also have the Scottish College for Educational Leadership (SCEL), who through their Leadership Framework and accredited professional development, seek to promote and support enquiring dispositions. Because this is so high on the national agenda, it is now further encouraged and supported by local authority policy, so teachers and school leaders almost have a mandate for this level of engagement. I know that other countries are also looking to promote enquiry dispositions amongst their teaching staff, but a lot of this is still very piecemeal or is being engaged with by 'outliers' in the system rather than being supported by the system as a whole.

These, then, are the considerations and conditions you need to be aware of before any engagement with practitioner enquiry. Get them all in place before you commence and you give yourself, and your school, the greatest opportunity to be successful. The list is not exhaustive, it could well be that you have more pressing issues to deal with before you can start your own journey. As a school leader, you get used to expecting the unexpected, and having to deal with this. As an example, during our own journey, another local school was badly damaged by a winter storm and we found ourselves hosting most of their learners, staff, and headteacher in our own school for a term. Whilst we were pleased to be able to help and support them, the disruption caused to our day-to-day operation meant that we had to put some aspects of our own development to one side for a while. Events like that can certainly deflect you and put your head in a different place. But, we had our vision and our plan for what we were trying to achieve, we always had our eyes on these, so that we were able to get back on track as soon as we were able to wave our visitors a fond goodbye! That's why a flexible and adaptive plan is essential in mapping out your journey, to ensure you can give your school and teachers the best opportunity to succeed.

Hopefully, you now have more awareness of key issues and conditions to be addressed at the very outset of that journey.

Notes

1 McLaughlin, C., Black-Hawkins, K. and McIntyre, D., 2004. 'Networked learning communities: Researching teachers, researching schools, researching networks: A review of literature'. [Online] Available at: www.educ.cam.ac.uk/research/projects/super/publications/, pp. 6–21.

2 Timperley, H., 2011. 'A background paper to inform the development of a national professional development framework for teachers and school leaders'. [Online] Available at: www.enable.eq.edu.au/Supportandresources/Formsanddocuments/Documents/backgroundpaper.pdf

3 Fullan, M. and Hargreaves, A., 2008. *What's Worth Fighting For In Headship?*, second edn. Maidenhead: Open University Press.

4 Harris, A., 2014. *Distributed Leadership Matters: Perspectives, Practicalities and Potential*. San Francisco, CA: Corwin.

5 The General Teaching Council for Scotland, 2012. 'Professional standards'. [Online] Available at: www.gtcs.org.uk/professional-standards/professional-standards.aspx

6 Donaldson, G., 2011. *Teaching Scotland's Future*. Edinburgh: Scottish Government.

3 Carrying out an enquiry
The process

Introduction

To consider how to carry out an enquiry, and the stages involved in the process, we must first be clear about the purposes of such an enquiry.

Too often in school and teacher development we have been guilty of rushing into changes or new approaches without being clear about what it is we are trying to achieve, and the outcomes we are looking for, or have achieved. Right at the start of the process, it is well worth exploring the values and purposes that underpin your individual and school practice. So, let's begin the process correctly and be clear about what it is we are doing, why we are doing it, and how we will know if we are being successful? My suggestion would be that school leaders and teachers need to have conversations around these questions at the very outset of the process. Unless everyone is clear about what it is you are trying to achieve, and why, you run the risk of the process running aground later on in your journey. When you are clear about what it is you are seeking to do, and achieve, you can keep referring back to this collective vision in order to ensure you are still on track. This can also be a starting point for any self-evaluation processes, and against which you measure future actions.

Though practitioner enquiry is a development process that most definitely aims to produce ever-improving teachers, it is not one where the *main focus* is on the teacher, or teaching. This is not an enquiry into a teacher or their practice, but is one which is centred very much on the quality of *pupil learning*, and the impact each teacher has on this in their daily practice. Obviously, there is an interconnection between each of these elements, but the focus is on the learning, not the teacher.

Improving the learning experiences and outcomes for *all* learners, sits at the heart of practitioner enquiry. John Hattie in his work *Visible Learning for Teachers*,[1] produced after his years of looking at the outcomes of thousands of pieces of educational research across the world, stated that 'the biggest effects on student learning occur when teachers become learners of their own teaching' (p. 14). Of course, we are also very much concerned with the teacher as a learner, but this is teacher learning *for impact* and a definite and clearly understood purpose. That is to make each of them more effective practitioners, better able to tailor and support the learning of all their learners. It seems obvious, for why would we concern ourselves with anything that would make them less effective or which had negative impacts on learning? But, this needs to be clear from the start as an over-arching outcome for all participants. When teachers see practitioner enquiry as a process to improve learning for learners, they feel less threatened than if it presented as yet another process to make them better, because they are not good enough. The traditional deficit model applied to teachers and schools, i.e. tell them what they are not good at and focus on improving those aspects, hasn't worked and has had negative impacts on attitudes to professional development. Practitioner enquiry should be viewed as very much a positive model of professional development.

When considering who should be involved in the enquiry process, in an ideal model all teachers and school leaders would be active participants in this process. I have even experienced support staff and playground supervisors embrace the process, because they wanted to, not because they were told to.

Helen Timperley in her background paper for the professional development framework for teachers in Australia[2] identified that it was no longer sufficient for school leaders to merely support the professional development of teachers. She said it was essential that they also needed to be active participants in this process. I wholeheartedly agree with Timperley, so would urge school leaders to become enquiring professionals themselves, and to be actively involved in the enquiry process within their establishments. School leaders who are actively involved have a much clearer understanding of the demands and requirements of the process, which helps them to be better able to understand these and support staff. By being involved in the process, they are also much more able to identify when things may be starting to go awry, and when adjustments need to be made in any planned development process. They are also clearer about where teachers and schools really are in terms of their development, and can make more informed decisions as a result.

My advice to school leaders is to prioritise learning and professional development of your staff, and do everything you can to actively support this process from an informed and participatory standpoint. If you really understand and embrace the process of practitioner enquiry, why would you not apply the same processes to your own practice? Model what you seek and show you are 'walking the walk', not just 'talking the talk'. I have long understood that people really do judge you on what you do, not on what you say you will do!

What I present in the rest of this chapter are the steps required for teachers to carry out an enquiry of their own. For ease and understanding, I am presenting these in a relatively linear format. But, I would like everyone to be clear, that this is in *not a linear process* when put into action. Enquiry has identifiable steps, all of which are important, but these are very much influenced and affected by each other, as well as everything else that can happen in a school on a daily, termly and yearly basis, planned and unplanned. They are also at the mercy of teacher circumstances, personal and professional. Teachers and school leaders need to thoroughly understand and recognise this. Practitioner enquiry is very much an organic and complex process of development, not a simple and mechanistic one. It is one that will provide participants with a new way of thinking and being, which ultimately can reshape them, and their thinking, as professional educators. As long as you are clear about what you are doing and why, temporary circumstances and events may deflect, stop or reshape the process for short periods of time, but they won't deflect you from your ultimate goals.

The steps to enquiry

Various models for carrying out an enquiry into practice can be found. In the most common ones, emphasis is put on the process being one which is continuous, ongoing and interconnected. Some models used to illustrate this process as a spiral of activity, rather like the models used to represent the features and complexity of human DNA. This is to represent the connectivity between each of the stages involved in an enquiry process. I would refer you to the work of Marilyn Cochran-Smith[3] and the General Teaching Council Scotland and their website,[4] for further illustrations to represent the process involved. The Scottish College for Educational Leadership (SCEL)[5] is another good source for further information and graphic content.

As I have already stated, practitioner enquiry is not a linear, step-by-step process, but each aspect or stage is linked, and co-dependent on each of the others. What practitioner enquiry needs to be is systematic, with a clearly understood structure, and clearly defined elements. But, what are those elements?

The steps we identified for our enquiries were as follows:

- identify the issue and forming an enquiry question;
- identify a sample group of learners;
- collect data;
- carry out professional reading and research;
- identify interventions or strategies to be trialled;
- re-collect data;
- analyse results;
- identify next steps;
- share findings;
- continue the process.

You can see there are at least ten key aspects in carrying out an enquiry. I say 'at least' because it could well be that you identify more nuanced stages yourself, as you get more immersed into enquiry and deepen your understandings of the whole process. Developing that collective vision and understanding might be seen as the very first step in the process for yourselves and your schools.

We now need to consider each of these stages in more detail so that you have a better understanding of what each is, and what each looks like in practice.

Identifying the issue and forming an enquiry question

As I have already stated, the issues we are going to be focusing on through enquiry are centred on aspects of learning. So, it is the identification of learning issues that needs to be our starting point. I should say, that ourselves, and many others, have started with a common learning issue, rather than an individual one. This is a useful tack to take until teachers understand the process deeply. Then they can individualise their focus.

One colleague has described to me as thinking about 'what is your itch?' What she meant was, what is it that is bothering you about some aspect of the learning that is going in your classroom? Something you need to scratch to find out more about, and stop it from irritating or bothering you so much. My word of caution here is that you need to narrow right down *your focus* for your enquiry, and that's why the forming of an enquiry question is important. A common mistake made by many teachers undertaking an enquiry for the first time is that they make their focus too big and too wide. If your focus is too large you make the rest of the stages as large and complicated, and you will quickly find your enquiry becomes unmanageable, just adding to your workload and your stress levels, with less chance of producing positive outcomes. Any enquiry should fit relatively seamlessly into your daily practice. It should not be seen as another 'add-on' or unduly increase your workload. Keep it *manageable and proportionate* is a key message.

Some examples of making your focus too large might include something like 'I want to improve numeracy in my class' or 'I want my learners to write better' or 'I want to improve the exam results in my subject'. You may say, such aims are perfectly desirable, however, they can only be achieved by small steps of progress and through a process that is embedded and meaningful. Also, if you took any of those examples and then looked at the other stages of carrying out an enquiry, how could you possibly keep the whole process proportionate and manageable? You couldn't! Remember, first and foremost you are a teacher or a school leader, and that is your first priority. You are not an educational researcher, who can devote all their time, resources and expertise to large-scale educational research. You are a teacher or a school leader who is going to enquire and reflect into aspects of your practice, so that you may improve the learning experiences, and therefore learning, of your learners. Always keep that in mind, no matter how enthusiastic you become. Don't let your enquiry grow arms and legs so that you lose both focus and control, which will only lead to less impact for learners, with more stress for you.

We can still use the examples above to help shape our thinking about what a focused enquiry might actually be. So, you want to improve numeracy in your class? Numeracy is too wide a subject area with knowledge, skills, context and aptitudes all important and all at play. We need to narrow our focus down, so that we can enquire into and improve one aspect of numeracy, which will have an impact on overall attainment. You need to think about numeracy and what are the aspects that are really bothering you, or more importantly your learners. This is about deconstructing learning in order to identify issues to address. It could be that learners are not confident with their use, and recall, of times tables; it may be that they can't identify and verbalise strategies they use mentally; it may be that they don't recognise when they can use numeracy learning outside of the classroom; it may be that many of your learners have developed fixed mindsets towards numeracy and maths learning; it may even be one pupil or a few, who have got gaps in their learning and you are not sure how to address these.

All of the possible focuses that are identified above can be broken down into smaller and more manageable issues to consider and investigate further. Then you start to see the trees from the wood, so that you begin to identify steps you may take to improve the overall picture. That is the first skill in identifying and carrying out an enquiry. If you addressed any of the smaller issues that I have given as possibilities, and were successful in improving these, then numeracy in your class would have improved, and you will be able to demonstrate and articulate why. If you then apply the same process again, you could then go on to improve numeracy even further and in a sustained way, as part of a continuous process of improvement.

You can then take your narrowed-down and more precise focus and put this into an enquiry question. This is to help you understand what it is you are looking to do and to help the focus of all your activities in your enquiry. As an example, you may have identified that your learners are not secure in their knowledge and understanding of their times tables, and this is impacting on their numeracy and mathematical performance and confidence. You need to think about how you could put this into a question that will keep your enquiry on track and help you establish the impact of that enquiry. We liked to use questions that started with 'What happens when …?' during enquiry activities in my own schools. We would come up with something like, 'What happens when I use a range of different and new strategies in the teaching of times tables with Primary 6 pupils?' Primary 6 pupils in Scotland will be aged 9 or 10 years old. It may well be that you will find the formation of an enquiry question difficult at this stage, until you have engaged with some professional reading to discover what it is you don't have knowledge of, or the latest thinking in this area of learning. But, you can start to consider the question you might seek to resolve, and then tweak or change this if needed after the engagement with that professional reading and research. Often, initial research or enquiry questions change in the light of reading, discussion and further thought.

The more you engage with the process of enquiry, and the more you collaborate and share your experiences with colleagues, the better you will get at being able to identify a narrow, but meaningful, focus for your enquiry, then being able to formulate helpful enquiry questions.

Identify a sample group of learners

Given that any enquiry has to be part of a very busy professional life, and that it has to be based and supported by data, professional reading and research, we now need to turn our attention to a sample group of pupils. It is important that you can collect data and evidence in regard not only to the issue you have identified and your enquiry question, but also so that you can quantify and qualify the outcomes and impacts of your enquiry.

Again, the danger is you make this more difficult for yourself, and this then sets your enquiry to founder against the rock that is everything else you have to do as a busy teacher. The basic rule here is the same as for your focus, keep your sample small, and therefore proportionate and manageable. It is too large a group to be setting out to focus on a whole class or year group with your enquiry. Remember you are going to have to collect data about your sample, the larger you make this, the more data you are going to have to collect and deal with, and the greater the chance your data collection will be less valid. It is much better to sample a small group of learners, I would suggest no more than six, as this means the collection of data becomes more achievable and less onerous for yourself and more focused. One of the best enquiries I was involved with was actually focused on only one learner, but the outcomes were felt by all his classmates and others that followed them, because of changes in pedagogy made by the teacher and her deeper understandings around behaviours. Having visited a number of schools engaged with practitioner enquiry, such findings are not uncommon.

The identification of a suitable group of learners can be done in consultation with colleagues and school leadership to help ensure issues are carefully considered. It is worth pointing out at this point that you may wish to inform parents/guardians at this stage that you are carrying out a piece of classroom research as part of your professional development in order to improve learning. Then ask for permission to include children in this, pointing out that children will not be identified individually and all procedures will be ethically applied and monitored by senior managers. In my experience, parents are really interested in the process and outcomes, with very few prepared to object. In fact, more are likely to ask, 'why is my child not involved?' as they hear about what has been happening from other parents or their children. Generally, the more you keep parents/guardians involved and informed the better, this is good practice anyway in building and developing those crucial partnerships with parents.

Another consideration when selecting your sample of learners is, how easy will it be to gather data from the chosen group? Again, keep this as manageable for yourself as possible, but it still has to be meaningful. How you may go about collecting data is explored below. If you pick learners who are really struggling, for whatever reason, you may find the collection of data more difficult and problematic. That is not to say you should ignore such pupils, but you may have to adjust carefully how you collect data from them. I would suggest that focusing on those pupils is easier as you gain experience in the process. At the outset, you should aim to keep the processes and focuses as simple as possible until your confidence and experience grows. How you decide the composition of your focus group is up to you, but you should consider all the issues, both for the learners and yourself. What I will say at this stage, and will return to later, is that whoever you choose for data collection purposes, the impact of your interventions and changes to practice will probably be experienced by all learners in your class. Don't feel that some will miss out, they will all benefit from any improvements in your pedagogy and your understanding of learning. It is just that you will have narrowed the focus for the collection of your data, thus keeping it manageable but valid.

As with identifying the focus of your enquiry, you will get better at selecting your sample of pupils as you get more experienced. You will make mistakes, this is fine and to be expected, and you may need to adjust your focus group as you go, so don't be afraid to do this. This applies to the whole enquiry process. Not one enquiry I have been involved in or seen has gone exactly as planned and envisaged at the outset. How could they, when there are so many variables (people and circumstances) involved in the whole process? What is important is that you expect and accept this, then make necessary adjustments as you proceed, and that your understanding and insights develop as the process continues.

Collecting data

Now we come to the issue of data collection. By data I am not just talking about figures and percentages, though these can obviously form an important part of any data collection exercise, the process needs to be wider than that, and we need to find ways of capturing data that are meaningful and helpful to help us understand the issues, as well as to demonstrate the impacts we are having. When the schools I led first began to engage with practitioner enquiry, we had to have a number of staff development sessions around data collection, because most of us lacked confidence in how to go about the collection of this. I think many schools and teachers are still in the position of lacking confidence in all the ways they can and do collect data which is both valid and reliable. Some of the data we put most faith in, can often be the least reliable, especially considering the purposes we use it for. We were fortunate to have the support of Dr Gillian Robinson from Edinburgh University, an academic and researcher, who was able to point us in the direction with professional reading, and practice, around data collection, as well as ethical practices in such collection.

Before you can identify the sort of data you may wish to collect, you have to be clear what it is you are looking for data about. Is it achievement, attainment, attitudes to learning, subject specific, the impact of teaching? The list depends on what your focus for enquiry might be, and the enquiry question you have shaped. The methods you use to collect data need to be tailored and shaped as best you can to help provide information around this, not something else. Data collection methods and tools also need to be shaped and constructed to be appropriate for the learners in your focus group. How this looks in a primary, or elementary, setting will be different to a secondary one. You should also be aware of subconscious bias, and not construct or use tools designed to give you the answers you expect. Never go into any enquiry with an expectation of what you will find. Enquiry is at its most powerful when we gain insights and understandings that we were completely unaware of, and which compel us to change our thinking and our practice.

The starting point for data collection will often be the *teacher's professional judgement*. This is something that is often talked about in education, but which, in my view, is not given enough respect or validity. You know your learners, as learners, better than anyone, so you should not be afraid of using and utilising that knowledge to help you understand what is going on in their learning. You can quite easily formalise this a little for your focus group by putting down some initial observations and thoughts about them in relation to the focus of your enquiry. You can then reflect on these again towards the end of the enquiry, and see how they compare. These have validity and should not be underestimated. They are valid parts of a holistic learning picture you will have about your learners.

Also, within the daily and weekly activities in your classroom, and as part of the learning process, you will have a mix of *formative and summative assessments* regarding your learners, and these can provide some more information about your focus group and where they are in their learning. A lot of this will be quite general and of a larger scale than desired, but it could well be that you can drill down into some of this to find specific information relevant to the enquiry. You may have *standardised test results* that provide you with data and may point to why you selected a particular pupil, or pupils, for your focus group. Some of this can throw up trends and patterns that are useful to consider. Again, there are insights to be gained from such consideration of such data after you have introduced interventions, to see if there have been any detectable changes, positive or negative.

We start, therefore, very much with information and data we already have to hand. However, in most enquiries, this is not enough and not specifically related to your focus and enquiry question, to give you the specific data required, so you will have to use other data collection tools and methods.

The first we used were simple *learner questionnaires*. These are helpful in getting pupils to think about, and talk about, their learning and their thinking. The questionnaires can be quite simply constructed to explore the issue you are wishing to consider, remembering the cautions about subconscious bias, and making them ethically sound. They don't take long to put together and should not take learners long to complete. Designing these, or having them checked out, with a colleague can be helpful to you both. Depending on the age of your learners, these are also quite easily administered as part of normal teaching time, they are resource light. The results can be easily and quickly seen and collated in any way that you find useful and meaningful. There is a skill in developing closed and open questions, or a mix of both, which you use depends on the nature of your enquiry. Closed questions tend to be easier to collate and present the results of, whereas open ones are often more insightful in their revelations.

A development of learner questionnaires are *learner interviews*. In these you, or a colleague, sit with the learners and ask them a series of questions about their learning and the issue you wish to explore. Questions are constructed in the same way as for learner questionnaires, but now the writing of answers is removed as a possible barrier and their responses are recorded by the interviewer. This works best when the interviewer is yourself as the enquirer, but you can also use colleagues or classroom support, but resourcing in terms of time and people is greater in this method. You need to think about the questions, how they will be administered and by whom, and where and when this will take place. Logistically, there are more considerations with such interviews and more variables.

Recording learners answering questions or talking about their learning is another step. Again, this is fairly easy to organise, and now with smartphones there are not the costs, technical problems and issues we used to face. It is relatively easy to record learners either answering questions or engaged in learning activities and then having time to replay and analyse and transcribe some of these at a later time. The use of such recording means you can, if you wish, still be engaged with other learners and activities whilst this is happening. Such a data collection exercise will of course be dependent on the maturity, independence and self-regulation of each group of learners.

Moving on from just recording learners answering questions, you can also *film learners* during the same types of activities. Again, smartphones can be a big help here, but if you have access to other more sophisticated recording equipment, you can use this too. Filming learners is another tool that can be used with little disruption to classroom organisation, once it is set up, and allows you and others to view the results whenever is convenient to yourselves. With both the recording and filming of learners you may decide to transpose some of this into a written format, but remember to keep this proportionate and manageable. We tended to go for soundbites and quotes which helped inform, especially when looking to share our results. Original recordings should be erased after use, unless you have the necessary permissions from learners and their parents/guardians.

Another written tool that we have used often, and which have proven very powerful, are *concept cartoons*. These are available from various sources and consist of cartoon drawings of various learning scenarios. These will always include learners often with blank 'speech' bubbles coming from their mouths, and blank 'thought' bubbles coming from their heads. During one enquiry into the learning around reading, we used one which showed children in a reading group, being heard read, with their teacher, an activity that goes on in thousands of classrooms every day. The children were asked to write in the speech bubbles the sort of things they might be saying during such an activity. They wrote things like, 'Can I read now?', 'I think the main character is good' and 'She has missed a word'. They often struggled to fill the speech bubbles. Then they were asked to write in the thought bubbles some of the things they would be thinking during an activity like this. They wrote things like, 'This is boring', 'Why am I reading this again?', 'When's my turn?', 'I have read this whole book already' and 'Why are we doing this? I can read!' They found it a lot easier to fill in the thought bubbles. Imagine how teachers felt when they read some of these 'thoughts' that they were completely unaware of. It made teachers in the schools I led change their thinking and practice with regards to the teaching of reading, especially with our older learners. Often the simplest and cheapest of tools can give you the most powerful insights and data.

Another way of collecting specific data is by *observing learning*, and the conversations about learning, that take place in the classroom amongst your target group of learners. This is more labour-intensive and requires collaboration with colleagues so that you can support each other with your observations. This requires you to have dedicated time when you can observe your focus group in a learning situation and record what you see, and what you hear, in some simple but meaningful way. Some thought has to be given to how you set up such an activity, and in such a way that the observer does not skew the results of the data obtained.

No matter which tool you are using to collect data, you need to think about its use and its purpose very carefully. With many of the tools and procedures you decide to use, you will need to prepare the learners by explaining their use and purpose. You can give them a practice with the tool you decide to use, to allay fears and answer questions. In that way, they are more likely to give you the honest responses and information you seek, with higher levels of validity and reliability. Whichever methods you employ, they should be repeatable later on in your enquiry, so that you have another measure of the impact for learners. Your initial data collection allows you to establish a starting point or baseline, against which you can measure your impact. Too often we blunder into change in education from an unknown starting point, then wonder why we are unable to reliably and validly report on impact and progress after we have introduced such change. Practitioner enquiry should move us away from such practice.

One last thought regarding data, and data collection. Data, is just that, information. The really important thing about data is what you do with it, not the fact that you have it. As Professor Andy Hargreaves noted on Twitter in November 2016 'The data don't always tell you what to do.'[6] Schools and systems today are often awash with data, some of it useful and some of it less so. It only becomes useful when you can use it to inform actions. It is not useful if it is collected to show you have it, or to impress someone else with, or worse sit in a file or filing cabinet doing nothing. If data is valid and reliable, we should use it to help identify actions and inform practice, and for us to know we are having positive impacts for *all* learners. Which is why we need to combine the use of data with professional reading and critical engagement with educational research.

Carrying out professional reading and research

In truth, your engagement with professional reading and research can begin as soon as you have begun to identify the issue you wish to enquire in to, and are thinking about formulating your enquiry question. What I will say is that this is an essential component of any enquiry process and to which we should all aspire as educational professionals. Education practice has been guilty of being at the mercy of too many fads and trends that later have proven to be not as good as we were led to believe. We have to become a profession that is informed by critical engagement with data and research, not one which is continually seduced by the latest snake-oil salesman or pitch. I have long argued that we have been very busy in schools and systems across the globe for many years, but the impact of that busyness has not been in anything like proportion to the effort put in. The main reason for that has been our seeming predisposition to look for quick fixes and silver bullets, compounded by the gap that exists between what research shows us works and what actually happens in practice. This has to change. We need to think and act more professionally, as this puts our practice in an improved position, and enables us to better defend that practice against those who would think they know better from outside of the profession.

As Helen Timperley noted in her background paper for AITSL in 2011 'it is no longer acceptable for professionals in schools to do their individual best. Rather, it is expected that they will engage collectively with what is known to be effective in improving outcomes for pupils' (p. 1).[7]

It is my view that practitioner enquiry gives us a '*way of being*' as professional educators that will tackle all of these issues. We have to become a profession that is critically engaged and informed by research. To me, this should be a disposition of all professions, and one which teachers and school leaders need to adopt more than we do currently.

To carry out an effective enquiry into an issue you have identified, requires you to spend time thinking, reading, talking about and exploring that issue. We cannot just pluck a theory or an intervention out of thin air and then expect this to work, for us to be seen as credible in our professional practice. What I am not saying is that we should engage with every piece of research published around an issue, remember *proportionate and manageable*. Educational researchers don't help themselves at times by the language they use in academic works and articles. This can be impenetrable by those outside of the academic research circles, as they tend to write for each other in most of these. Of course, I am generalising here and there are many academics who have presented their research in a way that is accessible and understandable to those who may benefit from it in their daily practice, i.e. teachers. But, let's keep this real, teachers really don't have the time to be trawling through research bases, even if they are allowed access, to look for the nuggets they need to improve their understandings and practice.

So, what do you do and where do you go? The first thing I would say is that, if you don't already, you need to start reading. Professional development should happen over the full course of your career, and should become a disposition. You need to read to keep abreast of the latest thinking and research around education, learning, pedagogy and policy. Also, by reading you build up your ability to engage critically with writing and conflicting views and opinions. You also begin to identify those writers and researchers that have credibility and are worth listening too. Often these people will write books and articles in a way that is completely engaging and easy to understand, but which are grounded in years of solid research. Many of them have blogs and engage through social media like Twitter, as they recognise the need for them, and their research, to become more accessible. You need to identify who these people are and you need to start exploring writing and research that is specific to the issue you have identified for your enquiry. I would also recommend that you get on Twitter as soon as possible, if you are not there already, in order to develop a wider professional learning network and get up-to-date information about new research findings.

Once you have identified your issue, you can soon start looking around to see what you can find on this in professional libraries and online – not Wikipedia! Google Scholar can be useful, as can other online research bases, but you do need to know specifically what you're looking for in order to narrow your search. This is where your collaborative professional learning network (PLN) can come in very useful. I am lucky enough to have contacts in universities and online, via Twitter, who can point me in the direction of reputable sources for most issues. Professional organisations like trade unions, GTCS, SCEL, Education Scotland (in Scotland), AITSL (in Australia), The National College for Teaching and Leadership and the newly formed Chartered College of Teaching (in England) are all good starting points. You should look to build these further yourself. Whilst you are developing such networks there are still lots of ways you can start finding evidence-based resources and reading to help you explore the issue you have identified, with the internet and social media providing lots of new avenues which are a lot easier to access than before.

Identifying the interventions and strategies to be trialled

Out of this reading, and talking with colleagues, should emerge a better understanding of the issues, possible interventions and changes to practice that you may wish to try out, all to see if they bring about improvements for your learners. Another word of caution here, you are not looking to change everything you do already, you are looking to tweak and improve your practice by small incremental steps so that the learning experiences improve for your learners. In identifying the changes, you are looking to make, keep these proportionate, measurable and achievable. If you make this too ambitious, in identifying the interventions or strategies to be tried, then you set yourself up for disappointment or an unrealistic workload, neither of which are desirable or useful. There comes a great confidence in knowing you are trying something where there is already evidence that it has worked elsewhere, but also remember that context is crucial and what is truly powerful are the principles that lie behind any successful intervention or change. Whatever you decide to do, has to be adapted to your context and your learners at that time. When engaging with research you should always ask the question, 'under what conditions did this work?'

The types of new practice you may wish to trial depend very much on the issue of your enquiry, often these are pedagogical tweaks, but they can also be structural or curricular. What I would advise is that you apply the changes to the whole class or year group, but your focus for enquiry purposes remains very much on your target group of learners. They are the only ones you are going to collect data on. This comes back to keeping your enquiry manageable within your daily practice, but still valid. This is perhaps more reasonable than expecting teachers to be delivering something completely different to one group of learners, compared to others. It could also be seen as unfair, as presumably you will be trialling changes that you expect will improve learning. In that case, all should benefit. In my experience, this is what happens anyway, often the steps to improving what you do can have big benefits for all learners, not just your focus group.

When you introduce the changes to your practice in the area identified you need to keep on with them for some time to give them the best opportunity to have an impact. My suggestion would be a minimum of one full school term, about three months, preferably more, before you will then be in a position to meaningfully assess the impact of your changes and interventions.

Recollecting data and analyse the results

Having implemented the changes you identified for a period of time, the next task is to gather more data in order to identify what have been the impacts for the learners and their learning. Most often, and most desirable, this simply involves repeating the data collection exercises you carried out at the outset of the process. By doing this, you are able to make direct comparisons between where the learners were in there learning, some time ago, against where they are now. Knowing you are going to do this, is another factor to take into consideration when initially identifying the data collection methods you will use in your enquiry.

Repeating the data collection processes is only the first part of this element, you then need to analyse what this data is showing you, and what it is not.

All of the data collection devices and tools mentioned above have validity and should give you confidence in your findings. At this point you may have other data that you can also use, this may be comments or observations by colleagues or other professional visitors about your learners, and learning. It may be information and comments from parents or guardians. When you receive such feedback, you should get into the habit of noting down any bits that you think are significant, this is easily done in your daily diary or planner. This then becomes another part of your data and evidence base, to help support the conclusions you will come to about the impact of your interventions, as well as where you need to go next.

Hopefully, you will be seeing the signs of positive impacts from your interventions, but don't be despondent if you are not seeing this, sometimes the results can take longer to emerge. Have the results been consistent across all your focus group? If not, why might that be so? Were the results what you expected? What/who surprised you? What worked, what didn't? How has your thinking changed? How has your practice changed? How do you know? What will you do next? These are all good questions to be asking at this stage of the process. Perhaps most powerful is asking the learners what they think, and how they are feeling about their learning now? Again, discussion and collaboration with colleagues is very useful at this recollection of data and analysis point.

Identifying the next steps

So, what happens now? You have decisions to make at this stage of the process. You need to reflect on your enquiry and *your learning* from the process. This should be part of a continuous process of self and professional development, so where does the process go now? You may decide you need to continue with the focus of your enquiry for a longer period of time, or you may decide that you have gained enough insights, so that your thinking and practice has changed, and you have already determined to embed the changes trialled into your professional practice, so that they become a part of your professional identity. If the changes you have made have had positive impacts, you may decide you want to trial some more in the same area. It could be that as the school year has progressed another 'itch' has started to disturb your thoughts about learning, driving you to want to enquire into another area of learning, and your practice. This is entirely down to you. This is professional development and growth that is completely owned and directed by you. It is not something else being done to you. Conversations with colleagues and school leadership teams can help clarify and inform this decision, but ultimately, it's yours to make.

If you are fully ready to embrace enquiry for your professional development, you will recognise the continuous nature of the journey of professional growth and identity change you are now on.

Knud Illeris, a Danish professor of lifelong learning who has looked closely at transformative learning and identity has stated that, 'The concept of transformative learning comprises all learning that implies change in the identity of the learner.'[8] If you have truly been involved in professional learning that has been transformative to your thinking and your practice, then your professional identity as a teacher will have changed as a result.

Sharing your findings

This is another crucial element to the enquiry process. It is vital to individuals, to schools and to systems that we share insights and new understandings. We need to share the insights and outcomes from our enquiries to deepen our own understandings, as well as part of a collaborative process to help others who might be having the same issues in their own classrooms and practice, and to contribute to the educational knowledge base in the system in some small way.

How you share your findings can vary according to your context and setting, and your own preferences. This may consist of a two-way conversation and dialogue with colleagues. It may be through you producing a simple research poster which contains all the main elements and findings from your enquiry. It may be in the form of a PowerPoint presentation about your enquiry, or you might prefer to write up your results. You could write a blog or put something in a shared area online somewhere. I have seen teachers keep a learning scrapbook during their enquiry, which has photos and comments from participants. These then become a useful tool for sharing their work and findings with colleagues and others. Again, it's your choice, you must find a way that works for you.

At my own schools, we would schedule one of our first professional development meetings in any new school year for the sharing of everyone's enquiry results from the previous school year. That way everyone was aware of what had been happening and the impact for learners, and teachers could learn from each other. This becomes a powerful collaboration to help support whole school development and activity.

At first the sharing of your enquiry results and insights will be within your own establishment, but this can then be spread further, especially as you gain confidence in yourself and the process. We invited teachers from another local school, who were thinking about how they could use practitioner enquiry themselves, to some of our enquiry sharing professional development sessions. That way they could see and hear about the processes involved and the insights gained, straight from class teachers just like themselves. Most importantly they could ask questions and have any concerns or fears allayed. Teachers from our schools then visited them at their school and led a professional development session on practitioner enquiry.

Teachers have also visited other schools to take part in development sessions and share their experiences. I have spoken to all headteachers in my local authority about practitioner enquiry, I have visited individual schools to support professional development programmes for teachers and school leaders. I have engaged with school leaders and teachers in other local authorities and have shared our work through Education Scotland and the General Teaching Council Scotland, as we have sought to share our experiences, as part of what we recognise as our system leadership responsibilities and role.

The use of blogs by myself and teachers has been another way we have shared our journey with practitioner enquiry. This book is another expression of that responsibility to share those experiences and insights gained.

* * *

These then are the essential elements and components involved in carrying out any practitioner enquiry. As I said at the outset of this chapter, you may identify more stages yourself, because everyone's journey is individual and unique, and each context is equally unique. You start from where you are, then identify the steps needed to take you where you would like to be.

My last word of caution would be that there is no destination on this particular journey. If you are committed to career-long professional development, and truly see yourself as a life-long learner, this is a journey throughout your professional career, and your life, that is about improving in what you do, and deepening your understandings about how you may go about this. Not through big 'eureka!'-type discoveries, but through a continuous process of self-discovery and enlightenment, which benefits and changes you, but also all those you work with and for. Most importantly, it offers most hope to all learners, especially those who are at risk of otherwise missing out, because no one recognised or addressed their learning needs properly as they moved through the system. If this continues to happen, it is a damning indictment of those systems, and ourselves as educators.

The adoption of a systematic approach to improving what we do, which practitioner enquiry offers, can prevent everyone in the system being accused of dereliction of duty. It does not offer the solution to all that ails schools and education systems, but it does offer a systematic way to look at these, in order to identify solutions that may work.

Notes

1   Hattie, J., 2012. *Visible Learning for Teachers*. London: Routledge.
2   Timperley, H., 2011. 'A background paper to inform the development of a national professional development framework for teachers and school leaders'. [Online] Available at: enable.eq.edu.au/support-and-resources/professional-readings, p. 14.
3   Cochran-Smith, M. and Lytle, S., 2009. *Inquiry As Stance*. New York: Teachers College Press.
4   The General Teaching Council for Scotland, 2014. 'Practitioner enquiry'. [Online] Available at: www.gtcs.org.uk/professional-update/practitioner-enquiry.aspx
5   Scottish College for Education Leadership, 2016. 'Where to begin with practitioner enquiry'. [Online] Available at: www.scelscotland.org.uk/blog/where-to-begin-with-practitioner-enquiry/
6   Hargreaves, A. https://mobile.twitter.com/i/web/status/801958216133443584, 25 November 2016.
7   Timperley, 'A background paper'.
8   Illeris, K., 2014. *Transformative Learning and Identity*. London: Routledge.

4 The role of school leaders/ principals in practitioner enquiry

There is no doubt that to successfully undertake practitioner enquiry for individual professional development and school development, the role, influence and actions of the school leader are crucial. In the previous chapter, I touched on the importance of the school leader in this process. In this chapter, I want to consider the roles, influences and actions of school leaders in more depth.

Much has been written about high-performing school leaders and the challenges and responsibilities of school leadership. Fullan and Hargreaves have called for 'head teachers who can lead knowledgeably', and they go on to exhort school leaders to 'lead the change you want to see.'[1] Andy Hargreaves, Alan Boyle and Alma Harris, after looking at leadership in education and in different business and sporting organisations feel the very best and impactful leaders provide uplift for the people and organisations they lead in various ways, whilst still keeping their feet on the ground. They found in their studies that 'Uplift's emotional, spiritual, and collective social powers means that it also has the power to improve people's performance and results.'[2] Clive Dimmock, who has written on school leadership and the lack of empirical evidence and research as to what constitutes high-performing school leaders, still acknowledges that 'Good leadership has become the mantra for successful organisations in general and schools in particular.' He goes on to recognise 'that effective leaders are distinguished by the possession of specific traits, dispositions and attributes.'[3] John Hattie, as part of his *Visible Learning for Teachers* meta-analyses of educational research data, identified the three most impactful traits that school leaders can exhibit were 'believing in evaluating one's impact as a leader (effect size .91), getting colleagues focused on evaluating their impact (.91) and focusing on high-impact teaching and learning (.84).'[4]

These are just a few of the writers and researchers who have focused on, and recognised, the crucial nature of school leadership to school development and success. The consensus would seem to recognise the school leader role as challenging, complex and at times frustrating, but as absolutely pivotal in the success, or failure, of school development and change. National and local policy can support school leaders in their endeavours to keep improving their schools, or they can hinder. But individual leaders still, mostly, have the time and space to ensure they remain the key influencers in the performance of their schools. Too many national agendas are focused on accountability and performativity of schools and their leaders, but where leaders are able to use their knowledge, skills and understandings, they can still have massive impacts for schools, teachers and learners. I firmly believe that it is still possible for school leaders to focus on the right things for their schools and learners, and the best are able to 'exploit policy',[5] as Michael Fullan has called it, in order to remain focused on those right things.

It would be my contention that school leaders have to utilise many of the skills and traits that make them high-performing and effective during the introduction of, and support for practitioner enquiry approaches. This is not a quick fix or a panacea for school and professional development, the best leaders are not looking for those anyway. Like any learning that is deep and sustainable, practitioner enquiry is complex and messy at times, so it needs sympathetic and understanding leadership and actions to help it succeed and to have the greatest impacts. There are a number of key traits and dispositions that leaders need to understand and display during the successful implementation of practitioner enquiry. Some of these they may well have at the outset, and others will emerge during implementation, but all will be further developed and enhanced over the course of the journey. This is a journey with no end, as it is understood by the best leaders and learners as a continuous process over the course of their professional lives, and beyond.

So, what are these traits, dispositions and actions that school leaders are going to have to embrace and display? These have been identified by many teachers, school leaders, researchers and ourselves during our engagement with enquiry and should be considered by all looking to lead, and take part, in similar development.

The first thing that any school leader needs before embarking with enquiry is some *knowledge and understanding* of what they are undertaking before they start. I must confess that my knowledge and understanding was pretty limited when we began our own journey in 2008. I was always a school leader who read a lot and was interested in latest research and implications for my own practice and that of the teachers I led, but I had not heard much about practitioner enquiry. It was only through my meeting with Dr Gillian Robinson of Edinburgh University that I became more aware of the approach and the possible opportunities that lay in its application. She did apply the same method with myself as we were to employ later with teaching staff, in that she never mentioned the term practitioner enquiry when we first spoke. Instead we talked about informed practice, using research and engaging with professional reading related to areas we wished to improve, and to inform our actions. I think if I had known we were embarking on practitioner enquiry from the outset, I would have read more on this so that I would be helped and informed in order to plan and map out the steps in our own journey. Mind you, at this time we didn't consider this as the start of a new journey, more of a scoping exercise to try and identify our next steps. However, I understand why Gillian took the approach she did, as she was trying to get to know me, my thinking and my drivers, she also needed the same knowledge about all our teaching staff before we commenced.

I would advise school leaders to read about, and speak to others about, practitioner enquiry before embarking on their own particular journey. There is definitely more information and material around now than there was before we started, so it would be well worth spending some research and preparation time in getting to understand what it is you are engaging with and how you think this might pan out in the future. Being aware and prepared can definitely help school leaders and the teachers they lead, and is likely to reduce misconceptions and misunderstandings of all. I think we were very much piloting a different whole-school approach to development when we started, and our understandings and insights grew as we all made our way. It is my hope that this book is helping school leaders and teachers to start with more information, and a better understanding, than we had at the start of our journey. You will encounter different and similar issues to ourselves and, like us, you will deal with and overcome these as you go, and this should all be expected as part of the process of changing growing and developing.

The next understanding school leaders require is that the whole process needs to be *managed*. Now this might seem an obvious statement to any school leader, because most of them can find their days tied up with management type activities and little else. It does need some further explanation. Actually, the two roles of school leaders, *management and leadership*, are both at play here, and often it is difficult, if even desirable, to disentangle the two roles. The whole process of introducing practitioner enquiry needs to be managed, because if it is not then staff may feel overwhelmed by what they are being asked to do. If the process is not managed properly and sensitively by school leaders, staff will be overwhelmed. In order to prevent this from happening, you need to develop a plan for implementation, and this plan needs to be flexible, agreed and understood by all, and will require constant review and adjustment as you go. You have to identify the steps in the implementation process and expected timeframes for completion. It is then crucial that you create, and ensure, the time required is made available. Keeping everything proportionate and manageable is crucial to the success of your journey, and the well-being of yourself and staff. Of course, you also need in your plan expected outcomes for all, including learners, and how you will know if you are on track and have been successful.

The best school leaders recognise they will need to adjust plans and the management of the process according to context, circumstances and how staff are coping and responding. This is just like the best of teachers who are highly adaptive and who adjust learning experiences for learners according to their response and engagement with learning activities. School development, and the facilitation and support of this is no different. There were times, in our own journey, when we needed to stop, go back and slow down in the implementation and development of the practitioner enquiry process. This requires sympathetic and empathetic management from school leaders. I will repeat, this is not a one-size-fits-all approach, either for teachers or schools, and therefore it requires sound, responsive and flexible management of the process for it to be successful.

In my own schools, I was able to remove all other actions from our School Improvement Plan, so that everyone could focus on practitioner enquiry. I ensured there was time provided, in our professional development activities each year, for staff to spend on enquiry activities individually and collaboratively. Because professional dialogue was seen as increasingly important to the process, we also started to include planned and protected time for staff engagement and discussion. We also used management non-teaching time to help support staff with enquiry tasks, and provide further support. In all of these actions and decisions, we had full staff agreement on the changes we made in order to help and support them, and ourselves, so that we could best manage the implementation process.

All our actions and plans were driven by our *vision* for what we were trying to achieve. At the outset of the process, after Gillian and our senior management team (SMT) had met to explore the possibilities of what we might do, we then consulted with all teaching staff from both schools, to set out a draft proposal, and get their inputs and response. We laid out before them what we were proposing to do, after identifying issues that were causing concern, though we never mentioned the term practitioner enquiry. We pointed out that we had a plan that would help them, but it would require their agreement and understanding. I have long held the belief that deep, embedded change in thinking and practice cannot be imposed or forced on individuals. When this happens, all you get is compliance at a surface level, and reversion back to ingrained practices and thinking at the first opportunity. We had to win hearts and minds if practitioner enquiry was to succeed. So it is important you spend time engaging with your own staff to share your vision, answer questions and allay fears and misunderstandings. If you take the approach of 'this is what we are doing', with no discussion or explanation, you are setting yourselves up for failure. Investing time and energy at the outset, is time well spent by all.

As well as identifying how we could support and help them through the process, we also laid out some expectations of them. They would have to let us use all our small continuous professional development (CPD) funding for our work with Gillian. At that time, each member of staff had an 'allocation' of around £150 for CPD, so this was a big ask. The previous model for professional development was focused on attendance on courses, paid for by this CPD funding. A situation no one was particularly happy with, in terms of outcomes for learners or sustainable school or professional development. We explained that they would be required to spend time on professional reading and research, and then discussing this with ourselves and each other. They would also be expected to try out or trial new teaching strategies and to gather data about the impact of these. All of these activities would be fully supported by Gillian and ourselves.

They certainly liked what we proposed and readily agreed to our draft proposal, which Gillian and I went off and firmed up, as an agreement between ourselves and her university, and a plan for the two schools I was leading. This initial school development plan was to be only for one year, with a review at the end of that, before we would make any decisions about continuation beyond that initial year. We were definitely very much focused on taking baby steps as we embarked on this part of our development journey. During that first year of engagement it was crucial that we kept checking in with staff to manage the process and understand how everything was progressing, and how staff were feeling. We adjusted the plan accordingly when we identified times when we had moved on too quickly or circumstances changed, or couldn't be avoided.

Toward the end of the first year of engagement, we called all the teaching staff together to review the year and make decisions about the future. The response from all was overwhelmingly positive, and we were then able to put together a plan for the following year in order to continue our journey. Gillian, my deputy headteacher and I started to think and plan longer term than that, but we kept this to ourselves, as part of how we were managing the process at that time.

What was also emerging was a developing vision for what we were trying to achieve, and a better understanding of what we could achieve. Gillian had a vision for what she was trying to do in terms of meaningful professional development developed in partnership between a university and schools. I and the management team were further developing and imagining our vision for a self-improving school, with deep meaningful and sustainable change, informed by educational research and appropriate levels of data. Teachers were developing their visions of how their practice and thinking may be changing and improving, so that they could better meet the needs of their learners, and how meaningful professional development could support this. This was a massive step away from the previous situation where everyone was very busy, feeling overwhelmed by all the 'things' they had to do, and all the while thinking they were not making as much as a difference for many of their learners as they would have liked, or desired.

School leaders have to be *actively involved* in the practitioner enquiry process, not just as managers and leaders, but as enquirers into their own practice, thinking how they impact on learning. As I have shown in other chapters. Helen Timperley,[6] John Hattie and Michael Fullan have all noted, and shown, why high-performing school leaders should be active participants in school development activities. It is no longer acceptable that they just support these activities, the biggest positive impacts come, when they are actively engaged in the process. I would agree with this. There is nothing so enlightening about your schools, your teachers and yourself, than when you engage with them all in meaningful and thoughtful professional development. If you recognise this as an important aspect of your role, then you will prioritise and ensure you have the time for such engagement.

School leaders need to become enquirers too. We all need to enquire in to our own practices and thinking, and to consider how we might develop these as part of a continuous process of professional growth, but also as a way of keeping in touch with our classrooms and the learning going on in them. Headteachers and principals, in the face of increasingly complex and competing demands, have to stay connected to the learning and teaching going on in their schools. In my view, the more remote you become from this, the less impact you can have on learning. School leaders need to roll their sleeves up and get into the process. You will keep in touch with what is happening and how people are thinking and feeling. You will see the impacts, positive and negative, of any changes first hand and you will have a wholly deeper understanding about the whole process. I understand that the larger a school becomes, the harder it is for school leaders to be actively involved in everything. However, I would argue that learning and teaching is *the* 'core business' for all schools, or should be. It is when we take our eyes off that, that we create issues for ourselves, our school and our learners, and the systems we work in. Fullan has talked and written about 'right drivers' and 'wrong drivers' in education for many years. He, and many others, would identify learning and teaching as amongst the 'right drivers'[7] for activity in all schools and education systems.

The next trait school leaders need to exhibit is the ability to *gate-keep* on behalf of their teachers and protect them from the demands of others, and themselves. For as long as I can remember, both as a teacher and a school leader, schools and education systems have had to deal with a constant barrage of change and interference, most of which is imposed from above them in the hierarchies that still exist in most systems and many schools. Some of this does come from within, driven by school leaders, and their teams, who wish to implement each and every new fad or trend to emerge, and to be seen to be active and busy. Some have passed on demands placed on themselves, from above, immediately to teaching staff, and have actually seen this as part of their role. Michael Fullan describes this as 'initiativitis', which he explains is a tendency to engage with a continuous stream of innovations, that are often unconnected and which are impossible to manage effectively. This leads to continuously busy schools and teachers, but with little thought, or time, given to consider the impact of all this busyness. Others, who know their schools really well and have sound self-evaluation processes, have identified what they need to do next as part of a continual journey of improvement for their establishments. They are to be applauded for this, but they can often be deflected by the external factors that impinge on school improvement agendas. In Scotland, which I am sure is common to many systems, schools and their leaders have various levels of the system, and others outside of the system, adding to their agendas and telling them what they should be doing. We have the local authority development programme or agendas. These are then linked to Scottish government priorities and policy, which is further interpreted and added to by Education Scotland and the HMIE Inspectorate (Her Majesty's Inspectorate of Education). Both these organisations are directed by Scottish government, and each is supposed to be separate, but are currently under the same umbrella body. It never rains, but it pours, as they say! Add to this the General Teaching Council Scotland, various trade unions and other media and social commentators, and you have a whole plethora of agendas being set or suggested for schools and their leaders.

Too often we have been guilty of trying to please everyone and meet all of these agendas. This resulted in frazzled schools, teachers and school leaders, and little improvement for learners. We constantly asked for someone to gate-keep and protect schools and teachers from this continuous cascade of demands down onto schools, but to little effect. This has still not changed, therefore, school leaders need to determine to undertake this role themselves. For practitioner enquiry practices and dispositions to become embedded into the culture and ethos of teachers and schools, they need protection from all these competing, and sometimes conflicting, agendas. If school leaders have robust self-evaluation processes and understandings in place, they will know exactly where their schools are in their development journey, and understand deeply their local context and how this should be reflected in their activities. This should give them a strong position from which to prioritise and identify what are the right actions and drivers for their schools. I have shown elsewhere, that when teachers are engaging with enquiry, they are in fact connecting up all the main agendas and cannot think of one area or aspect in isolation, but will be considering them all as part of a continuous and connected process of growth.

What is required is for school leaders to be *professionally courageous*, values driven, and to be able to argue, from an informed position, using evidence and research, to justify them saying 'no' more often to those who would seek to impose the same changes and courses of action on all schools, and all at the same time. This is a ridiculous position we find ourselves in. Just as we need to differentiate learning for individual learners, we likewise need to differentiate school development according to the schools and their contexts. School leaders need to be prepared to fight the fights that are needed to protect their teachers and, most importantly, their learners. A fight for professional development that uses research, is informed by data and which can bring about deep and sustainable change in practice and thinking, is a fight worth having in my view.

School leaders across the planet, and system leaders, have had the *support and challenge* mantra as a key part of their remits for many years now. The problem is that as more and more systems have been infected by what Pasi Sahlberg[8] describes as the GERM (General Education Reform Movement) agenda, which is high on accountability and low on trust, it is the *challenge* aspect of this that has come to dominate in many systems and schools. The trouble with this is that it also plays into the hands of the many control freaks that still exist in systems and schools, and promotes more micro-management and top-down diktats. I do agree that we need to challenge our schools, their leaders and their teachers to be the best they can, and to keep trying to improve. However, in my experience, that is what most schools and their teachers are trying to do every day. They are constantly challenging themselves to improve and to develop what they do. Unfortunately, they are still then the focus of relentless challenge agendas set by some school leaders, by some system leaders, and by structures and systems created to hold them to account. Too many schools and their leaders spend too much time having to prove what they are doing, rather than spending that time improving what they do. We have to change such cultures and attitudes, and school leaders have a key role here. We need to develop more trust in the system at all levels. It is my contention that when we show we are consistently looking to improve, informed by research and data that we have critically engaged with, and show we can act, think and speak in a professional manner, then that trust may come. Especially, when we can evidence and demonstrate improved outcomes for more and more of our learners, and that we are taking real steps to close gaps and ensure our provision is equitable and fair. We are not there yet, but I believe enquiry approaches and dispositions equip us to make greater progress with all of this in the future.

We have lots of challenges already in the system, both intrinsic and extrinsic in nature, but perhaps a bit too much, and we have not focused enough on the *support* role of late. For practitioner enquiry to really succeed, school leaders need to provide a range of support to individuals, and for the collective vision and aims agreed by all. This should not be something that is delegated off to someone else. As a school leader, you need to actively support staff to succeed. When embarking on practitioner enquiry, teachers soon come to recognise how complex and challenging this engagement is going to be. They need to know their school leadership will protect them from other demands and is knowledgeable and skilful enough to understand and support them through the process. This means school leaders need most, if not all, of the traits and dispositions commonly identified in high-performing leadership models. To provide such support, school leaders need to thoroughly understand the process and the challenges presented by practitioner enquiry. They should have the skills and knowledge to switch between a coaching and a mentoring approach as necessary. Each individual will require differing levels of support, so it is crucial school leaders really know their staff, and their strengths and areas of development, as well as individuals knowing this about themselves. We all have them, and it is crucial school leaders are honest and sufficiently personally aware to recognise these in themselves, and do not expect to have all the answers to every issue. Instead they know how to coach teachers so that they can solve issues and develop understandings themselves, or mentor them with suggested possible courses of action when required. It is essential they promote and develop collaborative support structures and cultures within the schools they lead, and beyond these as and when necessary.

Sometimes you will need to be a 'sounding board' for teachers, sometimes you may have to don the 'mantle of the expert' and sometimes you will need to be a shoulder to cry on. Whatever is necessary to support teachers to achieve their individual and collective goals, and how to support these, has to mainly come from the school leader and their leadership teams. In the right culture, it is possible to develop such qualities and dispositions in all staff.

Another key aspect for school leaders to consider is their ability to *monitor and track* the progress with practitioner enquiry, and their ability to collect meaningful data and then critically engage with this to inform future actions.

A common aspect of many education systems at the moment is the constant desire to be 'driven by data'. As Alma Harris and Andy Hargreaves have demonstrated, instead of being 'driven by data' it is perhaps a lot more desirable that we instead become 'informed by data'. Hargreaves has gone further by pointing out at a conference in London in 2016 and repeating on Twitter, 'the data doesn't tell you what to do'.[9] Generally, schools and their leaders are now awash with data of various types and with variable validity. For some, the only data that has value is that which can be expressed numerically and be turned into percentages, percentiles and easily understood graphs and other data capture procedures. The trouble is that a lot of the data we have is not telling us what we think it is, and some of it we struggle to interpret. When you make standardised testing, and the production of data, high-stakes, then 'playing the game' or 'gamification' is an almost inevitable consequence for some. It is remarkable that many of the systems that purport to put so much faith in teacher's 'professional judgement' then go on to completely ignore this when it comes to assessing how good teachers and schools actually are.

Andreas Schleicher of the OECD is fond of repeating 'that without data, you are just another person with an opinion'.[10] What I have discovered, the more I engage with researchers and writers, is that even with data, you are *still* just a person with an opinion. Each person interprets data in ways that suit themselves and many of their biases, or ideological standpoints. Two people can look at the same pieces of data and information and come up with two diametrically opposing viewpoints using it. What is it they say about statistics and damn lies? I think we should take a similar view with much of the 'data' we purport to have and use.

The important thing about having data is to be able to critically engage with it, so as to understand what it is telling you, and what it is not. It is important to understand the validity of much of the data you will have at your fingertips as a school leader, and what it is telling you, both as a snapshot in time, and as an indicator of longer-term trends. There is no doubt that you need to be informed by data, but do not let yourself, your school and your teachers become awash with data, that does nothing, and only makes the picture you are looking at even more muddy and confusing. You need clarity of thought, clarity of action, and you need clear data, that is valid and proportionate, to help you make decisions about future actions. What is an absolute necessity for you as a school leader, is to be able to monitor and track progress and achievement with the implementation of practitioner enquiry, or any change. To achieve this, you will need to do two main things. One is to have data from the outset that provides you with a clear picture of where you are starting from, a baseline assessment. This evidence should be qualitative in nature and the collection and collation of this should be repeatable, so that you can look at the evidence of impact over time, and at various points during the process. The other thing you need to do is to again be actively involved in the process, so that you are gathering more formative and subjective views of how the process is progressing. You need to check in with participants, as well as commentators and observers from outside, and from your learners and any other partners, to give you an overall picture. I can remember thinking our own engagement was going really well, and having this confirmed by respected and trusted visitors, then someone making the statement, 'well that's all good, George, but I can't see where each person doing their own enquiry connects to your School Improvement Plan.' After getting over my initial annoyance, this comment did make me think about how we could demonstrate everything that was going on across both schools was part of a connected, collective and coherent process of continuous development. I had conversations along those lines with my senior management team and teachers, as well as Gillian, to see what they would say. Out of those conversations, came a clear understanding of what we were doing and how it all connected together, and as a result both schools and each individual teacher were more confident they were getting better, and were better able to demonstrate and articulate this. We were also clear about the evidence and data we had to demonstrate as well. Sometimes, it's good to have people challenge you, or question what you are doing, in order to refocus and ensure that you are still on track. That then becomes a valid part of your data collection and self-evaluation processes, and part of the monitoring and tracking of your progress. It is also a key aspect of the total and transformative learning process you are engaged in, and stops you existing in a bubble, or echo-chamber, of self-delusion.

Another key aspect for school leaders to consider is how they promote and support *collaboration* through practitioner enquiry. This might seem counter-intuitive with something called *practitioner enquiry*, as we might assume that the focus in this will be on each individual enquiring into their own practice, and that is correct. But, for such enquiry to have wider benefits, and so it can contribute to the development of a learning culture within and across schools, it needs to be more than this. It needs to be situated within a collective and collaborative culture, focused on development and growth of all, and for all. A key responsibility for an effective school leader is to develop and support collaborative working and sharing within the schools they lead.

They can do this by setting up structures and expectations around collaboration. In the two primary schools I led, we required teachers to plan collaboratively, across areas of the curriculum and the different stages of the schools. This was for a number of reasons. We wanted to have a progressive and connected learning experience for our learners. We wanted all teachers to understand the learning journeys their learners had been on, and how what they were planning fitted into that overall journey. We wanted to promote conversations and dialogue about learning between teachers, and we wanted them to talk about the enquiries they were engaged in, sharing insights and issues as they went. The other tactic we employed was for a member of the leadership team to sit in on these collaborative meetings to contribute to the discourse and to hear, and understand, the thinking behind what was being planned and discussed. This was an element of our monitoring and observation procedures, but was not formal in nature. It became just part of what we did. It was not about controlling such collaboration and discussions, it was about being an active and equal participant in these.

Flattening hierarchies in schools can contribute to the development of collaboration amongst all staff. So, as I have talked about already, we promoted and supported teacher leadership, dispersed leadership and teacher agency as we sought to develop teachers with high levels of adaptive expertise. When you develop these, and demonstrate this is how you wish to work yourself within the school and beyond, you are slowly developing those collaborative cultures recommended by Fullan, Hargreaves, Harris and others. Our belief was that we had enough expertise and agency within our two schools to solve most issues, and to keep the schools developing and moving forward. If we felt there were issues or development we needed further support with, this was where our collaboration beyond the immediate confines of our particular schools became so important. Working with, and speaking to colleagues in other settings, and different parts of the system, not only helps you develop your understandings and your practice, it also helps those colleagues in the same way. This is true system leadership, by all, and for the benefit of all.

The school leader has to believe in, and understand, how such collaboration can act and support powerful school development and change, then ensure these all become part of the school culture and expectations. When this is all just part of how you work, and is an expectation embedded into the fabric of everything you do, then the real power of collaboration is released. Alma Harris[11] describes this as the promotion and development of 'shared influence' amongst staff. When there is so much to do, one person cannot do it all. Our real power and strength lies in the fostering and nurturing of deeply collaborative cultures and structures.

The school leader needs to understand and embrace the concept of *system leadership*. Key to this is understanding the power of collaboration at all levels in the system in order to produce the self-improving system that many, including myself, believe is the way forward for our education systems and schools. When we have true system leadership, the system will be led by practitioners at all levels who have the necessary skills, aptitudes, attitudes and experience that allow them to develop an organic and growing system that is informed by research and evidence, but which reflects each unique context. When we reach such a point, perhaps we will not be so susceptible to the whims and ideologies of others who are not grounded in the profession, but who seek to impose their views and practices, and we who should know better than.

When school leaders have a system leadership understanding and mindset, they view everything they are involved in differently, as they recognise their responsibilities should be not just to the learners in their own schools, but to all learners.

You may ask, what has this to do with practitioner enquiry? My response to that is that through practitioner enquiry, you are beginning to develop the understandings and dispositions in teachers that will be required for system leadership to become a reality. Having an understanding of system leadership, allows the school leader to tap further into the power of practitioner enquiry to help support and develop individual teachers, and prepare them for the envisioned working environment and conditions they can expect in the future. At the very basic level, to have a self-improving system requires that we have self-improving teachers and self-improving schools. You are not only preparing teachers for the future, you are equipping them for now, so that they can be part of shaping that future.

The final trait and disposition required for school leaders to ensure the success of practitioner enquiry is that they must have a deep understanding of learning, both in adults and young learners. You may think this is a given, and something all school leaders will have already, before they get to the point of leading a school, or schools. However, in my experience, this is not always the case, nor as common as we would suppose. As I have already said, I have always read and tried to keep abreast of the latest thinking in regards to learning and cognitive development. I developed a level of understanding from my *teacher training*, for that was what it was in the 1970s, and my reading, professional development and thinking about the content, and sometimes being able to discuss this with colleagues. However, it wasn't until I really began to engage with practitioner enquiry, the work of my teachers, and working with Gillian Robinson, that I began to deeply understand learning, and how to promote this. Previously, I had been as guilty as many others of using teaching methods and practices, because I had always used them, or the school had always used them, and not because I *knew* they impacted deeply on learning, and how children learn. Through the years of engagement with practitioner enquiry I deepened my knowledge of learning, and gained more insight, so that I was better able to support teachers, and learners, as a result.

It is amazing how many times, as you carry out an enquiry, that you come to realise that what you have thought and practised for many years was not helping the learners, and may have been setting up most of them to ultimately fail. When that does happen, it is very powerful not only to your practice, but also to your thinking. What I certainly understand about all learning is that it is more complex than we sometimes think, not much of it is linear, though some of it is. When gaps occur in learning this should require teachers to rethink, and also know, how they are going to address those gaps, not just plough on hoping that learners will eventually get it. All learners learn and progress at different rates, we should recognise this by not trying to standardise everything we do to a common denominator or model. With all learners, young and adult, they are much likely to understand and get to grips with new learning when they understand the 'why' before they understand the 'what' of learning. A lot of learning is hard and needs persistence and resilience on the part of the learner, but when they understand why that learning may be important to them, and are able to connect it to their real lives, they are more likely and able to develop and demonstrate such qualities. I understand the importance of revisiting learning and giving learners the opportunity to use learning in new and different contexts, and I understand various hierarchical models involved in learning depth. I also can recognise that there is a change underway in how learners learn with the advent and development of technologies and platforms, and that this will bring about different understanding and practices for teachers and learners, some of which have not been thoroughly considered, identified or researched yet. I also understand myself as a lifelong learner, and that my understanding and thinking about learning will keep developing and growing.

I understand about intelligence, and something of how the brain works, and how it changes over time. I know that intelligence is not fixed and, with the right conditions, most people can learn and function at high levels. I had the pleasure of meeting Reuven Feuerstein in Jerusalem a few years ago, and taking part in some of his mediated learning and instrumental instruction programmes and training,[12] which taught me so much about the plasticity of the brain and how learning, and language, difficulties can be addressed for *all* learners.

It would be my contention that school leaders need to consider learning deeply and continually, in order to better support all the learners in their schools, and in order to ensure that they are not deflected or led off-track by strategies and practices that might be actually detrimental to the learning of all.

I started this chapter by considering some models of high-performing school leadership and leaders. I think you need to consider some of these yourself if you are a school leader or are aspiring to such a role. School leadership is not easy and presents various challenges. However, it also presents so many opportunities, I think practitioner enquiry could be one of those opportunities for so many schools and their leaders. When you and your schools are ready, you have the chance to reshape and configure the culture, thinking and practices across your school and beyond. You can make significant improvement and changes that will impact positively on all learners and contribute to deep and meaningful continual improvement of your establishments, whilst contributing to the development of the system as a whole. As with everything, this process can start with a few simple steps, and perhaps the first ones are to ensure you have the necessary skills and aptitudes to support your teachers and your schools as you all embark on such a journey together.

Clive Dimmock has taken an overview of the qualities, traits and dispositions required by effective and high performing school leaders. He identifies that such school leaders need deep professional knowledge, and they need a rich array of skills and techniques. Dimmock also recognises the need for such leaders to acquire and develop higher-order capacities, developed over time and in the light of experience, tacit understandings that all leaders develop and which are crucial. He recognises also that all of these are situated in, shaped and influenced by their school context. Michael Fullan has encouraged school leaders to work at de-privatising teaching, model instructional leadership, develop capacity, grow new leaders, divert distractors and become system leaders. Andy Hargreaves, Allan Boyle and Alma Harris have encouraged school leaders to dream with determination, to develop creativity and counter-flow, to collaborate, to use pushing and pulling forces, to measure with meaning and all the while have a clear vision but with their feet firmly on the ground.

As all these researchers, and many others recognise, school leadership is a challenging and complex undertaking. There are some certain commonalities though in what they, and others, have identified in high-performing school leaders. You will need most, if not all, of these to help practitioner enquiry to become embedded, and to succeed in your setting and context. You can also use practitioner enquiry to help you develop some of those same qualities further, and improve your practice as a school leader.

Notes

1 Fullan, M. and Hargreaves, A., 2008. *What's Worth Fighting for in Headship?*, second edn. Maidenhead: Open University Press, pp. 25, 51.
2 Hargreaves, A., Boyle, A. and Harris, A., 2014. *Uplifting Leadership: How Organizations, Teams, and Communities Raise Performance.* San Francisco, CA: Jossey-Bass, p. 4.
3 Dimmock, C., 2012. *Leadership, Capacity Building and School Improvement.* London: Routledge, pp. 4, 193.
4 Hattie, J., 2012. *Visible Learning for Teachers.* London: Routledge, pp. 153–156.
5 Available at: https://michaelfullan.ca/wp-content/uploads/2016/06/00_13_Short-Handout.compressed. pdf, p5.
6 Timperley, H., 2011. 'A background paper to inform the development of a national professional development framework for teachers and school leaders'. [Online] Available at: www.enable.eq.edu. au/Supportandresources/Formsanddocuments/Documents/backgroundpaper.pdf
7 Fullan, M. and Quinn, J., 2016. *Coherence: The Right Drivers in Action for Schools, Districts and Systems.* Ontario: Corwin Press and Ontario Principals' Council.
8 Sahlberg, P., 2012. *Finnish Lessons: What Can The World Learn from Educational Change in Finland?.* New York: Teachers' College Press.

9   Available at: https://mobile.twitter.com/i/web/status/801958216133443584, 25 November 2016.

10 Available at: https://www.theatlantic.com/magazine/archive/2011/07/the-worlds-schoolmaster/308532/

11 Harris, A., 2014. *Distributed Leadership Matters: Perspectives, Practicalities and Potential.* San Francisco, CA: Corwin.

12 Feuerstein, R., Feuerstein, R.S., Falik, L. and Rand, Y., 2006. *The Feurestein Instrumental Enrichment Programme.* Jerusalem: ICELP Publications.

5 The role of the teacher in practitioner enquiry

Having considered the pivotal and crucial role of school leaders in facilitating and enabling practitioner enquiry in Chapter 4, we now need to turn our attention to the key beneficiaries and implementers of such an approach, the teachers.

As its name suggests, practitioner enquiry involves practitioners, or teachers, looking closely and systematically at their practice, and their impact on learning, as they consider how they may continually develop this in order to improve outcomes for all learners. In that case, teachers are absolutely central to this whole process, because this is totally about their ongoing professional development and growth in order for them to improve their practice, to have greater impacts for all learners.

How important are teachers in the learning process, and why should there be such a focus on their impact and development? These are a couple of good questions to consider to start with.

Andreas Schleicher, the German scientist and statistician in charge of PISA (Programme for International Student Assessment, carried out on behalf of the OECD[1]) has famously said 'The quality of an education system can never exceed the quality of its teachers' and he uses this assertion in many of the presentations and talks he gives. No matter what you think about Schleicher and PISA, there is no doubt he, and the PISA programme, have great influence in many education systems across the globe. Given what he has said about the primacy of teachers in any system, it seems obvious that Schleicher believes that in order for systems and schools to improve teachers have to improve what they do first of all.

John Hattie[2] has written that 'teachers are the major players in the education process' and that they need to be 'vigilant about building expertise to create positive effects on the achievement for all students.' He too recognises the primacy of teachers in any education system and, therefore, calls on them all to be committed to professional development activity that is focused on achieving positive outcomes for all learners. He does go on to acknowledge the importance of school leadership and teachers working collaboratively to improve and develop what they do, and act more professionally. Stating that, 'professionalism in this school is achieved by teachers and school leaders working collaboratively' (p. 32) might be a good quality indicator for any high-performing school which seeks to demonstrate a commitment to improvement of what they do.

Another Australian educator, educational writer and trainer, Tracey Ezard in her book *The Buzz*,[3] looks closely at how school leaders and staff can create high performing learning cultures in order to support growth that has the biggest impacts for learners, states, 'Shift cannot occur in the classroom if there is not first shift in the staffroom' (p. 7). This is her own call to teachers to recognise their professional roles and responsibilities, and to commit to professional growth and development that impacts on mindsets, as well as their practice.

Brian Boyd, a former professor of education at the University of Strathclyde in Scotland, wrote in 2009[4] that 'the research community has only recently identified teacher impact as being central to the process of schooling' (p. 7). That was emerging only in 2009, so one really does wonder where the focus for learning and school improvement was before then. Probably, much as it still is in some systems today, the focus was on curriculum, structures, programmes, resources, leadership and policies, rather than the people, and their professional dispositions, who really make a difference to learning every day. The fact that so many were so slow to recognise and realise this, with some still struggling, resulted in the de-professionalisation of teachers and for them being viewed as deliverers in what was viewed as the 'technical' activity of teaching.

The now defunct General Teaching Council for England put teachers, and their professional development, at the centre of school and system development in 2010 and stated that, 'teachers should be able and willing to scrutinise their own and others' practice in the light of relevant theories, values and evidence.'[5]

Dylan Wiliam, too, has recognised the pivotal role of teacher actions, development and improvement in the process of improving and deepening learning for learners. He, and Paul Black, demonstrated the impact of pedagogical change in their work on formative assessment strategies and practices to support learning.[6] Wiliam has spoken for the last few years about the importance of all teachers continuing to grow and develop their practice and understandings, 'not because they are not good enough, but because they could be even better.'[7] Wiliam has recognised the complexity of teaching, but puts teachers, and their continuous professional development at the heart of school and system performance.

I could go on to cite various other researchers and writers all of whom would support, through their research and systematic studies, the primacy of teachers and their development in facilitating improvement in schools and education systems. No doubt you are already aware of many of these. What now needs to be considered is how we up-skill, or re-skill teachers so that they are able to take on the new roles, responsibilities and expectations that are assigned to them.

My contention would be that practitioner enquiry can provide a very effective way of achieving what so many seek. But this is not an approach that can just be taught and delivered, as research would show, neither should we expect it to be. It requires shifts in mindsets and the development of dispositions by all teachers, so that they are better able to take up those roles and responsibilities we see as crucial to moving forward.

Having thought long and hard about this, and through reflecting on my work over the last eight years with practitioner enquiry, I believe it is possible, and useful, to identify the traits, qualities and dispositions that teachers will need for any successful engagement with practitioner enquiry.

For such a successful engagement with practitioner enquiry to occur, teachers will require to display and develop a range of *personal and professional qualities and dispositions*. As with school leaders, teachers will require to *understand fully* the process they are engaged in. I suggest you read Chapter 6 of this book, if you have not already done so, then discuss this with colleagues and school leaders. Ask questions, of yourself and others, so as to begin to consider what the various stages in carrying out an enquiry might look like in your particular setting and context. This is the nuts and bolts of carrying out an enquiry into your practice, but you need to think about and understand why engagement in an enquiry process might be beneficial to you and your learners. Just carrying out an enquiry, progressing through the steps in that process, is not going to cut it on its own. You need to understand and think about the implications for you, as you consider *your vision* for the development of your practice. I am presuming you understand and are committed to yourself as a *lifelong learner*, and that you also recognise that your professional development is something that needs to be continuous, directed by yourself, shaped to your personal and professional context. In other chapters (especially Chapter 1), I have pointed you in the direction of research and reading around teacher professional development in general, and practitioner enquiry specifically. You may wish to look at those, then consider their content further.

At the outset of your journey with enquiry, it is worth investing the time to read some of the research I have used throughout this book, but also, I would urge you to seek out schools and teachers who have already engaged with enquiry to gather their thoughts and insights. Use your local networks and social media platforms, such as Twitter, to find these if you are unaware of any already. You can read as much as you like, but it is only when you begin to *consider and understand* what this may look like *in practice*, in your setting, that what is being discussed becomes more real. When you speak to others about enquiry, make sure you get the full picture, warts and all. I never try to fool anyone that, brilliant though I think the approach is, it is not without its complexity, issues and challenges. The more you understand about these, the better informed you are about what your own journey will entail. Some younger teachers are now coming out of university having employed practitioner enquiry as part of their courses and the way they worked and were assessed. This can only help them to engage with enquiry methods at the very start of their careers. It is good if you have such a background, but I would caution that the process is different, it has to be, when you are teaching full time and trying to carry out an enquiry into your practice alongside your teaching responsibilities. However, the results will have a more direct impact on your thinking and practice, as well as for real students, who's learning you now have responsibility for.

Make sure you are as *informed* as you can be about the process and demands, so as to shape your expectations and activity to keep these *proportionate and manageable* as you begin your journey. It goes without saying really, but I am still going to say it, that you need to approach practitioner enquiry with an *open mind*, prepared to accept what it throws up, and equally prepared to make changes to your thinking and your practice when required. This can sometimes be difficult for some teachers of all levels of experience to do, but it is a prerequisite. Going into the enquiry process with a closed or fixed mindset, as Carol Dweck[8] might identify, is not going to help you discover the steps you can take to get that little bit better each day in improving your practice, and the outcomes for all learners. Being open-minded and prepared for measured change, based on evidence and research, is really important. Some of the times I have seen practitioner enquiry fail are when people have been forced onto a course by headteachers or others who feel they need to improve their teaching; such participants often resent even being there, clouding their total engagement with the process. This just sets everyone up for failure. I have also witnessed participants who have arrived with such mindsets, but who have completely changed their views and their practice as they got more into the process and opened up to the possibilities. Either consequence depends on the dispositions of teachers and the skills of those leading such interventions.

I don't know how long you have been a teacher, or how long you intend to be a teacher, but your career could span thirty years or more. I can think of nothing so dispiriting as coming in each day, week, month or year, continuing to deliver what you have always delivered, in the same way you always have. That is not what I ever experienced during my own career, and it is not what *being and behaving as a professional educator* should be about. No one can force you to change your mindset or your practice in any deep and meaningful way. Only each individual can do that, and each person needs to determine that this is how they want to think and act as part of being a professional educator. They are looking to develop through development of *agency* and *adaptive expertise,* welcoming the responsibilities that go along with such freedom of action and thought.

It is really important that teachers, and school leaders, are *emotionally aware and intelligent*. The work of Daniel Goleman[9] has pointed to the significance of emotional intelligence and awareness to effective workplace and organisational working. We all need a level of emotional intelligence and awareness to function effectively as teachers and human beings. Education is a 'people' business or activity. We work with all kinds of adults and young learners on a daily basis, and the success of that work, and those interactions, is very much dependent on the strength of the relationships we create with them all. Relationships, are the glue to everything we do in schools. If you lack emotional intelligence or awareness, the maintenance and creation of positive relationships with colleagues and learners becomes very difficult for all involved, resulting in a reduced impact.

The successful implementation and engagement with practitioner enquiry, whilst maintaining an individual focus, is very much dependent on the strength of *collaboration* and relationships you have with colleagues and others. I have already said that enquiry is complex and challenging, emotionally socially and cognitively, so being able to engage with colleagues is crucial. The two schools I was leader of had involved all teachers in the process, so that they were able to share with and support each other as they went along. This was crucial, for as supportive and understanding as the leadership team and I tried to be, we understood we were not the ones having to engage each day whilst planning for, managing and teaching a class. Having other people to speak to who were experiencing all the same issues, as well as many of the same feelings, as yourself is so important to the success of the process, and individual enquiries.

Professional dialogue and conversations are crucial to deepening understandings and exploring the learning of all learners, teachers and students. It is important that you do not feel you are on your own, and that you have a peer support structure to turn to when needed. All this helps the process, but also develops the *learning culture* of the setting in which you work, which is another important element for everyone. When you are emotionally intelligent and aware it helps you develop the collaborative culture and practices you are going to require to get the most from the enquiry process. You need to be committed to collaboration within a culture of *personal and professional trust*. You will need support, and will be able to offer support. This is part of the enquiry process, as long as you can trust your colleagues to act professionally, and they you. Sharing the workload and exploring, and solving, issues is only really possible within a collaborative, supportive structure. This may be in place in your school or setting already, but it may need to be developed as part of your early engagement steps with enquiry. If you already work in a collaborative culture, great; but you may have to develop such structures to support this, you need to be an active participant and driver in this.

Alma Harris and her colleagues talk glowingly of the professional learning communities (PLCs),[10] and she and others have used these, or variants of them, very successfully to develop collaborative learning, promote learning cultures, and develop dialogue across schools. It may be a necessary step for yourself and your own setting to explore such structures to promote collaboration and develop professional dialogue around learning and teaching. A key aspect and consideration with enquiry is that you start from where you are, each person's context and point on their development journey is recognised as being different and unique. That is why it is crucial that you are *honest and informed* about exactly where you are.

I would also ask you to consider that engagement with enquiry is going to require you to be *thorough and systematic* in your endeavours. The real benefits for teachers from carrying out enquiries into their practice comes from the insights they gain about their practice and how they are impacting on the learning of all their learners. To gain those insights, you need to work systematically and thoroughly, so that what you discover is informed and valid. To achieve this, you need to think carefully about the process and have a *flexible plan* for how you will engage, and when. You are not trying to become a professional educational researcher. You are trying to become a professional educator who can research and enquire in order to improve their practice. Yes, you have to be systematic and thorough, but you also have to be reasonable in your expectations and be able to keep the whole process proportionate and manageable, yet meaningful. Hence the need for being systematic. As in all scientific approaches, the ones we use in practitioner enquiry have to be repeatable and to stand up to scrutiny. This gives our findings validity, gives us confidence about changes we have made and the impacts they have for all our learners.

What are *your values* as an educator? When was the last time you thought about or considered these? I would suggest that you give some thought to these. Again, I would suggest that you do this not in isolation, but as a collaborative activity at the outset of your engagement, repeating as you go during the process itself, when necessary. Understanding your values, and the principles that underpin your thinking and actions as a teacher, is important to understanding yourself and helping you find your way as an educator. If you profess to be fair, non-discriminatory, honest, authentic, compassionate and committed to justice for all, for example, are those values reflected in your actions as a teacher and as a person? If your actions do not match your spoken values, then they are not your values. Your values are reflected in what you do, not what you say you do.

I have always considered my own values as key in driving and informing my actions. This has caused issues for myself and for others at times, but they help me to sleep at night, knowing that I am taking the right actions for what I believe to be the right reasons. I have used my values as the first point of call in self-evaluation activities. Have my actions matched up to my values? If they haven't, why has this occurred, and what am I going to do about it?

At the same time as considering your values, you may wish to consider the *principles* under which you are going to operate as an educator. Principles are very close to values, but in education they might include a commitment to excellence, a commitment to do the very best for all learners, a commitment to work collaboratively and in partnership, to be concerned for others and to understand your responsibility for all learners. Again, I think it is worth taking time to consider these, and to revisit them from time to time, but especially at times of change, so that you are more self-aware about the underlying drivers of your actions and thinking, not just in deciding these but also in evaluating them.

Practitioner enquiry is challenging to your thinking and to your practice as a teacher, therefore it can be challenging to your personal identity and understanding of self. Any professional development activity that is worth engaging with, which is going to produce embedded changes in individuals, is going to be challenging and complex in nature. Practitioner enquiry is that. Understanding yourself and your motivations is important if you are to engage fully in the process and get the most positive benefits for yourself and the learners you teach.

In Scotland, teachers have to be registered with the General Teaching Council for Scotland (GTCS) which sets out a framework of professional standards for teachers and school leaders.[11] There are three standards, The Standard for Registration, The Standard for Career-Long Professional Learning and The Standard for Leadership and Management. It is not by accident that all three of the standards used by GTCS begin with a statement about 'professional values and personal commitment' as these are recognised as the starting point for any consideration of the role of teachers and school leaders in Scotland. In other systems like Australia with their Australian Professional Standards for Teachers,[12] England and the teachers' standards set by the Department for Education,[13] and Finland, where there are no formal standards as such, but where the whole system is underpinned by values and principles set out in 'Finnish Education in a Nutshell' provided by the Finnish National Agency for Education,[14] values and supporting principles feature strongly. This points to the importance of teachers and educators being values-driven and principled individuals who should think and act at all times in the best interests of all their learners.

Be clear of your own values, and those of your setting, before you embark with practitioner enquiry, this will help you through the process, enabling you to achieve the most from the process.

Teachers who are looking to engage with practitioner enquiry are often *inquisitive and reflective* practitioners already. That ability to self-reflect and consider your own practice, and to support others to do the same, are crucial to the process. Fortunately, the promotion and development of reflective practitioners is a lot more common now in many education systems and schools. This is a positive and early step necessary in the development of adaptive practitioners with high levels of agency. You need to be able to reflect honestly on your practice, and you need to commit to adopt and develop such a disposition throughout your career. This has to be a career-long commitment for all teachers and school leaders.

However, the disposition to reflect and consider your practice, having this embedded in all that you do, is not enough. What you do as a result of those reflections is more important. This is not simply a navel-gazing exercise, but one that needs to have outcomes in terms of your thinking and your practice. Alongside this disposition, you need to be *committed to improving* what you do and to *personal and professional growth*. Do not enter into engagement with practitioner enquiry without such an understanding and commitment, otherwise you will be just engaging in another 'tick-box' approach to professional development, and one which will make little, if any, difference to your personal and professional identity or practice.

To some, this might seem a harsh requirement, to others it may seem obvious and part of what you do already. I am not making any judgements here, because we are all a product of our experiences and circumstances. It is up to you to decide where you are on the continuum of personal reflection and commitment, and where you would like to be, then to decide what you need to do and when to get to that place. It may be that you are not in the place you would like or need to be to begin the next step on your journey, that's fine. But, you can still start making preparatory steps, so that when you are in a better place, you are not starting completely from scratch. These initial steps might just involve you becoming more aware of where you are and what you might need to do to prepare the ground through thinking, reading or talking to others. Such preparations will be moving your thinking on and contributing to your personal, professional development.

I don't know about yourself, but I entered teaching *committed to making a difference*. As a teacher, I succeeded with this for many learners – but not all – and this was still my main driver as I became a school leader. School leadership gave me my opportunity to make a difference for even more learners, not just the ones in my class as a teacher. As I came to better understand system leadership, I realised I was actually able to make a difference for even more learners, not just the ones I was directly responsible for in the schools I led.

This is a huge thought and responsibility when you step back and think about it. When you are working day-to-day, as a class teacher or school leader, you can sometimes lose sight of this responsibility, though you are engaged with such responsibility every day. The reason why I mention this desire to make a difference is because it is also important for teachers to recognise this, both for their learners and themselves as they engage with enquiry. You may also come to understand more about your responsibilities for all learners in a school as you develop as a *system leader*.

Through practitioner enquiry you are demonstrating your *commitment* to making a difference for all your learners. You are committing to looking scientifically and systematically at your thinking, your practice and the impact you are having on learning for all your learners. You will understand that this may mean you have to ask yourself difficult, challenging questions about what you currently do, and may have done for many years. You are going to face challenges to your thinking and your personal and professional identity. But, you will understand the necessity of all this in order to make a difference, or a greater difference, for all your learners. Your aim is to improve their learning and deepen their understandings so they are better able to make their own way in the world, then make a difference themselves. In my view, one of the central aims of education should be to better equip the current generation of learners to make sense of, and solve, some of the problems or issues previous generations have created, or failed to solve. To do that, so they can make a difference to their future is through the development of knowledge, skills, aptitudes and attitudes.

You are also making huge commitments to make a difference to, and for, yourself. You will make a difference to your practice and will better understand how to facilitate and support the learning of all, or at least more, of your learners. You will change your professional identity, which is a key component of truly *transformative learning* as identified by Knud Illeris.[15] The desire and commitment to making a difference for all is essential for all those teachers engaged with practitioner enquiry, as is the determination to truly transform their professional learning.

As a key aspect of practitioner enquiry is engaging with research, evidence and data, teachers need to *embrace reading* and discussing this. The number of teachers, and school leaders, who I meet who have stopped reading never ceases to amaze me. Now I know we all lead busy lives, personal and professional, but it is my contention that a professional educator has a responsibility to keep on reading throughout their career. By reading I mean all reading, fiction and non-fiction. How can we develop young learners as lifelong learners and readers if we can't even model and demonstrate this in our own lives and professions?

With practitioner enquiry, you have to develop the ability to read critically, as for every piece of research that says one thing, there will be another saying the opposite. You need to understand that and be able to make sense of it to help you and your learners. As part of any enquiry you will be reading pieces of research and professional writing. The fact that you are reading this book now shows you are already on that journey. As with any professional reading, I want you to read, then discuss, this book critically. You may find much that you agree or disagree with, but what is essential is that you read, think and engage with what you have read. Relate your reading to your current context, and consider how much applies and how much doesn't? What can you use, and what not? Which other reading have you engaged with that is similar, and which is different? These are all good questions to discuss and consider with colleagues as part of focused professional dialogue and collaboration. One of my best and most impactful professional development activities was as part of a professional reading group. In this we looked at the latest books and articles on learning, teaching, leadership and policy, then we discussed these amongst our peers, looking at what we agreed or disagreed with, as we considered the implications for our own practice.

As I stated earlier, practitioner enquiry is not about turning you into an educational researcher, so there is no expectation that you will be carrying out a full literature review for any issues you have identified, or writing up an extensive report on your findings. Remember, keeping activity proportionate, manageable and reasonable, is key. The more you read, the better you get at it, and the more you are able to identify people and research that give you confidence in their validity and reliability. I would offer further advice that you should be extra critical and suspect when there is a lot of hype happening around a particular piece of research or body of work. In my experience, when this happens often the original valid and sound piece of research mutates into something else very quickly, and as a consequence loses its original message and usefulness. Such overly hyped pieces of research often mutate into business opportunities, when everyone seems to be trying to sell you something, resources or training, linked to them. They can be quickly packaged and sold as the next 'panacea' or 'silver bullet'. I will not name and shame, but I am sure you will have experienced some of these yourself.

An issue with a lot of educational research papers and writing is that they have often produced for other researchers to read, not practitioners to use. The language and structure of much of this is inaccessible and becomes a barrier to practitioners. I often tend to use the *abstracts* at the start of research papers, and the *conclusions* at the end to decide if the piece might be of any help to me. If I think it will be, I will read further, if not, I don't.

A lot of the best research is then turned into more accessible books aimed at professional development, and these are a lot easier to access and understand. You will find many of my favourites cited in this book already. How much you read, and what, is down to you, your circumstances, and the amount of time you have available to do this. But you will need to read. If you are struggling to find time for such reading, you should approach your school leadership to see if protected school development time can be allocated for this to happen. You will also need time to discuss reading with colleagues. It is obviously desirable that the importance of such reading and engagement is recognised by all, then professional development time can be prioritised for such activity. I realise this will not happen everywhere, but, if you see this as a professional responsibility, you will find the time to do the best you can.

Reading is not something you only do at university, or during training, then forget. As a professional, you have a responsibility to read and keep your thinking and practice fresh, in order to keep improving. Doctors can spend seven years, or more, at university, but they still have to keep engaging with research and reading to update their knowledge and their practice throughout their careers, so should teachers. By engaging with practitioner enquiry you will be required to read then consider what you have read means for you and your learners.

I have spoken a lot throughout this book about professionals and *professionalism*. There is no doubt that many systems have, deliberately or accidently, de-professionalised teaching and teachers over many years. Teachers in these systems have become seen as mere deliverers of programmes, resources or pedagogies given to them. The thinking behind such an approach is one that seems to think that researchers and system leaders should identify what needs to be done to improve schools and teachers. This is then packaged and regurgitated in some way, so teachers can be shown how to deliver it. Then we put in accountability and monitoring measures to make sure they are doing it. I have seen this in operation in supposedly developed Western systems. I have also seen it in developing systems, especially where they have had lots of input from those Western systems to 'help' them improve. Such an approach views teaching as a technical activity, rather than a professional one. This is not my view of teaching.

As such systems have been shown to have failed a large proportion of their learners over many years, despite much activity and change, with falling attainment and achievement and widening equity gaps, we are fortunately starting to experience and see the emergence of a different view of teaching. In this, teaching is being recognised as more than just a technical activity that anyone can be 'trained' to do, and is being seen as a highly skilled and complex professional activity. Researcher after researcher has identified the quality of teachers and teaching as the most important factors in school and system performance, and that for teachers to develop and improve they need to be viewed and treated professionally. It is also necessary that teachers should be encouraged to act professionally and be self-improving in attitudes and behaviours. However, we are where we are, and there are many teachers in many systems who know no other way of working other than that of being told what to do and how to do it.

Shift needs to happen at system and individual level. Some take comfort in not having to think about what they have to do, and prefer having someone else identify all this for them. This is not how professionals operate, and it is not how teachers and schools should be operating. We have spent an absolute fortune on educating and preparing teachers; to myself and many others it would be a travesty not to utilise the skills, qualities and capacities such teachers possess to help them grow and improve, whilst at the same time contribute to similar growth in the systems in which they operate.

Professionals also recognise that meaningful professional development is grounded in their practice and their context. They understand that such development should be a professional disposition, an expectation throughout their careers. They view professional development as a continuous process or journey of personal and professional growth. Through meaningful professional development they develop *greater expertise*, having greater impacts for their clients – in our case, our learners. They do not view professional development as a series of disconnected activities to be done so that boxes can be ticked, and with no discernible impact on their practice, or for their employers and clients. They view their own professional development as part of their professional responsibilities and they ultimately control this. Done by them, for them, not to them in order to meet the needs and agendas of others.

We all need to take *more responsibility* and act more professionally, and this is expected of all participants in practitioner enquiry.

As a teacher engaging in practitioner enquiry, it is important that you embrace and understand *dispersed leadership*, *teacher leadership*, *teacher agency* and the power of *adaptive expertise*. I have already spoken about how practitioner enquiry, though individual in nature, needs to sit within collaborative approaches and structures. Enquiry involves teachers working together, challenging and supporting each other throughout the process. This is not a 'top-down' process of professional development, and it relies on individual teachers taking more and more *personal responsibility* for their own development. As you go through the process of carrying out an enquiry, you will come to understand how, and why, you need to take more control of the whole process yourself. Others will be around to support you, but you will come to recognise that you will have to take more and more decisions about your actions, and what may be required as you go.

This is not about school leaders abrogating their responsibilities, but about teachers recognising when it is necessary and appropriate to be making decisions themselves about actions that need to happen. This is about teacher leadership and agency. These might be individual actions, but they may be wider actions that involve more staff and are across wider areas of the school. When some of my teachers were carrying out enquiries, they often identified changes we would need. When this happened, they would often get together and start shaping these themselves before discussing with myself or my deputy headteacher. We would then often try to provide time for these teachers to work further on these aspects. But, it was never about us telling them what they had to do. It was about teachers recognising what needed doing, knowing they were trusted and would be supported to do what was required.

Some of the aims and expectations of practitioner enquiry are that it will develop and promote dispersed (or distributed) leadership, teacher agency and adaptive expertise dispositions in all teachers. Enquiry as stance is a disposition that facilitates individual, school and system development, and so you should understand where you are heading. Of course, you may feel a long way from that point at the moment, but this is okay and to be expected. 'The longest journey begins with the smallest step', to paraphrase a Chinese proverb.

There is no doubt that practitioner enquiry demands and expects a lot of classroom teachers. However, these demands and challenges develop over time and are supported through collaborative cultures. You are not alone, and there is no expectation you reach the desired positions I identify here quickly, if at all. But an understanding of what is involved and where you may be heading can only be useful, in my view. You may well surprise yourself, and others, by how quickly you achieve some of these desired outcomes. But, everyone is unique, and starts from where they are, so don't beat yourself up if others are further on or move quicker. This is a process of growth that should be controlled by you, and shaped by your context and circumstances.

With proper consideration of all the issues, as well as a determination to continually improve, you will soon find yourself in a different position, and able to support your learners in improving ways. Your thinking and your practice will change as part of a continuous process of professional growth.

Notes

1 Organisation for Economic Co-operation and Development, 2016. 'Programme for international student assessment'. [Online] Available at: https://www.oecd.org/pisa/pisaproducts/48852721.pdf, p6.
2 Hattie, J., 2012. *Visible Learning for Teachers*. London: Routledge, p. 22.
3 Ezard, T., 2015. *The Buzz: Creating a Thriving and Collaborative Learning Culture*. Melbourne: Tracey Ezard.
4 Boyd, B., 2009. *The Learning Classroom*. Oxford: Hodder Gibson.
5 Pollard, A. (ed), 2010. 'Professionalism and pedagogy: A contemporary opportunity'. [Online] Available at: http://dera.ioe.ac.uk/11320/8/TLRPGTCEProf%26Pedagogy_2redacted.pdf, p. 5.
6 Black, P. and Wiliam, D., 1998. *Inside The Black Box*. London: King's College.
7 Available at: www.dylanwiliamcenter.co./changing-what-teachers-do-is-more-important-than-changing-what-they-know/
8 Dweck, C. S., 2000. *Mindset: Self-theories: Their Role in Motivation, Personality and Development*. New York: Routledge.
9 Goleman, D., 1995. *Emotional Intelligence: Why It Can Matter More Than IQ*. New York: Bantam.
10 Harris, A., Jones, M. and Huffman, J. B., 2017. *Teachers Leading Educational Reform*. London: Routledge.
11 The General Teaching Council for Scotland, 2012. 'Professional standards'. [Online] Available at: www.gtcs.org.uk/professional-standards/professional-standards.aspx
12 AITSL, 2010. 'Australian professional standards for teachers'. [Online] Available at: www.aitsl.edu.au/teach/standards
13 Department of Education, 2011. 'Teachers' standard's'. [Online] Available at: https://www.gov.uk/government/publications/teachers-standards
14 Finnish National Agency for Education, 2012. 'Teacher education: Finnish education in a nutshell'. [Online] Available at: www.oph.fi/download/146428_Finnish_Education_in_a_Nutshell.pdf
15 Illeris, K., 2014. *Transformative Learning and Identity*. London: Routledge.

6 What are the benefits from the adoption of practitioner enquiry?

Introduction

Having considered the theory, conditions and practice of this different approach to *professional development*, we now need to be clear about what it is I am saying about the benefits of adopting practitioner enquiry. From my own experience, and the experience of many others across different systems, there is much to be gained. The gains are not just for learners, teachers and schools, but also can be substantial for education systems themselves. More importantly, the benefits are sustained, embedded, continuous and self-generating, providing the right approaches are used and correct dispositions are developed. For this to happen, all in the system have to deeply understand, and want to understand, the approach and what it offers.

Marilyn Cochran-Smith spoke to Scottish educators in Edinburgh in 2015 and she cautioned against the *mutations* that can happen to well-researched and evidenced strategies as they percolate through the different levels of the system. When they get into some hands they mutate into something that was never intended, and when this happens we lose many of the benefits we should be experiencing. Some in education want everything quickly and simply, leading to tick-box approaches and practices which are easy to observe and measure. I have had a number of headteachers contact me by phone and say things like, 'George, just give me six quick steps to introduce this practitioner enquiry thing'. After I finish banging my head on the table, I have had to slowly explain that I can't do what they are asking, but if they would like to visit me, or have me visit them, I could talk them through what is involved. For many who exist in a culture of having to produce results, and quickly, this is not what they want to hear. That is not their fault, but a fault of systems which encourage headteachers to think in this way. Just as many systems have de-professionalised teachers, they have done exactly the same to school leaders. If you find yourself in a top-down hierarchy with those above telling you what you must be doing on a daily and yearly basis, further de-professionalisation is a consequence.

But we do ourselves. and the approach, a disservice if we try to pare it right down and simplify something which can be quite complex to understand and deliver. Everyone has to commit fully, and that might first mean changing your thinking, approaches and your priorities.

Practitioner enquiry is very current and fashionable in Scottish education ever since the publication of *Teaching Scotland's Future* written by Graham Donaldson,[1] and the introduction of the new professional standards of the General Teaching Council Scotland (GTCS).[2] Both identify that teachers and school leaders need continuous and meaningful professional development, through which they develop as 'enquiring professionals'. I hear many speak about practitioner enquiry both at a local and national level, and am sometimes concerned about their level of understanding. Some see it just as another 'thing' to do, another fad or trend. If practitioner enquiry is allowed to become this, and is not given the time to become embedded into the culture of all that we do, any impacts will diminish, and will probably disappear quite quickly, if they happen at all.

Having added those cautions, I want everyone to understand what the big wins could be when enquiry is fully understood and embedded. These benefits exist for our learners, our teachers, our schools, and for our systems. If our political leaders really do want to leave a legacy of improved schools and education, with improved outcomes for learners and society, then they will miss an opportunity if they fail to take the time to understand what enquiry has to offer. They are then more able to support teachers and schools to develop the approach.

Benefits from enquiry

So, what are the big benefits and gains we can expect when we implement practitioner enquiry and thoroughly understand how to do this? These are the ones I have identified, though there may well be others that are particular to you and your context.

Raised attainment and achievement for all learners

At a time when it would seem that just about every education system across the planet is searching for improved *attainment and achievement* for its learners, and the closing of *attainment gaps* between the most advantaged economically and the most disadvantaged, practitioner enquiry offers an approach that can meaningfully address all of these issues. Research, and my own experiences, give me the confidence that the implementation of practitioner enquiry might be a solution to many of the issues that currently afflict many education systems.

As the fundamental aims of practitioner enquiry are about *improving learning*, learning experiences, and the continuous development of teacher practice and understanding about these, it would be expected that learner attainment and achievement would rise. What is also really exciting is that, when such approaches have been adopted, attainment gaps have also started to close. Indeed, the impact for those at the lowest end of our attainment levels and most at risk of missing out due to economic factors, may be even more significant than for the rest of the school population.

Helen Timperley, in her background paper for the Australian Institute for Teaching and School Leadership (AITSL) to support the introduction of a national development framework for teachers and school leaders in Australia, talks a lot about the power of *adaptive expertise* amongst teachers.[3] She describes teachers with adaptive experience as teachers who are constantly able and willing to evaluate 'the effectiveness of their activities' (p. 6). They are knowledgeable both about what they are teaching and the best ways of delivering this. She adds that 'engaging in ongoing inquiry and knowledge building cycles is at the core of their professionalism'.[4] To me, this is a further endorsement for using practitioner enquiry by Timperley and is supported by her research both in Australia and New Zealand.

In their 2010 New Zealand project,[5] she and colleagues worked with some three hundred primary schools, focusing on literacy, where she tested out the impact of developing and supporting adaptive expertise *dispositions* amongst teachers in these schools. She and her colleagues sought to develop teacher self-regulating learning capacities, so that teachers became responsible for their own learning, and to develop adaptive expertise alongside *teacher agency* (the ability to act and make decisions independently).

Timperley and her colleagues found important positive impacts for all learners in the schools they were working with. But, perhaps more importantly, they found that progress and gains made by students were even more significant for those who were considered in the lowest 20 per cent of achievers at the beginning of their work.

These results found by Timperley were very similar to ones experienced by two teachers in one of the schools I have been leading. They had both decided that they wished to look at aspects of learning in spelling, as both felt a lot of their learners were struggling with spelling and lacked a range of strategies to help them spell new and unfamiliar words. One was a P6 teacher (9 and 10 year olds), and the other was a P7 teacher (11 and 12 year olds). They gathered a mix of data about their learners, including pupil questionnaires which showed that the pupils did lack confidence in spelling, and many of them just thought 'I can't spell'. Having read around the area of learning in spelling and strategy acquisition, they introduced new methods, made some pedagogical changes, and decided to spend a small amount of time (15-20 minutes) most days devoted to a variety of mixed spelling activities.

One of the pieces of data they had to be able to refer to was our whole-school screening standardised test results for spelling, which we had for most of the learners from when they were in P2 (6 years of age). This gave their teachers a significant amount of information about individual learners, and about attainment trends over time. Learners had just completed this yearly screening before the two teachers embarked on their enquiry. When the same screening exercise took place again after a period of about six months, not a full twelve months, all the learners in both classes had made good progress with their spelling, and most were saying they enjoyed and understood spelling better now and felt more confident. However, it was with those pupils who were regarded as being in the lowest 20 per cent for spelling where the results were even more significant. Prior to the enquiry project, learners identified as being in the lowest 20 percent of attainers, tended to make only a few months progress in their 'spelling age' over a twelve month period. In less than half that time, their progress now ranged from 10 months of improvement to 18 months! This summative assessment picture was supported by the other data collection methods the teachers had been using to illustrate the impact of their enquiry and new interventions.

When the teachers shared their results and insights with colleagues, they initiated a complete change in the teaching of spelling across both schools, and for all learners. This was a win for pupils, teachers and schools, and reinforced the power of practitioner enquiry for us all. This was progress achieved through teachers focused on meeting the learning needs of their learners and enquiring into how they could use a mix of methods and resources to support this, rather than a single solution driven by one particular resource.

The first gain from practitioner enquiry then, is that you should expect it to *raise attainment and achievement* for all learners, and could go a large way to helping *close the gaps* for learners that still persist in many schools and education systems.

Making connections between all that we do

When the two schools I was leading decided to embark on our journey with practitioner enquiry, we did so for two main reasons. The first was that both teachers and management felt dissatisfied with the professional development (PD) activity we had been engaged in up to that point. Such development generally consisted of a mish-mash of different activities that teachers opted in and out of, or which were imposed on us from outside by our local authority, and which usually changed on a yearly basis, or when we got a new Director of Education. This all meant we struggled to see any sustainable impact in the schools and for our learners, and there was little chance for teachers to embed changes into their practice before they moved on to the next 'thing' to do. These activities were disjointed, some connected to school priorities and our development plan, but we struggled to see where many fitted in to where we were and what we were trying to do. This was a cause of growing frustration for me as a school leader, but also for staff who were incredibly busy and were feeling swamped by all the 'things' they were doing. Added to these frustrations was the realisation that we struggled to see the impact of all this busyness for our learners over any length of time.

The second reason we embarked with practitioner enquiry was that teachers felt overwhelmed by all they had to do. We were implementing the relatively new Curriculum for Excellence in Scotland and it was an incredibly busy time at local and national level. When is it not? This was in 2008–9 and it seemed the national bodies were issuing new 'support' documentation and edicts almost on a weekly basis, and then these were interpreted and added to by our local authority. We were informed that we were required to develop and shape the new curriculum from the ground up, developing new curricular pathways; we needed to think about how we assessed the new learning, using formative and summative assessments; we had to change our planning formats; we were to consider the changes necessary in how we reported to parents; and we were expected to change and improve our learning and teaching. Whilst dealing with these major pieces of work, we still had to be raising attainment and achievement, the closing of gaps, whilst considering how we were developing our learners as *effective contributors, successful learners, responsible citizens* and *confident individuals*. We also needed to consider how we would measure all of this and share the results with all partners. No wonder teachers and school leaders were feeling so overwhelmed, and generally frazzled!

Something had to change. The consequences if we didn't would be dire for everyone.

I had been talking to colleagues on our leadership team about these issues and one of them put me in touch with Dr Gillian Robinson from Edinburgh University. It was following conversations with her that I began to see a possible solution to these issues might lie in a completely different approach to that which we had been applying previously. This was the start of our engagement with practitioner enquiry and we quickly saw how, through the adoption of such an approach, we could deal with so many of the issues which were overwhelming us, and that it was possible for us to do this in a *connected, meaningful and sustainable* way,

The first thing I did as a school leader was to get agreement from staff for a new approach. Supported by Gillian, this was an easy sell by the way. We then said to them and our local authority that practitioner enquiry would become the sole focus of our new school development plan. Fortunately, we were given the time and the space to try this, but I still had one or two interesting conversations at the local authority and at director level, when they thought we should still be taking part in corporate development activity that all schools were expected to sign up to. We held our ground.

Actually, I thought it was quite easy to justify our actions and our position. If our core purpose was about learning, and through practitioner enquiry we were clearly focused on improving learning, we could not do this without considering all the various issues and aspects that were on the national, local and our own agendas. If we were wanting to improve learning, we could not do this without looking at the *curriculum* or *learning experiences*, and *pedagogy*. If we were looking at the curriculum and learning experiences, we couldn't really consider these without thinking about *assessment*, formative and summative, that we would use to support learning. If we were looking at assessment, we could not do this without thinking about how we would use this to *support learning* and also to *report* to various 'audiences', including parents. If we were looking at all these key aspects, we couldn't do this without thinking about the *planning* of such learning experiences, and at our *strategic planning* in the school. If we were looking at planning, we couldn't look at this without considering *evidence, data and self-evaluation processes*. If we were looking at all of this, we couldn't do it in isolation so we needed to *collaborate*, both within the schools and across others.

And so it went on. The teachers were quite wary at first because they thought we would still have other 'things' imposed on us from outside. But, I constantly sought to reassure them that this would not happen, and I fought the fights that were necessary to make sure that this did not happen. Teachers could see that we were dealing with every important aspect of school development, but we were doing so in a connected, measured and meaningful way. Each was being dealt with within a curricular or learning context, and out of the whole process would emerge practices that developed and grew in an organic way, rather than a mechanistic or 'tick-box' way. No longer were we focused on assessment one year, the curriculum the next and then pedagogy the following, for example. We were looking at all of these things all the time and our practices and understandings were constantly improving as a result. The learning and experiences of all our learners grew in a similar way.

I felt we were getting ever closer day by day to the development of self-improving teachers and schools, with adaptive expertise and high levels of teacher agency. As a school leader, and given the climate and conditions in our system, and many others, I think this is something we all should be aiming for.

Deeper learning and deeper understandings

For too long in schools and education systems we have focused too much on breadth of coverage, at the expense of *depth*. Curriculums and expectations have expanded and grown over time, whilst the time we have to cover all of this has either remained static, or has actually diminished. Our own Curriculum for Excellence at its very inception set out to increase the depth of understanding in our learners, and de-clutter the curriculum. This was as a result of the complaints by teachers and others that we had tried to cover too much in our previous '5-14' Curriculum, leading to 'surface-level learning' which lacked depth. However, over the years Curriculum for Excellence has grown and grown and become more and more crowded with *knowledge, content, skills, aptitudes, attitudes, Experiences and Outcomes*, and the recently added *Benchmarks*. Schools and teachers have got busier and busier, which means learners have got busier and busier, and all this has impacted negatively on the time required to deepen learning and understanding.

These issues apply just the same to teacher development and learning, just as much as they apply to our learners.

Practitioner enquiry gives us a way to *slow down* and deepen learning. When teachers are focused on the learning going on in their classrooms, and how they might improve this from an evidence base, they soon recognise not only the complexity of much of what they ask learners to do, but also the importance of giving them *time* to master new learning and understandings. When teachers engage with research and researchers, that are constantly making statements about the importance of taking time to enable learners to assimilate new learning, then more time to embed and deepen this, teachers cannot ignore that advice. When they see the results of doing just that, they are even less able or likely to ignore such advice.

Learning has slowed down in the two schools I was leading, but I make no apologies for this, because understanding and the ability to transfer that learning has improved. If we look at literacy and the teaching of language as an example, before we engaged with practitioner enquiry our practice would be considered 'good'. It is in a completely different place now. That is because teachers have a *deeper understanding* of how to teach reading, writing and to develop talking and listening. They know how to teach reading skills, and no longer just listen to reading. They know how to teach spelling to make it engaging and to provide learners with a suite of strategies to employ. They know how to immerse readers in different genres of reading and writing, to identify characteristics so that they are able to incorporate these into their own writing. They know how to use *dialogical* approaches to develop understanding, as well as talking and listening. They know how to carry out miscue analysis, which allows teachers to pinpoint the specific difficulties individuals are having in their reading, identify gaps in learning, then point to how these may be addressed. But most of all, they understand the importance of all of this and that it takes time, to give learners the best opportunity to succeed and to deepen their understandings.

All of this is as a result of practitioner enquiry and teacher engagement with research and *professional reading*, reinforced by their collective collaborations, relationships and focused *professional dialogue* around learning. They too have deeper understandings about learning and their impact on that learning. They are taking charge of their professional development, based on where they currently are, and the needs they have identified. All of this professional development is located in the particular *context* within which they are working, and though individualised, is collaborative in nature.

Many of the teachers I worked with, not all I would hasten to add, now have 'inquiry as stance' as Marilyn Cochran-Smith and Susan Lytle described it.[6] It is part of their professional identity and has become a disposition. They look at every issue through an enquiry lens, and will solve issues by utilising the strategies and interventions they have developed. They are not teachers who wait to be told what to do, or for someone else to solve issues for them. They have agency and high levels of adaptive expertise, as advocated by Helen Timperley and others.

Small changes have big impacts

With practitioner enquiry, our attention is always on learning and the focus of any enquiry is small and tight. This is to keep the whole process proportionate and manageable for already very busy teachers and schools.

By having a tight focus, and keeping the collection of data to an equally small group of learners, the process remains *realistic and achievable* for teachers, and fits easily into their daily classroom practice. However, this does not mean the impacts of an enquiry remain small and focused. They quickly scale up.

What we discovered from our own engagement process, was that improvements and insights quickly *scaled up* leading to greater *impact*. For example, when a teacher decided to enquire into aspects of learning in 'reading' with a small group of pupils to focus on, she engaged with a range of professional reading and research to explore the changes she could try. As a result of this she identified that she was going to introduce a new focus for her reading group and would identify exactly what it was she was going to teach, and what she wanted them to know by the end of her block of teaching. To achieve this, she recognised that she would have to give the group more focused teaching time from her during reading lessons. This led her to think closely about pedagogies that would support what she was trying to do, and to consider how she could manage the organisation of the class to allow her to trial what she wanted. This led her to consider all of her reading groups and what she was attempting, and the organisation of this.

As a result of this reflection, she changed her classroom organisation to use more of a 'carousel' or 'learning stations' approach, where she was based at one, but where there were meaningful connected learning activities for other children at the other points on the carousel of activities she provided. This meant she could give each of her reading groups quality and *focused teacher input* two or three times a week.

Though her focus was small, and she was only going to collect data for one of her reading groups, the changes she made had impacts for *all the learners* in her class. They all benefitted from the organisational changes and the new strategies she was seeking to implement. The enquiry proved very successful, with the teacher's understanding of how to teach reading skills and strategies improving, and all the children's performance improving over the period. But, what also happened was that the organisational changes worked so well in 'reading' that the teacher introduced them into other areas of the curriculum as well, and they worked equally effectively there.

So, whilst the focus was a narrow one around literacy, she was also able to bring about wider positive impacts in maths and numeracy teaching and learning as well. What is more, as a result of her enquiry, she changed and simplified her planning formats. These worked better for her as well, as they did when she tried them out in maths and other areas of the curriculum. Therefore there were much larger gains for this teacher and for her learners, than just her original focus in 'reading', and her small group for data collection. There were big benefits for all learners and across the curriculum. When she shared her enthusiasm for what had happened with colleagues, they too decided to try some of her changes in their own practice, so learners across the school were also benefiting.

This is just one example of something we saw happening on a regular basis from enquiry. Teachers would gain insights which changed their thinking and their practice, and which scaled up very quickly to have much bigger impacts than had been planned or expected. Once this had happened on a regular basis, we began to look out for and expect these bigger gains to occur, and they always did.

Evidence and research used to inform practice

In January 2015 I attended the International Congress for School Effectiveness and Improvement (ICSEI) in Cincinnati. This is an annual event that brings together researchers, practitioners and policy-makers from education systems across the globe. One of the main themes from that congress was 'how do we address the gap between the research base that tells us what works in education, and the practice that happens daily in our schools?' This is a question that has troubled researchers for many a year. Too much practice that goes on in schools, happens because it has always happened, not because it is grounded in any particular piece of research or evidence. That is not to say that both sides of this divide are free from blame as to why this should be the case. But, this too needs to change, not just for the benefit of researchers or practitioners, but for our learners.

We need to be utilising the best practice and methods we can, to provide the best learning opportunities and activities for all our learners, so that all have the very best opportunity to succeed and achieve their potential. To achieve this we have to be informed by *research and evidence* and we need to engage critically with this. Practitioner enquiry promotes this.

As Helen Timperley said in her background paper for AITSL: 'It is no longer acceptable for professionals in schools to do their individual best ... it is expected that they will engage collectively with what is known to be effective in improving outcomes for all students.'[7] But, as Dylan Wiliam has pointed out: 'Everything works somewhere, but nothing works everywhere.'[8] This is why *critical engagement* with evidence and research is what is key. No longer should teachers be seen as mere deliverers of the practices, programmes and resources given to them by others. They have to be active and critical consumers of research, as well as creators of some of this themselves. We should seek to promote more teacher agency throughout our schools and systems. I have often stated that teachers are not educational researchers, and neither should they seek to be, unless that is where they see their career heading. However, they have a professional responsibility to ensure that their practice is informed, current and the best it can be. This means they need to read, engage with and discuss educational research and evidence. They need to consider how it can support their own practice and understanding, and how it can be shaped to their context. As with everything, I recommend how they do this has to be *proportionate and manageable* as their main focus has to remain on learning and teaching their class or learners every day.

Teachers who engage in practitioner enquiry, not only read, they begin to understand how to critically engage with research and use this to inform their practice, as well as the professional dialogue they engage in with their colleagues and others. They are more able to explain what they are doing and why, and are more open to reflecting on and changing their practice and thinking. Timperley and other researchers, from John Dewey, through Lawrence Stenhouse and so many others, encourage, if not demand, that teachers engage with research and evidence to inform their practice. Equally, there are more and more practitioners like myself, who have seen the power, and the need, in being engaged with research and evidence to develop our practice and thinking. Hopefully, this will become more widespread, because it equips ourselves as a profession to defend practice that we know has high levels of efficacy, and to argue against practices being imposed that may well be detrimental to our learners.

The promotion of collaborative practices, teacher leadership and dispersed leadership

Michael Fullan has spoken and written for many years about the power of collaboration in school development. Like Timperley, and others, he has long argued for teachers to stop solely focusing on themselves as individuals, and that we need to break down *silos of practice* that exist in many classrooms, so that we are better able to collaborate. Silos are characterised by closed classroom doors and where teachers get on with doing the best they can for all their learners, with little professional contact or collaboration with others. Fullan's research about high-performing schools and teachers has identified that *focused collaboration* is a common feature of them all. Teachers in such schools recognise the power of collectively and focused collaboration.

In his short but powerful call to arms, *What's Worth Fighting for in Headship?* first published in 1992 and in later editions with Andy Hargreaves, Fullan comments that, 'We have known for a quarter of a century that focused collaborative cultures generate greater student learning' (p. 18).[9] If you accept the power of collaboration in schools and systems, then any practices that develop and improve such collaboration are to be welcomed. Practitioner enquiry is an ideal vehicle to promote collaboration around a common purpose. If you are lucky, like I was, this may be across whole schools, or it may be across departments, or it may be amongst willing individuals, all circumstances and contexts are different. The key is that all should be welcome and supported to grow and develop their understanding and practice.

An essential characteristic of collaboration, as recognised by Fullan, Hargreaves and others, is that such collaboration needs to be *focused*. Practitioner enquiry provides teachers and schools with a common focus and a common language to help promote collaboration and the development of a deep *learning culture* within a school.

Timperley and Fullan are also believers in and supporters of *teacher leadership*. This concept can be controversial for some, who argue that leadership is the responsibility of those who are being paid to lead. Teacher leadership is not about titles and payment it's about everyone making valuable, and appreciated, collaborative contributions to school development and growth. It is about the flattening of hierarchies that traditionally exist in many schools, in order that all may contribute and be valued. To me, teacher leadership is about teachers having agency within a culture that supports them to make decisions based on evidence, and their own professional judgement and experience. Leadership is not about titles, again it's about dispositions to collaborate and understand when it is appropriate to make decisions about actions, not in isolation, but as part of a collaborative culture that supports learning for all. The Scottish College for Educational Leadership (SCEL) has carried out a lot of research into teacher leadership and offers more information and programmes to support this on their website, which is well worth a visit.[10]

As we seek to develop *self-improving systems*, we need to first develop *self-improving teachers* through the promotion of enquiry, adaptive expertise and agency. Practitioner enquiry engagement supports the development of such dispositions and qualities. I have always believed that the qualities that are required for high-performing school leaders, and the qualities required for high-performing teachers are very similar anyway. We should be looking to promote and develop these through initial teacher education courses and throughout a teacher's career. In that way, we are not only developing ever-improving teachers, we are growing and preparing future leaders and helping to produce meaningful *system leadership* at all levels. It is heartening to see that many local authorities in Scotland are asking newly qualified teachers (NQTs) to carry out an enquiry during their induction year into the profession.

Dispersed, or *distributed leadership* is very much promoted through practitioner enquiry, as I have indicated above. When talking about the development of leadership in such ways, I much prefer Clive Dimmock's use of 'dispersed leadership'[11] rather than the more common 'distributed leadership'. Using 'dispersed' more reflects my own experience, and preference for, teachers, and support staff, taking up leadership roles and responsibilities because they wanted to and it felt a 'natural' thing to do in the culture we created. Rather than 'distributed', which can feel like school leaders handing out jobs and activities to chosen people, mainly because they didn't have the time or inclination to do them themselves. To me, dispersed leadership is a natural outcome of a supportive and collaborative culture, with high levels of *trust*. It is possible to impose a form of distributed leadership, but I know which is most effective, and which helps identify and prepare future school leaders. For more information and research on distributed leadership, or dispersed leadership, I would refer you to Alma Harris[12] and Clive Dimmock.[13]

What is generally agreed by many respected researchers and academics is that high-performing teachers, schools and systems are commonly characterised by high levels of focused collaboration, teacher leadership and agency is commonly seen and promoted, as are dispersed or distributed leadership practices. The common theme to all of these is that organisations and individuals are stronger and able to support developments better when they work together, rather than when they work as a collection of individuals. American management writer and advocate for situational leadership Ken Blanchard is often quoted as saying, 'none of us is as smart as all of us'.[14] I would amend this slightly to 'none of us is as powerful as all of us' certainly in terms of professional and school development.

Anything that promotes and develops such collaborative and shared practices, becomes very powerful for school and professional development. In my experience, practitioner enquiry promotes, and enhances, such cultures.

I would say that we were quite good at working collaboratively before we embarked with practitioner enquiry, and I had worked hard to build such a *culture*, and build *trust*. But I have no doubt that these characteristics were enhanced further through practitioner enquiry. When we all had a common focus, i.e. the learning happening in each classroom and across the schools, we were brought together more closely in terms of our working, our thinking and the professionally collaborative practices and discourse found in both schools. In fact, this was commented on by many visitors to the schools, including local authority staff, other teachers and school leaders, colleagues from the General Teaching Council Scotland and Her Majesty's Inspectorate.

One of the schools I led had only been engaged in practitioner enquiry for six months, when we were inspected. The managing inspector said he could see the impact of the work we were engaged in already. He saw this through examination of the learners' work and through conversations with learners, parents and ourselves. Lots of visitors have noticed conversations about learning happening spontaneously between teachers and support staff in classrooms, staffroom and corridors around the schools. This was a visible indicator of the collaboration that was happening around learning and the deepening of the learning culture developed in both schools.

System leadership developed and enhanced

I touched on how practitioner enquiry can contribute towards the development of *system leadership* above, but I think it is worth looking at how this happened through our implementation and how it may happen during your own engagement.

System leadership has for many years been seen as a desirable aim to be achieved by school leaders and teachers. In 2011, Robert Hill produced a commentary on a piece of research, from 2009, for the National College for School Leadership in England,[15] which identified school leaders as engaging in system leadership 'who work within and beyond their individual organisation; sharing and harnessing the best resources that the system can offer to bring about improvement in their own and other organisations; and influencing thinking, policy and practice' (p. 3). He went on to say that this was all done with the desire that school leaders recognised their responsibilities to improve life chances for all learners, not just those in the schools they led. This is a key plank of system leadership, that leaders, and skilled teachers, recognise and accept their responsibilities to consider and work for the benefit of *all children* in the system, not just the ones in their particular schools or class. Through the promotion and development of system leadership, the ultimate aim is to develop a self-improving system, which provides benefits for all.

There are of course many challenges for such a vision, but nevertheless it does seem that it is one that is still seen as desirable by many researchers, writers and educators in systems across the world. It is a key feature of leadership development, at all levels, in Scotland as well. Given that it a desirable position and situation to aspire to, how does practitioner enquiry support such a vision?

By having a collective and relentless focus on learning and teaching, and through the development of this in a collaborative way, you immediately switch teachers to thinking about all learners in a school, not just the ones they teach. We certainly found that teacher focus and conversations about learning moved from 'the children in my class' to *all* children. Teachers in the upper school wanted to speak to and learn from their colleagues in the early years classes, in order to better understand children's learning journeys. They also wanted to understand more about literacy and numeracy learning and teaching at different levels, so that they were better equipped to deal with gaps in learning that still persisted for some learners. All of these are necessary steps on the journey to the development of system leadership practices and mindsets.

Our next step was for teachers to work with teachers from other schools, both in their setting and ours, to share our experiences with practitioner enquiry and the insights gained from individual enquiries. This involved our teachers recognising a responsibility, and having a desire, to support colleagues locally, so that they were able to better support the learners in their schools. That is, teachers thinking about, and recognising, how they could support other learners in other settings through the sharing of experiences with colleagues outside of their immediate setting, a true characteristic of system leadership.

At the same time, I was writing about what we were doing and speaking to colleagues, at local and national level, to support them in developing their understanding about practitioner enquiry. I was also working with organisations like SCEL, GTCS, Education Scotland and Edinburgh University, to support teachers and school leaders in other areas and from other countries. We all started sharing and working across sectors as well, so our teachers helped and supported both primary and secondary colleagues, as did I.

Through our work, we were able to support learners at cluster, local, regional and national levels. We were doing all this as a natural extension to the activity we had been engaged in, and, of course, we managed all of this engagement in such a way as to spread the load and keep everything proportionate and manageable. There were plenty of times when we had to say 'no' so as to protect everyone from unreasonable extra demands and commitments. Sometimes, we all needed protecting from our own enthusiasm and our desire to support others.

Of course, the benefit of this engagement worked both ways. Yes, we were supporting others and contributing to system development at various levels, but we were learning so much through this collaborative engagement ourselves. Helping others deepened our own understanding of practitioner enquiry, but also helped us gain insights of how we would change approaches in different contexts and circumstances. The value of engaging in professional dialogue with colleagues, to help develop shared understandings about learning and the challenges faced, cannot be underestimated, and continues to this day.

Protection from fads and trends

As I have noted elsewhere, education has been subject to, and a victim of, various fads and trends over many years. I am sure we can all recall a number of these during our careers. Fairly recently we have been exposed to learning styles, brain gym, personal learning plans, lollipop sticks, traffic lights and more. All of these have been quite commonly seen in classrooms everywhere, and indeed were expected to be seen by many, and yet they are based on little evidence or research as to their efficacy or some of the claims made for them. In addition, we also have various mutations of sound pieces of research and evidence, which became a series of actions, strategies and gimmicks, so that they lost their initial purpose and impact. This is a consequence of people not having the time, or inclination, to look closely at the initial research and thoroughly understand what it says.

A few of the latest examples of this are with formative assessment, growth mindsets and visible learning. I am sure Paul Black, Dylan Wiliam, Carol Dweck and John Hattie are disappointed by how their research and recommendations have been interpreted by some.

Engagement in practitioner enquiry can help protect you, and your staff, if you are a leader, from much of this. Through practitioner enquiry you develop practices and thinking that can help you sort out the wheat from the chaff in terms of potential and possible school development activities. As you develop as a critical consumer of research and evidence, you encourage questioning and reflective dispositions to shape your practice and your thinking. You are better able to assess proposed changes and 'new' approaches that others may be trying to get you to sign up to. You are in a stronger position to ask the right questions and to seek evidence that what is being proposed might actually be useful and helpful to your practice, and most importantly for your learners.

The other protection it gives you is from those who would ask for you to be resource- or programme-driven in your practice. When you engage deeply with learning and curriculum, you better understand and recognise that every learner is at an individual point on their particular learning journey, and that the learning experiences you provide need to be shaped to recognise and reflect this. When you engage deeply with learning, you really understand the *complexity* of the processes involved, which leads you to question many of the practices and activities that are common to many schools and systems. I have had very interesting, and often short, conversations with representatives of companies who have the latest resource that they claim can deliver all our learning needs. Learning needs are recognised and met by teachers, not resources and programmes. Any resource or programme is only as good as the teacher using it to meet those learning needs.

To deepen learning and to develop teachers so that they know how to provide this for all learners in ways that are engaging, thoughtful and which have impact, is one of the most powerful results of engagement in practitioner enquiry.

Increased teacher agency and confidence

As a consequence of all the above, teacher *confidence and agency* are improved through practitioner enquiry. Teachers are used to being told about all the things they are doing wrong or could be doing better, and using a '*deficit model*' to drive school and professional development. As a consequence, they are often reluctant to admit what they don't know, in case this becomes another stick with which to beat them and increase their workload further. We have de-professionalised teachers over many years, and so many have come to view them as mere *deliverers* of programmes and resources. Indeed, some teachers and school leaders have welcomed and liked this approach, because it requires less thought and is easier to understand. But, is this what is required or expected of a profession and professionals? I think not. Therefore, we have to reframe school and professional practice and development.

Delivered within the right school culture, and with the appropriate levels of support, practitioner enquiry allows teachers, and school leaders, to reflect deeply on their practice and how they might develop and improve it. If everyone is involved, so much the better. It becomes okay to admit what you don't know or don't understand, and to then work out how to address this. Let's face it, most initial teacher education (ITE) programmes do not equip newly qualified teachers to deeply understand learning and pedagogy. They can't, because they don't have the time for this to happen. A lot of teachers enter teaching after only one year in ITE. For this reason alone, it is vital that teachers continue to develop their practice and their understanding throughout their careers. But this needs to be an expectation for all teachers. When they do this, their confidence in themselves and their practice, and their ability to explain and justify this, improves. No longer will you hear comments like 'we have always done it this way' or 'because that's what we all do' when asking teachers about the rationale behind certain practices and activities. With increased confidence, comes the ability to explain your practice from an evidence standpoint supported by a necessary level of data.

When teachers are more confident and informed, their teaching improves and thus the learning in their classrooms improves for all learners. Learners are very quick to detect a lack of confidence in a teacher, and various problems then ensue as a consequence, and not just learning ones. Teachers are better able to form positive and non-threatening partnerships with school leaders, colleagues, parents and other agencies in order to better support the learning of all.

Another disposition that I have always sought to develop in all teachers has been that of agency. I have always wanted teachers to think and act professionally, and as independently as possible. That is not to say I was looking for teachers all doing their own thing, collaboration is key to each of them developing, and their schools developing also. But I did want them to feel they were able to act and make decisions, about their own practice and the improvement of learning, based on their professional expertise and experience. I never was, and never will be, a micro-manager. If you have confident staff, steeped in learning and committed to continual growth and development, there is no need for micro-management. Such practice is more a sign of school leader insecurities than anything else. What there is a need for is to show them you trust and support them, and that you will be there for help and advice, as well as to sympathetically challenge their actions and decisions when required. When teachers have agency, and a culture which supports this, you are getting ever closer to self-improving teachers and self-improving systems as a consequence.

Improved professional development practices and dispositions

In systems where for many years the power of *professional development* has been recognised, but the shape and impact of much of this has been questionable and dubious, practitioner enquiry provides an opportunity to reframe this in a more positive way. This is professional development that is identified and controlled by the individual and shaped to meet their needs and context. This is not a one-size-fits-all approach to professional development. There are no boxes to be ticked here.

Just like a class of learners, a cohort of teachers will consist of a mix of abilities, aptitudes and attitudes. Professional development, then, has to be tailored to meet each individual's needs as well as the school's priorities. Getting the balance right in this respect leads to individual and school development that has positive impacts for all learners. Getting it wrong leads to a disjointed approach and little sustainable impact over time. Through practitioner enquiry, we ensure we are *keeping the main thing as the main thing,* and that development is very much focused on learning and impact. We also ensure that the complexity of professional development is understood and allowed for, so that we create the best possible conditions, to give such development the very best opportunity to succeed. We also recognise that sometimes actions won't work as well as expected or projected, but accept this as part of a complex organic process of meaningful development activity.

For many years, teachers have seen professional development as merely a matter of signing up for and attending a mixture of courses that they thought might be interesting, useful or helpful. Many of these took place away from the setting in which they worked, and most took no notice of that setting or their particular circumstances. Is it any wonder then, that such professional development activity had very little impact on thinking, practice, or indeed learners?

We need to reframe professional development as a disposition, and a continuous and connected process of professional growth. It is not a one-size-fits-all approach, but more a *one-size-fits-one* approach. This is professional development grounded in your particular context and circumstance, and which is controlled and done *by you, not to you*. Every other profession requires practitioners to be constantly updating their knowledge and understanding throughout their careers, teaching should be no different.

We are not looking for a tick-box approach, but one which is deep and meaningful and which makes a difference. It is my view, that the adoption of practitioner enquiry can support us in this reframing of what it means to be a professional and to engage in meaningful and sustainable, professional development.

Professional identity and dispositions changed and developed

Perhaps the greatest benefit to be experienced by individual teachers, schools and systems engaging with practitioner enquiry is that the professional *identity and dispositions* associated with it are changed permanently. Individual teachers not only change their practice and their thinking to better meet the learning needs of their learners, their learning is truly *transformative*. Knud Illeris, has carried out a lot of research, thinking and writing about truly transformative adult learning, and he feels that learning becomes truly transformative only when a change occurs in the *personal and professional identity* of the learner.[16] What I would say is that the teachers I have worked with, who have what Cochran-Smith and Lytle described as 'inquiry as stance' because of their engagement with practitioner enquiry, are different teachers and individuals than they were before that engagement. They have become deeper thinkers about their, and their learners', learning. Their practice has improved, and continues to improve and develop. Their confidence in what they are doing, and their ability to solve learning issues and address gaps has similarly grown and improved.

They are better able to identify, and meet, the learning needs of all learners and to deal with gaps in learning. They take more responsibility for their own professional learning and are able to engage critically with research, evidence and data in order to support learners. They are less likely to be swayed by latest fads and trends and have improved understandings around what works, and what doesn't, in their particular contexts and with their learners. They understand thoroughly the power of collaboration and look to support colleagues, both in their own setting and farther afield. They have high levels of agency and see themselves as problem-solvers who are not afraid to take action, when they recognise this is required. They are reflective and critical in everything they do, but they are able to stay positive and keep actions proportionate and manageable. They measure everything they do in terms of impact for learners, and understand why this should be so. They make connections between this and everything they do, and they are committed to authenticity in their practice and their dealings. They will no longer tolerate practice and activities that have few positive impacts on learning, and for which there is no demonstrable evidence or research to support such practices. They are informed in their practice by research, evidence and data, but are not driven by this.

They are different professionals and understand their responsibilities as professionals, because of all the reasons given above. They also recognise that there is no destination to their personal professional development journey, and that this is a continuous process of growth resulting from constantly enquiring into their practice and their impact on learning.

Not all the teachers who I have worked with are in the same position as those with inquiry as stance, but every single one of them has developed and improved their practice and understanding as a result. As a school leader, to have teachers, who are growing their practice day by day, and continuously, is as much as you can ask for. You should accept that they will not all improve at the same rate, and some will not achieve the levels of others. But, that is life and what real learning looks like.

John Hattie said in his book *Visible Learning for Teachers*,[17] 'the biggest effect on student learning occurs when teachers become learners of their own teaching' (p. 14). I would endorse this, having seen the changes in the teachers I have worked with, and in my own thinking and practice as a result of practitioner enquiry. This continues and remains a work in process for all. What they are also modelling is attitudes and dispositions as life-long learning that we should be seeking to develop in all our learners.

One experienced teacher said to me at her professional review and development (PRD) meeting, 'last year made me really recognise the gaps in my understanding, and changes I could make to my practice, in the teaching of maths'. Whilst that may seem a bit negative an observation, the power lies in the fact that it was the teacher herself who had gained this insight from her enquiry. This process was completely controlled by her, and the issue had been identified by her. It was not imposed on her by someone else saying something like. 'you need to improve your teaching of maths'. Deep and sustainable change can only happen when an individual recognises a need themselves. Such a change cannot be imposed or forced on someone by an outside agent, such as a school leader. When that happens, all you end up with is surface-level compliance, but no real change in thinking or practice.

There is no doubt there will be other advantages for other teachers and other contexts, after all each person and context is unique. What is clear is that there are clear and important benefits to be obtained from practitioner enquiry for all in the system, and the system itself. How great these are, and their extent, will very much depend on the level of understanding about the process and the cultures that pervade to support such endeavour. I believe such a focused endeavour is well worth the effort and may offer an antidote to some of the seemingly intransigent problems and issues schools and systems have faced for many years.

When you engage with practitioner enquiry in your own context, you may discover and identify further gains to be made. What is certain is that the learning culture will have changed positively in many respects for individuals, and the schools in which they work. Given further time, such gains will also begin to accrue at a system level too.

Notes

1 Donaldson, G., 2011. *Teaching Scotland's Future*. Edinburgh: Scottish Government.
2 The General Teaching Council for Scotland, 2012. 'Professional standards'. [Online] Available at: www.gtcs.org.uk/professional-standards/professional-standards.aspx
3 Timperley, H., 2011. 'A background paper to inform the development of a national professional development framework for teachers and school leaders'. [Online] Available at: https://enable.eq.edu.au/Supportandresources/Formsanddocumnets/Documents/backgroundpaper.pdf
4 Timperley, H., 2011. *Realizing The Power of Professional Learning*. Maidenhead: Open University Press, p. 6.
5 Timperley, H., Parr, J. and Meissel, K., 2010. *Making a Difference to Student Achievement in Literacy: Final Research Report on the Literacy Professional Development Project*. Wellington: Learning Media Ltd.
6 Cochran-Smith, M. and Lytle, S., 2009. *Inquiry as Stance*. New York: Teachers College Press.
7 Timperley, H., 'A background paper', p. 1.
8 Available at: https://www.dylanwiliam.org/Dylan_Wiliams_website/Presentations_files/2014-09-06%20ResearchED.pptx, slide 4.
9 Fullan, M. and Hargreaves, A., 2008. *What's Worth Fighting For In Headship?*, second edn. Maidenhead: Open University Press.
10 Scottish College for Educational Leadership, 2017. 'Teacher leadership'. [Online] Available at: www.scelscotland.org.uk/?s=Teacher+leadership
11 Dimmock, C., 2012. *Leadership, Capacity Building and School Improvement*. London: Routledge.
12 Harris, A., 2014. *Distributed Leadership Matters: Perspectives, Practicalities and Potential*. San Francisco, CA: Corwin.
13 Dimmock, C., *Leadership, Capacity Building and School Improvement*.
14 Blanchard, K. and Bowles, S., 2001. *High Five!: None of Us Is As Smart As All of Us*. New York: William Morrow and Co.
15 Hill, R., 2011. 'The importance of teaching and the role of system leadership: A commentary on the Illuminas research for the National College'. National College for School Leadership [Online] Available at: http://dera.ioe.ac.uk/10431/1/download%3Fid%26filename%3Dsystem-leadership-illuminas-research.pdf
16 Illeris, K., 2014. *Transformative Learning and Identity*. London: Routledge.
17 Hattie, J., 2012. *Visible Learning for Teachers*. London: Routledge.

7 Case study of a whole-school approach to practitioner enquiry

Throughout this book I have used my own experiences in the two schools where I was leader to illustrate aspects of engagement with practitioner enquiry. I think it is really important for you to read about and understand our own journey with practitioner enquiry, so that you can see what this begins to look like in practice for school leaders and teachers. In Chapter 8, I look at different case studies of schools which have engaged with practitioner enquiry in other ways and for other purposes. I have read too much theory and research where I have struggled to match the main messages, principles, or findings to the daily activity of very busy schools, with all that entails. When I speak to teachers and school leaders a common response is along the lines of 'this all sounds great, but how do I/we fit this into everything else we have to do?' I understand those feelings, because they were very similar to my own at the outset of our own engagement.

In this chapter I hope to answer some of these questions, so that you can consider what practitioner enquiry could be for you, and in your setting. You will hear how we juggled the demands of everyday practice and activity, with a desire to do something different in terms of professional and school development. I am not saying you should, or could, lift everything we did and drop it into your school, or schools, and get the same or similar results. In fact, I doubt if we started again in the schools I led that we would get the same results. Time and people move on and, as I have said many times already, you have to start from where you are, not where you would like to be. What I do hope is that by reading about our journey in detail, it will help you in your own deliberations and on your own journey with enquiry. Each person's journey will be different, as will each school's, but the underlying principles and insights are transferable, and can help each person and each school on their own journey.

As you may remember, my own journey began some eight years ago. At that time, I was headteacher/principal of two primary schools in the Scottish Borders. These two schools, Ancrum and Parkside, were joined in a partnership whereby myself, my deputy headteacher (DHT) and our principal teacher (PT) had responsibility for managing and leading both schools. Children from Ancrum transitioned into Parkside after completing their Primary Five year of schooling, when they were about ten years old, so there was a connection already between both schools before we went into the partnership working model.

Parkside is situated in the town of Jedburgh, and Ancrum is in a small village, with the same name, some four miles to the north. During the time, when we had been engaging with practitioner enquiry, Parkside had a school population of around 350 pupils, including two to four nursery classes of 3- and 4-year-olds, whilst Ancrum had around 40 pupils on average, with no nursery provision. Parkside tended to have a little more of an itinerant school population with a small but steady flow of pupils in and out of the school over the course of any school year. Our staffing was relatively steady and consistent over most of this period of time. Though this did change in the last few years, due mainly to teachers having babies, and Parkside having a regular newly qualified teacher placement with us, for one year at a time. There tended to be ten class teachers in Parkside over this period and between two and three at Ancrum, as there was a significant difference in the size of schools. The number of classes did fluctuate over the period, from three to two at Ancrum, and from ten to nine at Parkside. Our nursery provision changed over the last two years, from four classes to two.

The pupil population at both schools was mixed in terms of demographics. Parkside was surrounded by a mix of local authority housing, private and some quite affluent housing and households. The Scottish Borders is quite a rural area, and Jedburgh and Ancrum are surrounded by the rolling Border hills, countryside and forestry. The River Tweed is a geographical and scenic feature that winds down through the Borders along the border with England. Farming and rural activity tends to provide a lot of employment, but Jedburgh also benefits from the location of a couple of quite substantial industrial manufacturing businesses which are economically vital to the town and are significant employers in the area. Tourism is also very important to the local economy and provides more employment opportunities in the town, and surrounding areas. Pupil and family demographics are very similar in Ancrum, though here there is an older population, which is becoming more and more common in smaller Borders' villages, and is impacting on housing and schooling in the village.

In Jedburgh, there was one other primary school, a little smaller than Parkside, and the children generally moved on to the small local secondary school, Jedburgh Grammar School, at the end of primary school, when they were 11 or 12 years of age. Though called a 'grammar' school, this was non-selective and was fully comprehensive in nature and organisation. The grammar school only had a cohort of around 250 pupils, so was quite small for a secondary school. But it still offered as full a curriculum as possible, often tailoring options to meet the needs of individual pupils, which perhaps larger secondary schools would find more challenging. All the primary schools, and the secondary, were part of the Cheviot Learning Community or Cluster. This linked them to another secondary as well as six more primary schools in Kelso for collaborative working and development activities.

I had become headteacher of Parkside in August 2007, then, following a re-organisation of the service, I was also appointed headteacher of Ancrum in 2008, as the two schools were organised into a new partnership model. Headteachers becoming leaders of more than one school was becoming a little more common at that time, driven mainly by financial pressures, lack of applicants for posts and a desire by the local authority to remove any teaching commitment for school leaders, so they were more able to focus entirely on the leadership and management of those schools. Having previously been a 'teaching-head' in another school, I understood the frustrations of that role, where you felt you were unable to fulfil either role, class teacher or headteacher, satisfactorily.

In my first year at Parkside I worked hard to build relationships and begin to change the culture of the school. The previous headteacher had been very traditional in her approach and was very directive in her leadership style. I didn't operate like that and very much wanted to flatten hierarchies, build trust and develop teacher agency. It took all of that first year to begin getting somewhere with this, as a lot of staff were suspicious of my intentions, also some were quite comfortable happy in being told what to do, as well as how they should do it. Anyway, I felt we were starting to get somewhere with moving the culture on in Parkside, when I found out I was going to have to lead another school as well, as the partnership with Ancrum was formalised. This brought another dynamic into the mix and I had to begin a similar process of culture change there as well. In addition, I had to be acutely aware of the sensitivities amongst staff, parents and community in Ancrum, who were determined for the school to maintain its unique identity, and not feel it was just becoming another three classes of a larger school in Parkside. The local authority provided me with another DHT at this stage to help manage the process, so we were able to allay fears and to demonstrate that both settings were still unique and that they would be learning from each other.

In that first year of the new partnership we all worked hard to develop staff and parental confidence in what we were trying to do, whilst working hard at maintaining the individuality of both settings. That first year was a very busy one for me, because I now had two of everything to attend and do. So, two parent council meetings a month, two school improvement plans, two lots of staff meetings, two lots of parents' nights, two Christmas performances, etc, etc. None of this was helped by the fact that I lived some 27 miles away from both schools, in an even more remote part of the Borders. But, we were also working at and thinking about how we could apply economies of scale between the two settings, bringing some aspects closer together or aligned, whilst still preserving each school's unique identity. It was a busy time with lots of challenges, but I actually enjoyed it all, figuring out how we could make it all work better for the benefit of all, but especially the learners in both settings.

As we bedded in the new arrangements at both schools, we were also very busy working on school development activities, most of which were related to our engagement with the relatively new Scottish Curriculum for Excellence (CfE).[1] We were very supportive of this new approach to everything we were doing in our schools. Although it was described as a new curriculum, it required us to look at everything, not just content. We were looking at new guidelines on curricular development, on assessment, on pedagogy, at planning, at partnership working, at reporting, and how we combined all of this to raise attainment and achievement, and support and promote the health and wellbeing of all our learners. As you can imagine this was a massive undertaking, made more so by the fact that it seemed everyone had 'directions' and 'support' they wished to provide us with about all of this. That might sound helpful, but all this help and support was being offered by people who had never had to work this way before themselves, and who seemed to construct their 'advice' and 'requirements' as they visited more and more schools who were actually working away at implementing the changes.

This only led to a confused and demanding picture becoming even more confusing and demanding for schools and teachers charged with bringing this new vision to fruition. Central to the ethos and principles of CfE was that this new curriculum would be developed from the ground up, based on principles that sought to develop Scottish learners as 'Successful

Learners, Confident Individuals, Responsible Citizens and Effective Contributors'. This was to be achieved by having learners who were actively engaged in the learning process, who would experience learning still based on knowledge acquisition, but who would also require the development of skills, aptitudes and attitudes that they would need to demonstrate the 'four capacities' mentioned above. This was described as the Broad General Education, and would run from pre-school through to S3 (third year) in secondary school. Learners would then move into an exam phase and structure, that was still to be determined at that time.

Because there was little idea of what all this might actually look like by those charged with overseeing its implementation, schools and teachers, were swamped by '*advice*' and '*guidance*', as well as demands and expectations, from both national and local bodies, to such an extent that we were all feeling overwhelmed by everything we were being told we had to do. The constant timescales being imposed on us for completion from those above us, and outside of schools, was a particular irksome feature to myself. Such direction, seemed to assume all schools were in the same place. They weren't, and never will be! CfE was quickly becoming a monster of compliance and tick-box approaches, that were leading to confusion and despondency for many in the profession, as well as reducing the original and well-intended impacts.

It was within this backdrop that we had decided ourselves, that something had to change, or CfE would be dead in the water, as would many staff and their initial enthusiasm for the new reforms. Added to all of this was our growing dissatisfaction around professional development activity as it existed at this time. This had traditionally consisted of a mixture of activities decided upon by teachers themselves, plus some others identified for everyone by the local authority, who were our employers. Common complaints by school leaders and teachers alike were that such activities kept everyone very busy, but were not linked to where schools were in terms of development, tended to be ad hoc, often one-size-fits-all, were not given sufficient time to embed and address issues, and, most damning of all, had little or no impact for learners. We all recognised that this situation needed addressing and had to change, otherwise we were letting down large swathes of our learners.

Both as a teacher and as a school leader, I had always read a lot and engaged with research. Everything that I read and experienced was telling me that the approaches we were using at that time, whilst keeping us all very occupied and busy, needed to change if we were to have more impact for our learners. I was reading about professional development that was collaborative in nature, situated in individual and school context, that impacted on teacher practice and which utilised research and evidence to bring about meaningful and embedded change which benefitted all learners. This was far from our own experience or situation, so I and the leadership team were determined to do something about it. We also had a responsibility for the wellbeing and effectiveness of our teaching staff so that they were better able to meet the needs of all our learners, and this was another responsibility we were very aware of and needed to tackle.

Whilst we were talking about this amongst the leadership team, one of my DHTs mentioned Dr Gillian Robinson from Edinburgh University. She said that Gillian was looking to work with schools who were interested in taking a new approach to both school and professional development. This sounded interesting, we already were aware of Gillian as she had been a DHT in a Borders school herself previously before moving into academia and initial teacher education. My DHT assured the rest of us that she was still very much grounded in practice and the practicalities of working in schools. We had all met and experienced academics and researchers who seemed to have little experience or memory of what it is like to work in a school every day, with the constant pressure on priorities and attention. Hearing that Gillian would not be like this was a positive start. We agreed to set up a meeting with her so that she could hear what we had to say about our issues and concerns, and we could hear her thoughts about how she might be able to help and support us with these.

The initial meeting with Gillian was very interesting and she listened sympathetically, and non-judgementally, to our issues and our concerns. She then told us that she thought she had an approach that might help us find a meaningful way forward. No mention of practitioner enquiry was being made at this time.

Staff had told us that they were feeling particularly concerned about aspects within the teaching of reading and writing, and that they would welcome some high-level support with this in school. This is Gillian's area of expertise, and she said immediately that she could help support staff with this. However, she was offering us more than just this high-quality support in one aspect of the curriculum. She said that if she came in to work with ourselves and staff, we had already decided that everyone needed to be part of this journey, then staff would have to do quite a bit of professional reading and engagement with research around the areas she would work on. We needed to understand, as school leaders, that we would have to create time for this, and the collaborative conversations that would be needed after they had read various papers or books. She indicated that she would ask, and require, staff to look closely at aspects of their own practice and how they were impacting on learning. They would also be asked to focus on a small group of pupils to gather data and evidence about the impact of changes they would make. All of this would be shaped to meet the needs of the two schools and the learners in them, taking account of context and point on their development journeys.

That initial scoping meeting was music to my ears, as well as to the rest of the leadership team. We agreed that Gillian would go ahead and draft up a plan for the following academic year. We would speak to teaching staff, and we would also consider the structural changes we would be required to make if we went ahead with any proposed plan. We would have to consider our school improvement plan (SIP), our collegiate activity time (CAT), resources in terms of money and time, and the local and national improvement priorities that were going to be imposed upon us from above. It was going to be quite a challenge to bring all these elements together, and we could already begin to identify some of the issues and challenges we would face should we decide to go down this radically different development road to ones we had previously wearily trod.

We spoke to staff. Laid out the issues we had all identified and been struggling with, and then told them of the scoping meeting with Gillian. We reassured them that we had not made any decisions, because this needed to be a collective commitment. We acknowledged that they needed to hear about, and question, the proposals, then to think about them before we reached a consensus. Many of the questions they asked initially concerned how I, and they, would deal with the outside pressures to keep doing lots of other things. I simply told them that if we thought this was the right thing for our schools, and our learners, I was prepared to defend that and protect them from any other pressures or workload demands from outside.

They agreed to meet with Gillian and hear what she had to say about how she could help and support us. Gillian sent me a rough outline of a plan for a year of engagement with her. We took this, and her, to meet all our teaching staff. She laid out the support she could give with the teaching of aspects of literacy, and the expectations she would have of them in return. She and I answered all their questions and concerns as best we could, then asked them to take some time to think about what was being proposed and the implication, then let me know if they wanted to take this forward. I thought the general response to that initial meeting with all teachers and Gillian was positive, but you don't want to count your chickens until people had a time to chat and think, without any direct influence from ourselves. A week later, we had another meeting with staff and they all said they wanted to go ahead and were really excited to have Gillian's input with their language teaching. We told them the next step would be for us to meet again with Gillian to firm up a plan for the year ahead and for us to consider the implications for our SIP for the next session.

I and the leadership team met with Gillian to firm up our plan. This was to involve Gillian attending a couple of in-service days, up to four of our collegiate activity time (CAT) meetings, which happened after school, one day a week, and to come into school for a few half days to work with us and teachers both in and out of classrooms. This was quite an amount of time from Gillian and the university, and there would be a cost to us, which was fairly high in comparison to previous one-off activities or development days. However, I had a plan for how we could meet these costs, especially as we were convinced about the level of support we would be getting and the impact this could have across both schools. We also agreed that Gillian's focus would be on supporting teachers with the teaching of reading, in various genres, as this was where the teachers were saying they would most like some initial support. She laid out, then we planned, how she would manage her input, as well as her expectations in terms of professional reading and dialogue from ourselves and staff. There was deliberately no mention of practitioner enquiry at this stage, as Gillian wanted to take small, but important steps, to where she thought we could be, and where she would like to help us get to.

I then took the plan to the teaching staff to seek their approval and views. They were very enthusiastic, and were keen that we start as soon as possible in the new school year. I pointed out the costs involved and explained that, if they wanted to give this new approach a start, then they would need to allow me to use all our continuous professional development (CPD) funding for this purpose. At that time, we received an annual allocation for CPD of about £125 per teacher, which was usually spent on their attendance on courses or activities identified for themselves. They immediately agreed to this. I pointed out that this engagement with Gillian was going to be our only action in our development plan for the next year, as we would be looking at all elements required through our focus on reading. I also said that the majority of our CPD time would be allocated to this work, and I would gatekeep and stop other agendas being imposed on us from outside. At that time, teachers were expected to carry out a notional extra 35 hours of CPD in their own time, and were expected to account for this each year, as part of the professional review and development (PRD) process. I told them that, because of all the reading they were going to have to do related to our work with Gillian, this would easily account for all these 'additional' CPD hours, and I would support this. I laid out the draft school improvement plan, to show them the time allocated for all this activity, which included protected time for them to work individually and collectively on this development. They were relieved to see what was in this, but were a bit sceptical if we would receive approval from the local authority for what we were proposing. I reassured them that this would be my problem, and I would sort this out, so that we gave ourselves the best conditions we could to help us succeed.

The next step was to firm up our school improvement plan and submit this to the local authority. I must admit that I used the system we had in place then to ensure that our plan went through with no problems. So, it was submitted just before the start of our summer break, which meant no one could challenge anything in it until we returned in August, that is if anyone actually bothered to read these plans at all. My view was, that if we had agreed as a staff to our improvement plan, based on our self-evaluation procedures, and this had not been challenged by anyone, that was it. This also gave us a level of protection from other demands being imposed from above. As the national and local priorities were around all the elements of CfE, and there was growing recognition that schools couldn't address everything at the same time, I believed the plan we submitted was easy to defend and explain if necessary.

We returned in August 2009 and, once the school year was underway, we began working on our new plan. We started with a CAT session with Gillian, followed by an in-service day in November, where we began to look at teaching and learning in aspects of reading, as teachers began to explore issues and research around this. Staff were enthusiastic and motivated during all our work with Gillian and one of the first tools she showed us, and which we read about, was miscue analysis, after staff had identified that they knew some learners were having problems with their reading, but they weren't sure what to do about this. Gillian asked the first of many challenging questions. 'How do you know they are having difficulty? What is the nature of that difficulty?' Staff really struggled to verbalise and provide useful evidence about what the nature of their concerns were. That led us into the use and consideration of miscue analysis. This was just the beginning of the challenges and provocations from Gillian, but they got us deeply thinking about our practice and how we could improve this to help and support all our learners.

At this early stage of moving towards practitioner enquiry we were very much taking a collective and collaborative approach. We were all looking at the same issues and elements of our curriculum, as Gillian helped demonstrate a model for tackling these. This was certainly necessary as we built our confidence and our understanding, supported by Gillian. The leadership team and I were focused on speaking to her regularly about issues, helping to manage the whole process, as we constantly tested the atmosphere, or 'mood music' as I call it, across both schools. This was important to the whole process and led us to one of our first, and most important, insights about the whole enquiry process. This is that the process has to be managed and, if necessary, stopped and steps retraced when required. Enquiry is not a simple step-by-step linear process of development, and school leaders and supporters need to recognise and understand this, then manage it appropriately. We reached a point early in 2010, that we were seeing that we had travelled a little too quickly with our new work.

Staff were so focused on the exciting work we had been doing with Gillian that they, and ourselves as leaders, had neglected other important areas of our practice or aspects of learning. We needed to stop a while and remind staff about these other areas of our work which still needed our focus. We had some very frank discussions about priorities for ourselves and our learners, and what was necessary to keep our work with Gillian deep and meaningful, but not at the expense of other vital areas. This taught us all a lot about managing the change process within an already very busy workload. You have to recognise this then adjust expectations, collectively and individually, according to changing circumstances, as well as the ebb and flow of a year in school.

The year progressed steadily, with a few hiccups, as we made good progress with our plan. I had few issues from our local authority as I was able to show that we were looking at all the aspects of curricular, teaching and school development in a connected way. We were looking at *pedagogy, planning, curriculum, assessment, attainment* and *achievement*, all through the lens of reading and language. We were also able to demonstrate how improvements we had made regarding learning in reading had also filtered through into other areas of the curriculum. Teachers soon discovered that when they gained insights about improving learning in one area, these could then often be transposed into other areas, with similar impacts. I got better at making this case as the year progressed, and I was able to fend off 'requirements' from outside by pointing out we were already doing this, or 'as it wasn't in our development plan, these would have to wait'. I think it was about then I developed a reputation with some as being 'awkward'. However, I believed in what we were doing, I knew all my staff were working hard at what we were trying to do, and that I needed to protect and defend them when necessary, to give them space to see and realise the possibilities.

One of my schools, Ancrum, was inspected by the HMIE in February 2010, and the managing inspector said he could already see the impact of our work, through conversations with the learners and inspection of their work. This was great to hear, as it was the first outside recognition or validation of what we were undertaking. Gillian and we were convinced that the learning experiences for learners were improving in both schools, and we had our own evidence and data to back this up, but it was good to get that recognition from an outside source that we were heading in the right direction, with positive impacts for all our learners.

As the end of that first academic year approached we spoke to staff collectively once more about what we had been doing and to gather their impressions. They acknowledged that the work had been challenging, more so for some than others, but that the results had been positive for them and their learners. We asked if they would like to continue our work with Gillian in the next year and the overwhelming response was that 'yes' they most certainly did. This was great to hear, but we understood one or two had some reservations, as they were finding the approach very challenging to them intellectually as well as around their sense of 'being' as a teacher. I was okay with this, indeed I expected it. They were all different people, with different strengths and at different points on their journey of development. But, what I was sure of was that every single one of them had developed and improved their understanding and practice to some extent. Some more than others, but they had all improved, and as a school leader, when you can look back over a year and identify all your staff have grown their practice, this is as much as you can expect of them all.

We had covered a lot of different genres in reading, and the learning and teaching of this during this first year of engagement. Staff now identified that they would like to turn their attention to writing during the second year. Gillian and I were fine with this, and drew up plans accordingly. We were able to provide a range of data and evidence to support the positive impact for what we had been doing, including simple studies of groups of pupils by teachers, and this had been acknowledged by the local authority representatives. We were still ploughing our own furrow but I think they were now quite interested to see how we got on as we progressed into another school year.

The school year 2010–11 started and this was the first time we explained or mentioned the term *practitioner enquiry*. Gillian had explained it to me towards the end of our first year. We determined that now was the right time to start talking to staff about this. We were still looking collectively at the same aspect of learning. But now Gillian wanted them all to focus more systematically on an aspect of this with a small group of learners, so they could collect more data about that particular group, as well as the impacts they were having on their learning. They were told they would be enquiring into their impact on learning with this group in particular, and that they would prepare a little report at the end of the year to share their insights and their work with colleagues. Obviously, some were a little reticent about this, but Gillian was great in reassuring them about the whole process and how she would be supporting each of them throughout the year with this.

One of the first inputs Gillian gave us in this second year was not about writing, but was around data collection techniques. We were all a little unsure of the ways we would be able to do this, whilst still keeping everything proportionate and manageable, but Gillian was able to show us lots of meaningful ways we could do this. We all appreciated and benefitted from the time spent on this key aspect of the enquiry process. Gillian introduced staff to all the key elements of an enquiry into practice, as well as giving them very high-level input around writing and genre. Gillian met with each teacher on an individual basis each term to check in with how their enquiry was going and to support them through the process. This second year was as challenging as the first, probably more so, as each teacher was having input around writing, but also having to carry out a deep enquiry connected to this as well.

It was during this second year that we noticed more and more visitors to the schools commenting on the number of conversations about learning happening around the schools. They said they heard these in corridors, classrooms and staffroom, often qualifying their observations by noting that it was unusual to see such spontaneous conversations happening so naturally. This was great to hear, and perhaps we had not spotted this, or its significance, ourselves as we were so immersed in the busyness of working schools. We were developing and enhancing the learning culture throughout both schools, which is a prerequisite for developing a self-improving school in my view. The other key insight and recognition in that second year was that we could actually achieve more, and in more depth, by *slowing down, not speeding up*. I had a conversation with a teacher in a corridor and asked her how she was feeling about our work. The interesting thing she said to me was that compared to the previous regime, before I had arrived, 'we do less but achieve more'. I pushed on this to find out what she meant, and she explained they were previously always very busy, but that nothing really changed, before they moved on to the next piece of busyness. 'Now, we seem to be doing less, but I feel I am having more impact for my learners, and the school, than we did before.' I had been as guilty, as the previous headteacher, of trying to do too much and too quickly, a common feature of school cultures. I now saw the power of slowing down and giving enough time for deep, embedded change to occur. A lesson I have applied in my leadership practice ever since.

At the end of year two, all the teachers shared the results of their enquiries with colleagues. How they did this was left to themselves. Some produced a PowerPoint presentation, some wrote a brief report, some made a poster and a couple had kept scrapbooks and used these. This was a very powerful CAT session as it allowed everyone to see, and reflect on, the work that had been going on across both schools, and for them to share gains and insights with each other. We made such a sharing session an essential element of every year's activities from that point on. What also happened, as part of our own self-evaluations we did at the end of that second year, was that staff indicated that they had used aspects of language learning as the focus for two years, and now wanted to turn their attention to learning in mathematics and numeracy. We readily agreed to this and arranged for a colleague of Gillian's, Dr Susan McClarty, who had expertise in this area, to come in and support the teachers with this. Gillian would still be supporting teachers with their enquiries, and it was agreed that they would all carry out an enquiry into issues around learning in mathematics.

Most decided they would like to focus on learning in problem solving and the children's ability to use mathematical skills and concepts to solve problems, especially in unfamiliar contexts. We also said that we would like each teacher to produce a *research poster* based on that year's enquiry. Again, we reassured them that they would be supported fully with these at all stages of the compilation of these posters. We wanted to have evidence for them, ourselves and others, as to the impact of the work they were engaged in, and the high-level of thinking and practice they were displaying. Gillian was to provide us with some templates so that these posters could be produced electronically, and we were going to have them professionally produced and reprinted by the university reprographics department. The results of some of these, including my own effort, are included in the appendix at the end of this book.

The impact for individual teachers of producing these posters and then having them produced professionally was fantastic. Teachers were so proud to see their work displayed in such a way and have its importance recognised and validated by other professionals. They were able to use these posters to share with their colleagues. In addition, teachers and I have used them as we have shared our work with other schools and to other audiences.

Towards the end of our third year we had attracted some interest for our work from the General Teaching Council Scotland (GTCS) and we invited some of their representatives into school to interview the leadership team, as well as teachers, about what we were doing and to assess the impact. They were able to provide a lot of information and further evidence about how staff were perceiving our work, but also on the impact for learners. This was all very positive and very informative for Gillian, our leadership team, the local authority and myself. These evaluations were also to lead to a little financial support coming our way from Education Scotland, which further helped us with our costs, including having both Gillian and Susan working with us over the course of this year.

Some interesting extracts from those interviews with different teachers by GTCS when teachers were asked about the impact of our work on their professional identity and practice, were as follows:

> I used to just sit there in a meeting and think what someone is going on about and you think oh ok [laughing] I actually don't know and I will just ask someone later what that means. All that has stopped for me and it's the same with my teaching anything I didn't understand, it all stopped and I started asking, that's what I did.

It gives you the increased confidence with the things you choose and the stuff you have difficulty with or find frustrating ... Because I knew I was doing my enquiry project and I had planned activities it made me far more rigorous with my formative assessment of the children, which I thought I had done.

I think the main impact on me from the professional enquiry is I have become more adaptable with my teaching, thinking about the lessons a lot more and thinking about the learning/teaching that is going on.

It is really hard to quantify it [laughing]. I think the fact is that George and Alison [DHT] are very open and there is an ethos in the school where it is ok to make a mistake, its ok to say you don't know, its ok to take a risk, its ok to try something out and if it doesn't work, no one is going to be critical. They are going to be saying 'ok so that didn't work, what could you do differently?'.

It's been different to any other CPD experience I have had and where its been useful is that it is based on what you are doing in your classroom and it impacts on the children in your classroom. Because you are doing it over time you have a chance to embed it into your practice.

The transcripts from these more formal interviews with staff demonstrate powerfully the impacts on the thinking and practice for the teachers involved, all of whom, at this time, were very experienced and had been teaching for a minimum of six years.

As a result of these evaluations, and the research posters they had produced, six of our teachers received professional recognition by GTCS, because of the high level of work and its impact, and received awards from GTCS as a result. Some of the teacher enquiries and their stories now feature on the GTCS website section that aims to help all teachers engage with practitioner enquiry.[2] They have used some of the posters and quotes from the interviews as well.

For the first three years of our engagement, we had definitely been led and supported by Gillian, but over that time we had all grown in knowledge, understanding and practice. This applied to myself, just as much as it did to our teachers. We were all in a completely different place in our understanding and this was the time we felt we would be ready to fly solo.

In year four, we reduced Gillian's official input into our work as my DHT and I now provided more of the support to individual teachers, as we better understood how to give such support. Gillian remained available to us for consultation and to check in with how we were doing, but it was important to us all that we made this work self-sustaining and embedded in the practice of both schools. We also had similar thoughts about our teachers, so in the fourth year they chose the focus of their enquiry themselves. Some chose learning in aspects of language, some in mathematics and one or two tried looking at specific learning issues that crossed different areas of the curriculum. This was the stage where I thought we were truly embracing practitioner enquiry in its purest form. Where each individual was beginning to look at aspects of learning, and their practice, identified by themselves, but were still doing this within collaborative structures, in order to help and support others, not just themselves.

In our fourth year, there was no expectation that teachers produced research posters to share with others, though they were still expected to be able to share their findings with colleagues. We, of course, continued with one CAT session where teachers shared their work, though we moved this to the start of the next session, as it gave teachers more time to consider how they presented their work, but it also started the new school year on such a positive note. I and my DHT had to devote more of our time to supporting individual teachers with their enquiries, but this was time well spent. It let us more deeply engage with the process of enquiry and it told us so much about individual teachers and the learning going on in their classrooms. It became another vital part of our monitoring and evaluation activities, though this was not its main purpose. This is another example of other gains for teachers, schools and their leaders from the engagement with the enquiry process, which are really a byproduct or consequence of such engagement, but which are none the less significant to all.

Another important point made by a teacher, during her interview with the GTCS when asked about her research poster was:

> It's a summary of your research, it's not the poster, it's the process that gets you to the poster, but it's nice to have one.

This is a key message about enquiry, it is really not about a poster or an ending, it's about *the process* as you develop an enquiring disposition towards your practice and impact on learning, Marilyn Cochran-Smith and Susan Lytle describe this as 'having inquiry as stance'.[3]

By the end of our fourth year, we had at least six teachers who had this inquiry as stance. The disposition was so embedded in their practice, thinking and professional identity, their way of seeing themselves as a teacher, that it became their default position for any issues or changes to their practice they wished to address. Part of my role became about stopping them from trying to go into every issue that came up in such depth, in order to help them manage the demands and their workloads.

Since that fourth year we have continued to further embed and develop our approach to practitioner enquiry. As with everything, this has not been without challenges and issues. One of the factors that leaders have to deal with is staff changes and turnover. What happens when new staff arrive, and what happens when staff move on? We had a small turnover of staff, mainly due to having newly qualified teachers (NQTs) allocated to us, as well as some staff on maternity leave. In our early years of engagement, it was quite easy to get new members of staff up to speed in what we were doing, especially when we had Gillian's input. As the years have gone on, this has become harder. We tended to give new members of staff, who would be staying for more than one year, a year to settle in and get to know and understand the school culture and ethos, then we would expect them to start developing enquiry approaches from their second year with us. Some engaged quicker than this as they tapped into the zeitgeist. It was helpful that NQTs often came from university where enquiry was common practice. Our local authority also required all NQTs to carry out an enquiry as part of their first year. This definitely advantaged those who were based with us.

When staff have moved on to other posts, I am pleased to see and hear that they have taken this approach and associated dispositions with them. How could they not? When they have changed their professional identities and practice, they are permanently changed. Some have helped their new schools to develop in similar ways. Others have found it more challenging, and have found themselves in schools which are not as far on in their development. However, they have the skills and experience to deal with such situations, and still use their new stance to inform their own practice and actions.

As enquiry has become more and more just part of how we operate and function, so have we been able to take on more system leadership roles in order to support others with enquiry. During our fourth year, I was asked to tour Scotland, with Gillian and representatives from the GTCS, to speak to school leaders about enquiry. This was part of a very early national engagement, through policy and structures, with enquiry approaches, and was perhaps too early for some of the audience. I have since worked with headteachers across Scotland, individually and in clusters, to support their own engagement. Teachers from our schools have worked with other local schools to speak about their journey and to offer support. We have had educators visit us from Germany, China and India as we have shared our work with them, as an example of how professional development, and our approaches to it, are starting to change and evolve in Scotland. I have also spoken to headteachers and researchers in the USA, England and Wales as part of the process of helping others to understand our own journey, and to hear about their own approaches and views.

In the next chapter, I am going to look at some other case studies, to help you see how practitioner enquiry can be used in different ways, and across different settings to further professional and school development. All of them have taken a different approach to the one we used, and each is no less interesting as a result.

Notes

1   Education Scotland, 2016. 'What is Curriculum for Excellence?'. [Online] Available at: https://education.gov.scot/scottish-education-system/policy-for-scottish-education/policy-drivers/cfe-(building-from-the-statement-appendix-incl-btc1–5)/What%20is%20Curriculum%20for%20Excellence
2   The General Teaching Council for Scotland, 2014. 'Practitioner enquiry'. [Online] Available at: http://www.gtcs.org.uk/SearchResent.aspx?search%20posters&Submit=GO
3   Cochran-Smith, M. and Lytle, S., 2009. *Inquiry As Stance*. New York: Teachers College Press.

8 Practitioner enquiry across contexts

Case studies furthering professional and school development

Introduction

From Chapter 7, where I looked at the journey with practitioner enquiry for me and the two schools I led, I now want to consider some more case studies. I think it is important that you read about different applications and iterations of practitioner enquiry by other schools, settings and leadership teams, so that you have a better picture of what this may look like for you and your own setting. In this chapter, I consider how enquiry has been used by schools and their leaders in order to develop the schools and individual teachers within them. They are all different to my own engagement, which is to be expected given that each setting is different both in context and on its particular point of development. None of these schools have used practitioner enquiry in a pure way, as laid out in the various pieces mentioned elsewhere in this book. All have taken a pragmatic view of practitioner enquiry and how they can use it to suit their particular context or the issues they wished to address. As a result, there are some common gains, but there have also been individual gains and failures. All of this is to be expected, as each setting reflects its unique characteristics. What we should all be wary of is the possibility that the systematic nature and principles of practitioner enquiry mutate into something else, where schools are calling what they are doing 'practitioner enquiry' when actually it has become something else. What that 'something else' is depends on the schools and how they view and use enquiry. It may well be that even these 'mutated' versions could be a step forward for particular schools and individuals. But, I would argue, the more we retain of enquiry in its intended form, the greater the positive impacts for all will be; and the further a model moves away from this, then the less the impact and the sustainability.

I would ask you to look closely at each of the schools, and their context, then look to understand the journey taken by each, the gains each school made, the challenges they had to overcome, the insights they gained about themselves, and their attitudes to professional development for teachers. Each of these case studies is different, but they are all set in a Scottish context. I have spoken to school leaders and educators who are engaged in similar approaches in other countries, and I am sure you may be able to find some closer to yourself. My advice would be to make contact with any schools that are engaged with this approach and begin a dialogue with them. This actually helps them, as much as it will help you. It is my experience that schools who are engaged in enquiry, and who have the cultures and ethos that support such approaches, are very open and welcome giving support to others taking their own first steps.

All of the headteachers and leadership teams I spoke to for these case studies, said they enjoyed the opportunity to talk about and discuss their work. This helped them understand further what they had been doing, but also to recognise the gains they had made, and how much they had moved on, as well as what they still needed to focus on, or where they were heading next. The focused conversations you have with colleagues are a key element of any enquiry process, and at any stage in that process.

The successes achieved by some of these case studies are mixed, as I have already said, this is to be expected as each is a different iteration, as well as each context being unique. However, I have always felt that we can learn as much, if not more, from our mistakes as from our successes. You can learn more about yourself and others, when things go wrong or are challenging, rather than when things go as expected. Some of those who have embraced enquiry achieved fantastic career and school-changing results, others struggled with the challenges. But all were continually learning. I think it is important you read about both experiences to help you with your own understanding, as well as to learn from others. The aspects that were not so successful taught the schools and their leaders a lot about themselves, and where they were at. School leaders and teachers gained insights that they would have lacked if they had not engaged. Every school moved their practice and their cultures on through engagement with enquiry, but perhaps some needed to spend a little more time on preparing the ground, in terms of their cultures and practices, before they plunged into practitioner enquiry. I have spoken to headteachers who said that the cultures and practice in their schools were so far from where they would like them to be, that they decided to dive straight in with practitioner enquiry in order to begin to change cultures and practices, with some staff almost dragged kicking and screaming into the process. It's an approach, but I wouldn't recommend it myself!

Anyway, let's learn about the stories from some of the schools I visited, or worked with, and see what they had to say, then you can make your own mind up about the lessons to be learned. Again, discussing your thinking with others can be very illuminating for all concerned.

Case study 1: Using enquiry in four small rural schools to create a mutually supportive network

In this case study, two headteachers, who each led two small rural primary schools, sought to develop a mutually supportive professional development network amongst the four schools they were leading. They had struggled for some time to support meaningful school and professional development because of their small size and relatively remote and isolated locations in the southeast of Scotland. Their aim was to develop a professional learning community amongst the teachers of all four schools, which was systematic and research-rich, in order to support teacher professional development, with the expressed aim of positively impacting on the learning of all the children in each of the schools.

Anyone who works, or has worked, in a small, and often quite isolated, rural setting will understand the difficulties, as well as the opportunities, to be found in such settings. Amongst the difficulties or challenges is supporting school and professional development when the load falls on such a small number of teachers and their leaders. In this case, the schools averaged 2.5 teachers per school, but the expectations and demands for these schools were no less than those for larger settings with more staff to share that load. There were no deputes, but most of the schools had a principal teacher as part of their management structure. Both headteachers had struggled for a number of years to develop the schools and their teachers, keeping the workload and expectations proportionate and manageable. Capacity was limited and the headteachers were wanting to explore ways in which they could increase that capacity by developing learning cultures, as well as support structures, amongst all four schools rather than one or two of them. Both headteachers were leading two small schools and had no teaching commitment. This had brought some advantages, compared to when the schools were operating individually with teaching-headteachers. However, they were still limited in capacity and speed of change because of their size. Teachers in all the schools had also expressed frustration in having so few colleagues to interact and collaborate with.

Both headteachers recognised and understood the power of collaboration, and had already established informal links to support each other. However, they wanted to develop these a bit more formally, in such a way that allowed all staff to collaborate and support each other across the four schools. They recognised school improvement as a social process, so they met with all the principal teachers to explore the concept of working together to mutually support each other in order to ensure benefits for all learners. The plan developed would involve teachers from the four schools coming together to work collegiately, and they would use practitioner enquiry as a vehicle to provide a common focus for collaborative and individual activity. Another key aim emerged during their discussions, that was to support and encourage teachers to engage with research and professional reading, which they did not do much of at the outset of their joint working.

They laid out their plan to the teachers in the four schools towards the end of the 2014-15 school session, aiming to start with the new approach in August 2015, when the schools returned after the summer break. For the launch event with all staff they invited myself and two colleagues from the General Teaching Council Scotland (GTCS) to come and speak to their teachers about practitioner enquiry and the power of collaborative working. We tried to make this high-level and engaging, and were pleased to hear from the headteachers how enthusiastic everyone was afterwards about the prospects of beginning to work in this way. The two lead headteachers were able to link this work further to the GTCS professional standards, and the professional update process,[1] as well as other areas of national policy, so that teachers were able to see the connections that were being made to all of these.

One of the headteachers, who was undertaking a fellowship programme at the Scottish College for Educational Leadership (SCEL),[2] wrote a paper about their work as they came to the end of their first year. In this, she refers to the impact of their work for all the schools and teachers. The two headteachers had effectively increased their management teams from themselves and a principal teacher or two, to two headteachers and three principal teachers. This immediately meant that there were more people available to lead and support development, as they shared the workload across all four schools. They were able to have monthly support meetings where teachers would share progress with their enquiries and discuss the professional reading they had been engaged in. A lot of this professional reading was found for the teachers by the headteachers, who also gave their teachers time to read and discuss this. They felt they had to do this in order to support teachers and to help scaffold the process.

They thought it too early at the end of their first year to judge the long-term impact for learners, but they could show evidence of the impact for teachers. They were enjoying sharing workloads and support, and being able to engage with more teachers than they had previously. They all appreciated having more colleagues to share and collaborate with in order to help themselves grow and develop their practice. Teachers had already made significant pedagogical changes in their practice and were a lot more focused on the impact of all their work for their learners. The only negative comment from teachers in their initial evaluations was that they would like even more time during the following session for collaboration and focused professional dialogue.

For the next session, 2016–17, the two headteachers planned that they would have to go on supporting all teachers with their enquiries and to keep evaluating the impact of this work, especially in terms of outcomes for learners. Following a request from another colleague headteacher, whose situation was very similar to theirs, they agreed to include another two schools into the network, so there would now be six schools in this collaborative network. This would bring in another headteacher and at least another six teachers. Whilst they recognised possible benefits of this development, they expected that this would present more challenges too.

Both headteachers were also beginning work to support other school leaders, through a local professional learning group, as they sought to develop system leadership roles, and the impact of their work was recognised by the local authority.

I checked in with them at the end of the school session 2016–17 to see how the work was progressing. The teachers at all the schools had recently had a collaborative collegiate activity time (CAT) session and had been sharing where they were with their latest enquiries. Teachers and headteachers, had been very positive about the ongoing impact to their thinking and their practice. Some quotes from written evaluations by school teachers were:

> great to share with and reassure one another

> good to share workload and have positive discussions

> we need to spend more time to implement developments rather than trying to assess impact when not yet fully embedded

> big is beautiful, but small is powerful

> found critical reading very motivating

When I interviewed the lead headteacher again she was feeling a little frustrated at the end of the second year. She and her colleague headteacher had both experienced a difficult year in one or both of their schools, when most of their energies and attention had been deflected onto behavioural issues and working with parents. She was feeling a little guilty that neither of them had been able to devote the time they would have liked in supporting teachers during their second year of enquiry. They had been joined by the other two schools and this had brought another dynamic into the joint-school working that they had to consider and deal with. Fortunately, teachers from the two new schools had been engaged in a practitioner enquiry training programme run by the local authority, so they quickly understood what they would need to do, and how to collaborate to achieve this. She and her colleague had managed to give teachers a little more time for 'learning visits'. In these, they visited each of the six schools over a number of Friday afternoons to hear about the work going on and to have discussion and sharing sessions led by the principal teachers. Because she and her colleague were being distracted by other issues, they felt that teachers had been required to take much more of a leading role themselves, but that they had stepped forward willingly into this. She had been so pleased to hear the fantastic discussions that had taken place at the recent CAT session, where teachers had been sharing the work around their individual enquiries.

She could now see great benefits beginning to emerge, and be developed by all the teachers. They had not all progressed or engaged to the same extent, she acknowledged, but she had recently carried out some professional review and development (PRD) meetings and quite a few had spoken about how they no longer felt on their own, they enjoyed sharing and hearing about different practices and that they were developing common understandings. She felt that there were definite signs of teachers developing enquiry as stance, saying that it was just how they thought about issues, and how they operated now. She noted that teachers' views around professional development had certainly changed. They no longer viewed this as being about going on courses. As a result of all of this collaborative activity, there had been benefits for all learners in that, their learning experiences had improved, and were more tailored to where they were in their learning. The work they were producing, and depth of learning, was improving across the curriculum. This had been identified and acknowledged by visitors to the schools as well. They had evidence of raised attainment in numeracy, pupil participation in their learning, and in the development of critical reading skills, which had formed the focus for a number of teacher enquiries.

Of course, there had been issues and challenges to overcome. She had already mentioned the issues that she and her colleague had experienced, which had deflected a lot of their attention and energies, but staff had stepped forward and continued to develop the practitioner enquiry model anyway.

Time was still a major issue. Staff were asking for more time to be devoted to joint working and collaboration, but she and her colleague were feeling under a lot of pressure to find time for local authority priorities as they moved into the third year. The lead headteacher is moving at the end of the school year. She was unsure of the impact a new headteacher would have for both of her schools, each of whom would also have a teaching commitment, on the joint working and the practitioner enquiry process. But, both she and I recognised, that this, and the issues she had faced over the year, were part and parcel of school leadership and operation. Which is why we need to ensure change to practices and thinking are embedded for individual teachers and schools. In that way, there is more chance that, when such issues come along to deflect our attention and our energies, we can get back on track as soon as possible because we know and understand this is the right thing to do.

It was interesting to note that, whilst there had been a lot of initial interest from her local authority in what they had been doing over the first year of their work, this had disappeared in the second year, as they had moved onto other 'things' to do. This to me, is another reason why we need to ensure we have self-improving schools and teachers, so that they are constantly working intelligently to improve what they do, rather than being at the mercy of shifting sands of support from local authorities or others. School improvement needs to be embedded and sustainable, so that issues like this do not deflect us from the direction of travel we have identified.

Looking at this model of using practitioner enquiry, I could see the benefits of its adoption to the schools involved. I do think it is too early to say they are there with the embedding of the approach, and the school leaders did talk about practitioner enquiry as though it was another 'thing' they were trying. It had been successful and they want to continue, but whether the approach is embedded yet, I am not sure. They have made great strides forward in quite a short period of time. However, it will be interesting to go back and see where they are in a few years times, especially given leadership and staff changes. Changing cultures in a large school would seem to be more sustainable, as teacher turnover does not have such a great impact. In a smaller school, it only takes one or two teachers to move on, to have massive impacts on school cultures, as you have to start afresh with a complete new staff.

Case study 2: A single primary school

This second case study centres on a single primary school which was led by a headteacher who had worked with me in the past as a DHT at the outset of my own journey with practitioner enquiry, and who had put me in touch with Dr Gillian Robinson from Edinburgh University. She was with us for our first two years of engagement with enquiry, so she understood and was completely aware of our own early steps. She also knew Gillian well and so it was natural that she would look for support from Gillian, and ourselves, when she sought to take a similar direction in her school. This school was also situated in southern Scotland, and had similar demographical characteristics to Parkside, one of the schools I led. The management and leadership in the school consisted of the headteacher and a principal teacher. Over the period of their engagement with enquiry, they had six mainstream classes and a nursery class.

The headteacher had taken over after a period of uncertainty for her new school, following the retirement of the previous long-serving school leader. She set about getting to know the school and the staff in her first months in the post, but quickly determined that she wished to use practitioner enquiry to improve learning and teaching across the school in order to raise attainment and achievement for all learners. Having worked with Gillian both in school, and at the university, having been so closely involved in our own journey with enquiry, this headteacher was well-versed in the process and principles of practitioner enquiry.

By August 2017, her school had just completed three years of engagement with enquiry and it is interesting to get the headteacher's perspective and thoughts on where they are now, as well as the perspective of some of the teaching staff. It is especially interesting to note how the approach most definitely worked for some of her teachers but not all of them, and to consider the reasons why this may be so.

Their engagement with practitioner enquiry was aimed at all teachers in an effort to improve learning and teaching in a way which was systematic and informed by research and professional reading. The first two years involved a lot of direct input and support from Gillian as she led a number of CAT sessions specifically on the process of carrying out an enquiry and supporting the teaching of reading, which was their common focus in the first year. Practitioner enquiry formed a major part of the school improvement plan, with time allocated for teachers to carry out tasks related to their enquiries, as well as having time out of classroom for one-to-one consultations with Gillian, the headteacher covering classes to allow this to happen. During this year, one teacher looked carefully at two children with selective mutism, one at boys who were reluctant readers, one at developing metacognition through reading, and another looked at developing reading comprehension through use of picture books. There were another two teachers, who were unable to engage with the enquiry process because of ongoing health issues during the year.

The headteacher noted the positive impacts on all the teachers involved. She acknowledged that some had engaged more fully than others, but all had grown their practice and their understandings in some way. One teacher had commented that he had liked that he had choice in terms of his focus, and received individual attention and support with this. She had noticed that he was more willing and prepared to do the reading required, which he expanded himself. She felt this was because he had identified his focus himself and was more motivated because of this 'ownership'.

During the second year, there was still input from Gillian, but this was focused less on CAT sessions and more on providing one-to-one support for teachers with their enquiries and with aspects of learning. There were three sessions on data collection and tools for achieving this. The headteacher noted that because the focus was on one-to-ones, and time had been allocated for these, she was now able to sit in on these sessions, which she found very informative. It had also been agreed that at the end of the school year, all staff would share and present their findings in the form of *'research posters'*. I, and a couple of teachers from Parkside and Ancrum, visited the school to speak to staff to share our own experiences with practitioner enquiry as a way of setting the scene for their own journey. The headteacher noted the positive impact of this contribution for her own staff and felt it gave the process more credibility as we showed how we had made it work for us and our learners.

The range of enquiries in this second year was quite wide and very interesting. One teacher, a newly qualified teacher (NQT), looked at working with parents to develop children's learning. The work she did was to lead to more meaningful engagement with parents across the school. Many of the insights she gained, and tools employed, were used later by teachers elsewhere in the school, and helped inform new policy and practice. Another teacher looked at using visual supports in story writing, for pupils who had good reading and word recognition skills, but who were reluctant writers. She developed a talking-frame for a particular child, using plasticine, developing dialogic approaches to the teaching of writing. She also looked closely at the impact of displays in supporting learning and was to go on and lead CAT sessions to support her colleagues with this work. One teacher also looked at the development of dialogical approaches to learning and did some very interesting work on using a 'story-line' approach in developing learning in maths-in-context. He observed that the results with this approach varied amongst the children, but there had been great progress and success by one child in particular, who had previously struggled in this area. The teacher produced his poster and used this to share his findings and insights with colleagues.

Another teacher looked closely at spelling and the development of useful strategies that would actually make a difference for learners, especially those who found spelling difficult. He worked with the learning support teacher to develop a range of useful strategies to support spelling and they produced a booklet to share with colleagues. Another teacher looked at number conservation and collaborated with a teacher from one of my schools, to develop some games and activities to support her learners with this. Another teacher looked at the development of metacognition amongst learners, and the range of strategies children possessed when working mentally with number. He introduced a systematic and more regular approach to mental maths activities giving the pupils more time to share orally the strategies they used. He helped them all develop a range of different strategies they could fall back on when working mentally with number. Though this teacher moved on to another school, he was able to complete his research poster to share with colleagues and had definitely improved his practice and understanding in this area of learning. One of the teachers who had been ill the previous year, began looking closely at characterisation in reading, using some of the principles of enquiry. The headteacher thought that carrying out a full-scale enquiry, and the production of a poster was going to be too big a step for her, but she readily shared her insights verbally to colleagues at their sharing CAT session.

From all of the above stories, we can see how teachers were beginning to develop their own thinking and their own practice, but we can also see how the work they had been engaged in was having positive impacts for colleagues across the school, and beyond.

This school has just completed the third year of its engagement with practitioner enquiry. The approach has continued for most teachers, again personal circumstances and staff changes have led to some adjustment of expectations were necessary for one or two. But the nature of the enquiries is really interesting. One enquiry has involved a teacher looking at evidence from developmental psychology to better understand motivation in learners. He has explored theories and research around why particular children become disengaged from their learning, and has been able to use this to enable him to better support one of his learners in particular. What to do when children experience blocks in their writing was the focus of another teacher's enquiry. He has worked all year to explore why some children find writing more difficult than others, and how to support them, with benefits for all learners in his class. Another NQT focused on children's participation in exploratory talk through the use of picture books. She used a detailed rationale for her work and was able to present her results not only to colleagues in the school, but with other NQTs across the local authority. Finally, a teacher looked at a group of girls in her class who she felt had negative attitudes to work and closed mindsets. She developed a games-based approach in maths to improve their engagement, and to help them see that they could successfully engage with this learning.

These are a rich array of different enquiries over the three years, and some of the work and insights gained have been of a very high level. I asked my colleague to assess the overall impact of this engagement with enquiry and she was very honest, as well as informed, in her assessment. She said the impact had been greatest for the teachers who had been at the school for the full three years of engagement. They had seen tremendous professional growth and she could definitely identify three who had developed 'inquiry as stance' as identified by Marilyn Cochran-Smith and Susan Lytle.[3] I think this is a good return for three years of engagement, with a staff of six class teachers and a part-time support for a learning teacher. The headteacher felt all other teachers had also developed their practice, but for various reasons, had not progressed as much as others. This reflected my own experiences. She felt there had been big benefits for individual teachers and their learners, which was the main point of their engagement.

The teachers themselves provided some very powerful comments and thoughts as to the impact of their work:

> This has helped me to develop as a teacher, getting at more definite things that are needed rather than pluck ideas out of the air … I am more aware of what it is in my practice that needs to develop and can focus on these with the help of professional reading … gives you a way into the answer, through trying new ideas but with better understanding.

> Participating in practitioner enquiry heightens one's professional status. The teacher is recognised as somebody who can be trusted to undertake significant research and enquire into his/her practice to make a difference to the children's learning experiences … They [strategies] are very important for comprehension of a text … However, the strategies apply to life in general, for example making connections between new information and old, inference, monitoring understanding, these are very valuable teaching tools … We often make assumptions about what children know/can do.

> I would always start with professional reading now, once I had identified an issue or question in my mind. Practitioner enquiry has changed the way I work from now, rather than trawl the CPD directory randomly for interesting courses.

What these teachers show is their changed perception of what and who they are as teachers, as well as their approach to professional development. Every single one of them has grown and developed over the three years of engagement. Every one of them has a systematic and clearly understood approach for continuing to develop their practice. Each one of them can demonstrate improved outcomes for all their learners, and for particular individuals. This is backed up by the data held by the headteacher that shows rising attainment and achievement across her school. She describes the culture of the school as one that is 'using research to build understanding and improve outcomes for learners.' She talks of the learning culture in the school being changed for the better, with teacher agency continuing to grow. I asked her what she thought were the important conditions necessary for practitioner enquiry to succeed and she said, 'go slowly, provide and get support, provide time and space for teachers to engage, and keep your focus small'.

Knowing this colleague, and her school, as well as I do, I am able to endorse many of her findings. There is no doubt that she has made an impact of changing the culture within the school, and getting teachers to focus on their practice to improve learning experiences. Some of this has been at a very high level, but was not so for others. She faced some opposition and entrenched views and practices. However, she was committed to drive the improvements through that she believed the school needed. There is no doubt that those who were open-minded and embraced what she was trying to achieve gained the most from the process. The ones with the fixed mindsets made some progress, but this was reluctant and not properly understood by them. This will remain an issue for many school leaders, and they will have to decide the right way forward for them and in their context. This headteacher could have given more time to developing collaborative working and cultures, and she may have achieved more. As a school leader, you have to decide on how much time you give to preparation and setting the conditions to give enquiry the greatest chance to succeed and be embedded. For some teachers and leaders, you may never reach that ideal state, so some school leaders will have to go with it, accepting the gains you get, as well as the challenges, as a result.

Case study 3: A secondary school experience

In this case study, I look at a secondary school situated near Edinburgh, Scotland. This school currently has nearly 900 pupils and a teaching compliment of around 70 teachers. The school is in an affluent locality serving a coastal town and surrounding area on the Firth of Forth within easy travelling time to Edinburgh. With the building of new housing in the area, it is expected that its school population will grow by a further 50 per cent in the next few years.

I am often asked by secondary school staff and headteachers how they can use practitioner enquiry, as they point out the difficulties faced by these much larger settings. I understand that the challenges of adopting such an enquiry approach can be greater in a secondary school setting, but they are not insurmountable. There are strategies that the secondary sector can use to get where they would like to be. In my view, the principles of high-level learning and teaching experiences, and how you may look to develop these, are the same in both primary and secondary settings. I also believe it is incumbent on teachers and school leaders in both types of settings to be trying to get better and improve what they do, in order to improve learning experiences for all learners. There may be considerable differences in terms of school structure and organisation, but the basic fact still remains that teachers and their performance are *the* crucial element in the impact of, and improvement in, secondary schools, just as much as they are in primary ones.

I met with the headteacher and her deputy, who had responsibility for professional development as part of his remit, to talk to them about how they took forward enquiry in their setting. I was fascinated to hear how they had paved the way for such engagement, and how they had overcome difficulties related to the size and structure of their setting. The school is organised into faculties, each with a faculty head, and there are two DHTs and the headteacher who form the senior leadership team.

Their journey to where they are now really began six years ago when the headteacher recognised that she needed to change and develop the learning culture in the school. She wanted to create a culture that was more collaborative and focused on learning and teaching than she had found it when she took over. They had begun this process by getting teachers to work in trios, across faculties, to help promote collaboration with a focus on learning and teaching. They found that their early attempts to promote such collaboration were a good, and necessary, step towards where they were wanting to be, but that those early attempts did lack focus, and it was difficult to pin down what had actually been achieved for learners through them. The main outcomes seemed to be that teachers got to know each other better and were having some general conversations around learning and teaching. They needed more focus.

As part of his Flexible Route to Headship (FRH) course, which is a qualification that many aspiring headteachers take part in across Scotland, the DHT had been looking closely at what really worked and made a difference in professional development. He was particularly taken by the impact of coaching and professional learning communities (PLCs)[4] in promoting collaborative professional learning that would impact on individual teachers, their thinking and their practice. As a result, the trios of collaboration turned into PLCs, which teachers could voluntarily decide to join, from across the different faculties. These were to be focused on *'problems'* the teachers identified in their practice. The use of this term caused a few issues for the DHT, as some teachers took umbrage at the use of this term and some barriers went up as a result. He learnt a lot from that initial experience. The PLCs were intended to help shift the culture, so that teachers, and school leaders, recognised that they needed to be constantly looking at their practice and trying to improve this. As Dylan Wilam has said 'not because they were not good enough, but because they could get better'.[5]

The headteacher and deputy saw the formation of the PLCs as the first step towards what they called 'collaborative professional enquiry' amongst their teaching staff. The senior management team were well aware of practitioner enquiry and its place in the professional standards for teachers and school leaders from the General Teaching Council Scotland (GTCS).[6] They read more about enquiry and used the GTCS website as another resource for further information. The DHT had also attended a conference with Alistair Smith[7] focused on developing coaching cultures in schools. As an outcome of this, it was arranged for all staff to attend an introduction to coaching session, provided by the local authority. About half a dozen staff also took part in a series of sessions with Mark Priestley and Valerie Drew from Stirling University who were working across the local authority and schools focusing on collaborative enquiry.[8] This support, combined with the leaderships team's knowledge, helped other teachers in the school with little understanding of enquiry to understand the process and its systematic nature.

The leadership team now had a vision for professional development across the school, which was to develop a culture 'where teachers were collaborating, observing and coaching, as they enquired into aspects of their practice' as the headteacher described to me. Both the DHT and the headteacher felt that having external input and support was important in giving such development validity and credibility amongst staff. 'It wasn't just us saying this.' The DHT recognised that he may have pushed a little too hard at the start for people to sign up for a PLC, as he was feeling under pressure himself at that time to show what he had been doing, and the impact, for his FRH course. When he gave teachers an evaluation to complete at the end of the first year of operation of the PLCs, two of the questions he asked them were: 'What had been the impact? And, how pressurised did they feel to take part?' This was very brave of him, but it also gave him a powerful insight into how such collaborations should work. He discovered that he could correlate quite easily the teachers who said they felt the most pressurised to take part, with those who struggled to identify any positive impacts for learners! This convinced him and the headteacher that engagement in such high-level professional development activity has to be willing and voluntary for the greatest impact. Winning hearts and minds is vital if you are going to see the greatest impacts.

I was struck by their openness and honesty during my visit. The DHT referred to the well-known Thomas Edison quote, "I have not failed. I've just found 10,000 ways that won't work," where he talks about the number of ways he's found for light bulbs not to work. He said that was how they now felt about a lot of professional development. They had discovered lots of ways that professional development didn't work and had little impact for learners. But, they saw this as a necessary part of the process of them coming to a better understanding about what does work and would make a difference.

The PLCs have continued operating and the leadership team and teachers keep tweaking and improving how these function in the light of each year's experience. The DHT felt he was frustrated at times that all the teachers didn't engage or move their practice and thinking at the same rate, but understood that this was always going to be the case. Each teacher was at a different place in their professional development, and each worked in different ways, so they would never develop in the same way or at the same rate. He had learnt to accept the realities and the limitations of the approach, or any approach. Teachers had said they still felt they did not have enough time for PLC and enquiry work, so the SIP for next session had been changed to give them more time. The headteacher said they had to do this to demonstrate their commitment to the process of enquiry for professional development, then to allow the teachers the time necessary to carry it out properly. They had also created an online staff area for professional development activity and resources, this provided more information and links regarding enquiry and professional development that they and teachers could add to as they went along. I thought this was a great way to develop a whole-school resource for staff that would be useful to them all, as well as new members of staff coming into the school.

I asked them if they were able to quantify the impact of the PLCs and practitioner enquiry. They immediately identified that many of their teachers had made changes to their practice and their thinking as a result of enquiries. They had changed their practice to improve learning experiences for their learners, and they better understood how to address issues of concern that they had identified, by using the enquiry process and collaborating with colleagues. Some of the individual enquiries had scaled up and had impacted on other teachers across faculties. They illustrated this with two examples.

In one a teacher of French looked at how she gave feedback, and what learners did with her feedback. As a result of changes she made, and the positive impacts these had for learners, her strategies were now being used across the faculty. Also, other faculties were beginning to implement similar changes too as a result of her findings. In science, one teacher had looked at how he could support learners with note-taking and how to improve this. The changes he had made had impacted positively on learners and his strategies were now being used by other teachers after he had shared his findings with colleagues.

The school leadership thought it vital that teachers from the various PLCs to share their work and their insights with colleagues. Each year a CAT session is arranged where this can happen. These are quite informal, with teachers sharing what they have learned with colleagues from other PLCs in any way they feel appropriate or are comfortable with. Both senior leaders also recognised this was not about 'sharing good practice' but more about *sharing principles and insights* that colleagues might find useful to their own thinking and practice.

The culture across the school had changed and developed as a result of their PLCs taking forward collaborative, and individual, enquiry. The DHT described it as a 'normalising of discussion about pedagogy' and noted how often conversations were heard around the school about learning. Colleagues were often overheard engaging in spontaneous discussions around learning and this was a reflection of the deepening learning culture that had been developed. He understood the power of individuals coming to recognising themselves the aspects of their practice they could develop and improve, and how when this happened deep embedded change happened.

He thought a key approach was to 'prise apart the person and the practice'. He noted how many teachers, especially the most experienced, saw their practice as an extension of themselves as a person. So, any question being raised about their practice, was seen as a question about them as a person. It was important that teachers understood such insights were not a questioning of them as individuals, but a focus on how they could develop their practice as part of a career-long development process.

As a result of individual teachers improving their thinking, and developing their practice, there were improvements across all areas of the curriculum for the learners in the school. The learning experiences were developing and improving in each faculty, as a consequence learning was improving and learners had deeper understandings. The DHT also acknowledged that the teachers were being completely open with students and parents about what they were doing in looking closely at their practice and how they could improve this. This meant many of the teachers were modelling true professional learning for all their learners, so that they better understood that learning continues after school or university, and is something professionals engage in throughout their careers.

Teacher attitudes to professional development have changed too, and they understand better the process of continually examining their own practice and taking positive steps to develop this further. They have a reconceptualisation of what it means to be a professional educator, not accepting of the view of teaching as merely a technical activity that anyone can be trained to do. It requires high degrees of professionalism and intellectual rigour, dealing with complex social and intellectual activity, and requires teachers with high degrees of reflection, enquiry and agency.

Whilst participation in the PLCs and professional enquiry remains voluntary for the next session, the expected uptake rate by teaching staff is expected to be in excess of 50 per cent. This professional development will remain a priority for the school and the leadership team, as they are convinced it is making a difference to all that they do. They expect more teachers to come on board as they see the impact for learners and colleagues. If they are not part of this process, they do still have to demonstrate their commitment to professional development, and how this is impacting positively on learning and learners. They also have to commit to contributing to the school improvement plan priorities. This year these were to raise attainment in literacy, improve the mental well-being of learners, in addition to the PLCs and enquiry.

Whilst I have included some quotes from the headteacher and her deputy in the narrative above, I think it is also useful to hear from teachers who have participated themselves as well.

> The big thing is that it made me take a window of time to think about a specific bit of my classroom practice. It's normally so hard to make that time, with all the pressures on us teachers.

This was part of the feedback for one teacher, and points not only to the impact, but also to how the process of enquiry is not about looking at everything you do and changing it, but rather a process of reflective, small steps to improvement.

From another teacher's enquiry came this insight:

> It was when [a student] asked me for more options that I suddenly realised I could produce marking templates to allow them to evaluate their own essays.

Another noted that they:

> felt clear that coaching had been very successful in reframing the issue of the girls' lack of motivation, from 'what is wrong with them?' to 'How can I change my practice to improve their motivation?'

An honest and powerful insight by this particular teacher, which also points to the power of coaching running alongside an enquiry, as another tool for helping teachers reflect on, and pin down, issues.

Hearing a pupil talk about homework and her attitudes to it, made another teacher reflect:

> talking to her, made me reflect on the homework I give out to my classes and made me think about whether it is really positively impacting on my pupils' learning? If a pupil is constantly achieving very low marks in homework tasks is there any way to improve the situation, how can I motivate my pupils to see the benefits of homework?

This reflection, and identification of an issue for the teacher was to lead into an enquiry, and professional reading around the issue. She identified steps which could be implemented to try to improve this issue for all learners. Her pupils liked her ideas and they were all motivated to try them out, with a resultant improvement in homework tasks and motivation. The DHT had visited this class and the teacher to speak to her and learners:

> Regardless of the evidence of impact on attainment (which was strong), it was clear to me that every pupil in the class had taken on board the message that notes matter.

He could see that she had identified one change to her practice, that was having significant impacts for her learners.

I feel that the impact of the changes made to professional development can be seen in the narrative above. Both the headteacher and the DHT commented that often it was difficult to pin down, quantify and measure some of the important differences that had occurred. These were often small, almost imperceptible changes to thinking, attitudes, practices and dispositions. But, they had no doubt the quality of the learning experiences for all in the school were improved, and would continue to do so. They deeply understand the process they are engaged in, and the time required for this, but are committed and convinced as to its efficacy. Their role is to support and provide time and structures so that teachers can engage meaningfully in a process that they see as transformative for individual teachers and the school. Such thinking is also required of school leaders in primary settings. The scales are larger in secondary settings, but the principles, and the gains, remain the same.

Case study 4: Another primary story

Another primary school sits in a small town in the south of Scotland and has its own unique setting and context. This school has been known as a 'grammar' school for many years, though it is completely non-selective and is managed by the local authority. It is situated in a quite affluent rural township, with a high proportion of high-value private housing, with some local authority and social housing on its outskirts. Some two hundred yards or so from the school sits a private school that attracts fee-paying students and their families from across the region and beyond, primary and secondary. The primary school in this case study is operated by the local authority and has a very active and vocal parent engagement. The school itself has been growing considerably over recent years as new private housing has been built within and around the town. The main building is an open-plan one, with few walls or corridors separating classrooms or learning spaces. Because of recent growth, the school took over the former old primary school which was being used by the local authority, to provide space for further classrooms. The school population has continued to grow and is not far from requiring a complete rethink and possibly a new school built to meet this growing demand. The building of a new railway link to Edinburgh, has only pushed on demand even more, and is contributing to further growth.

I have known the headteacher for many years and she has always been interested in the work we have been undertaking with practitioner enquiry. We used to catch up at headteacher meetings and conferences, and she would always ask about how we were getting on. For a number of years, she had told me that she was interested in developing a similar approach at her own school, but that the school wasn't ready for what we were doing yet. Since she had arrived at the school, she had been working hard to develop the learning culture and to work with staff to help the school move forward. She had felt there were crucial and more important basic issues that she needed to address before the school, and its teachers, would be in a place where they could engage with and benefit from using practitioner enquiry. I respected and understood her position, but always said to her that, when she did feel she was ready to take this forward, I would be more than willing to help and support in any way I could.

She got in touch in 2016, towards the end of the 2015-16 session, and said she now felt they were in a position to move forward with practitioner enquiry. She had a new deputy headteacher (DHT), who had worked at one of the schools I led, as an acting principal teacher and understood what we had been engaged in. She felt his input would help support what they were looking to do and she was wanting to see if a couple of my teachers and myself would be available to come across to speak to her staff at the start of the next session. This we did, and my principal teacher, another class teacher and myself visited the school for a CAT session and to introduce practitioner enquiry to the staff.

The fact that we had both teachers and myself there helped considerably. I started with the high-level introduction to, and the research base lying behind, practitioner enquiry. I told them about what the process was, what it looked like and identified some of the key elements and expectations in this level of professional development. I think they might have been put off if I had been the only one speaking to them because some of them said immediately things like, 'this is going to be like being back at university' and 'where we going to get time to do all that, and everything else we have to do?' I tried to reassure them, supported by their headteacher and DHT and my two members of staff. But, it wasn't until the two teachers were able to describe what the process looked and felt like for a teacher, and the impacts it had made to their thinking and their practice, that the teachers stopped panicking, and recognised the benefits and gains they might find for themselves and their learners. My headteacher colleague was also able to step in and reassure them about how time would be created in all their CATs and in-service days for them to work on their enquiries and be supported with these. I, and my two teachers, also offered to be there, or at the end of a telephone, to help and support in any way we could.

I must admit their initial reaction can be a common one, when people first hear about an engagement with practitioner enquiry, especially from a headteacher or principal. The theory and the details can seem quite daunting for many, particularly if it is presented, or understood as, just another 'thing' to do on top of everything else. But, once they hear and see the practicalities of that engagement, and understand that this is a new way of thinking about, and carrying out, school and professional development, many of their fears and apprehensions fall away.

I was reassured to hear from my colleague that, after this initial meeting, staff were overwhelmingly supportive of moving forward with practitioner enquiry for their own professional development, and in their own context. They were going to work on what the focus of their enquiries would be, supported by the DHT and herself, and they were all looking forward to seeing the impact, during this first year of engagement. I was equally interested to see how this had all progressed during their first year.

I re-visited in June 2017 to hear about that first year and to find out what had worked, and what had been the challenges for all involved. I was to meet with the headteacher and her DHT, but unfortunately, she was called to cover a class, which I am sure a lot of headteachers will recognise as a common scenario, so most of the feedback was provided by the DHT. However, I had forwarded some initial questions, and they had had some time to discuss these before my arrival, so that the headteacher was able to contribute to their evaluations.

Though they were only at the end of their first year of engagement with practitioner enquiry, and various events during the school year had threatened that engagement, they remained upbeat and positive about its impact for all in the school. This school has thirteen classes, a couple of which were covered by job-share arrangements between two teachers. They had another two part-time curriculum support teachers (CSTs) who all took part in the practitioner enquiry engagement. At the commencement of the year, they had some staff who had previously engaged with practitioner enquiry as part of their own professional development activities. But, this was the start of a process that would involve the whole school.

They now felt that they needed an approach to staff and school development that offered something for all staff members, and which could be differentiated according to where each member of staff was in their professional development journey. Some were just starting out as newly qualified teachers (NQTs) and others were very experienced and were perhaps feeling 'we have seen it all'. The teachers and school were generally recognised by the local authority, and Education Scotland, as displaying high levels of practice, the headteacher and her deputy had spent time developing a collaborative culture that sought to promote learning for all.

After the initial input from myself and teachers from my schools, which they saw as important in setting the scene and giving the approach credibility with staff, each member of teaching staff had identified a focus for their enquiry. The headteacher created time in the school development programme for teachers to work on their enquiries and they had four CAT sessions over the school year where they shared what they were doing and updated school leadership. Practitioner enquiry was one of three main priorities in their school improvement plan (SIP). The other two were: to develop a new school vison and aims statement; and to raise attainment and achievement in literacy and numeracy. I could immediately see how practitioner enquiry could support these other two priorities, and so did the headteacher and her deputy over the course of the year.

Further support over the course of the year was obtained via the GTCS website[9] information on practitioner enquiry, as well as professional reading sourced by the school leadership and teachers themselves. There were two NQTs and they, along with all other NQTs in the local authority, had to carry out an enquiry during their probationary year. They received additional support via the local authority, though they felt this was confused at times, as the support was being organised by the authority, but delivered by external personnel. However, they were receiving ongoing input, and they were able to help support more experienced staff who knew very little of the practitioner enquiry process.

The DHT admitted she and her depute had not been able to provide as much direct support as they would have liked during the year for various reasons, but they had still achieved their main aims for the year. These had been to get teachers engaged with practitioner enquiry as high-level professional development, and to have them positively motivated by the process. They felt they had achieved this and more. They had faced a level of resistance initially, mainly amongst older members of staff, but that once staff had become engaged in the process, all staff had become very enthusiastic and wanted to continue next year and beyond. I asked how they achieved this with those staff who showed reticence or resistance, and the depute told me it was a question of 'just sticking with it, and when doubters began to see the positive impacts for learners, they were happy to engage'.

I asked him if they could quantify the benefits that had accrued as a result of their engagement, and he immediately pointed to the impacts for individual pupils who had been struggling. He felt it was too early to say what the long-term impacts would be for all learners, but both he and the headteacher had seen and documented improvements in learning experiences, attainment and achievement for some pupils already. He noted that the leadership team and teachers had all commented on and noticed how 'small inputs had produced really big impacts for learners'. Teacher confidence had really improved over the course of the year, both in the process and its impact. There had been positive impacts for their learners, themselves and the school. Teachers have already said they want to continue next year, but that they need more time for their enquiries and to collaborate and share with each other.

He spoke of a teacher who had enquired into engagement in reading with boys, and as a result of this the school had listened more to learners about what they like to read, and had replenished reading resources on the back of this. This was an example of how one enquiry had impacts for all teachers, and more learners. Another had focused on behaviour. The insights gained, and strategies used, from this had been shared with all staff: 'if another teacher comes across the same or similar issues, it means we have ideas and strategies they can use that have been tried before in our school, and worked'. He qualified this by stating that there are no guarantees the strategies will definitely work again, with different pupils, but at least teachers had a starting point.

Teachers still lacked confidence in being able to collect data and evidence to show the impact of their interventions. He said they had talked about this, and they did have data, but were unsure as to its validity in backing up their professional judgements. This would be something they would look at with teachers over the course of their second year. He also identified that the leadership team had to prioritise the discussions and dialogue around practitioner enquiry next year. When teachers wanted to talk about aspects of their enquiries, he felt that it was important that he and the headteacher spent the time on these conversations, and not let themselves become sidetracked as much as they had been during the first year. Staff had commented that other 'things' were still deflecting them all from their enquiries at times, and that their enquiries should be given priority over these other 'things' that might be parachuted in. In the new professional development timetable, they have tried to identify and protect time for enquiry and dialogue. Discussions about enquiry progress are to become a standing agenda item in meetings about pupil progress between teachers and school leadership.

I also asked him about the conditions he thought were necessary to successfully implement practitioner enquiry. He identified three. The first was the development of a culture of learning. He felt they had this in place before their engagement, but that practitioner enquiry had enhanced this further. He identified conversations about learning that were happening across the school, in lots of different situations as just part of what happened now. The second condition would be that there needs to be a clear focus on practitioner enquiry, and that this should be reflected in the SIP and professional development activities and programmes. They recognised they needed to give more time for this. The third condition would be that time has to be given to share enquiry work, ensuring that value is given to the process at all levels, with gains and insights shared across the school community. He finished by stating that in their view practitioner enquiry is an incredibly powerful tool. 'We feel so positive about where we are on our journey and can see that it will have positive impacts for our learners and practitioners.'

We finished by looking at written evaluations completed by teaching staff about their year of engagement with practitioner enquiry. The depute noted that not every teacher had gained as much from their engagement as some. I reassured him that this was normal and reflected my own and others' experiences as well. I include some of the teachers' comments from their own evaluations below.

Teachers were asked to identify ways in which practitioner enquiry had impacted on their learning and teaching:

Engagement in the process of taking a research based approach to a problem.

It has made me think about the process of teaching, self-assessment, meeting learners' needs through doing this, and the importance of recognising gaps.

1:1 learning conversations with a pupil to find out more about her thoughts on learning, and the strategies she uses. Implementing elements of choice into teaching and learning.

Has encouraged me to be more reflective.

Understanding pupil difficulties – complexities and exploring strategies. Realistic – doing what you can do within the demands of class.

Allowed me to have one to one conversations with a child, so I know exactly how he feels and what he thinks his next steps are to progress further.

Made me more aware of the needs, drive and motivation of more able readers and the need to give them some ownership in taking their learning forward.

The teachers were then asked to identify the impact their enquiry has had for learners:

Three pupils now writing without any adult support.

Learners are developing their understanding of their learning and the importance of meeting their own needs by choosing a self-assessment technique which suits them.

Confidence – a pupil has told me she is now proud to show off her work. Better relationship with pupil, better understanding of learner and needs.

One pupil has become more confident in his own abilities/more keen to participate.

Pupil less anxious, has more time allocated to tasks when required.

Some other learners have followed the 'finger guide' to number reversals. Also used to patterns with success.

Greater engagement from less able/less motivated individuals when outside, particularly with hands-on learning.

Every single one of the teachers also expressed how they felt their confidence had grown over the school year. They were more confident in the process of enquiry, they had increased confidence in themselves as teachers, and their ability to identify then address individual learning needs as a result of their enquiries. I think there are some pretty powerful messages and insights here from these teachers, emerging from one school year's engagement with practitioner enquiry. I think it is messages like these from practitioners that really make the impacts of practitioner enquiry come alive.

* * *

As you can see from these case studies, each school setting took a different approach to their engagement with practitioner enquiry. They had their own different motivations and reasons for engaging with enquiry, and each had a unique context. Every one of them has had a different journey to my own, as detailed in Chapter 7. But, what should be clear is that every level of engagement produced benefits for the schools, the teachers and the learners, and ultimately the system. Some of these were planned for, and some were unexpected, but all of them were powerful for individual teachers, learners and schools. Teachers have moved on and developed not only their thinking and their practice, but also their ability to impact positively on learners. As a result, schools have developed in a powerful way. Professional development has become deeper and more focused on sustainable impact for learners. All of these schools are developing self-improving teachers with high levels of agency. They are developing staff who are not waiting around for others to identify issues, and solutions to them. They are growing their adaptive expertise and positively changing their dispositions as professional educators.

Imagine, if all systems were populated by teachers and leaders with similar attitudes and attributes, what could we achieve for all our learners?

Notes

1 The General Teaching Council for Scotland, 2012. 'Professional standards'. [Online] Available at: www.gtcs.org.uk/professional-standards/standards-for-registration.aspx
2 Sanders, L., 2016. 'Developing the capacity for improvement in small rural schools, through creating a small schools network'. Scottish College for Educational Leadership. [Online] Available at: http://www.scelscotland.org.uk/wp-content/uploads/2016/06/Sanders-Louise-Area-of-Enquiry.pdf
3 Cochran-Smith, M. and Lytle, S., 2009. *Inquiry As Stance*. New York: Teachers College Press.
4 Harris, A., Jones, M. and Huffman, J. B., 2017. *Teachers Leading Educational Reform*. London: Routledge.
5 Available at: http://www.dylanwiliamcentre.com/changing-what-teachers-do-is-more-important-than-changing-what-they-know/
6 The General Teaching Council for Scotland, 'Professional standards'.
7 Smith, A., 2011. *High Performers: The Secrets of Successful Schools*. Carmarthen: Crown House.
8 Drew, V., Priestley, M. and Michael, M. K., 2016. 'Curriculum development through critical collaborative professional enquiry'. *Journal of Professional Capital and Community*, Volume 1, Issue 1, pp. 92–106.
9 The General Teaching Council For Scotland, 2014. 'Practitioner enquiry'. [Online] Available at: www.gtcs.org.uk/professional-update/practitioner-enquiry.aspx

9 Pedagogical changes

Throughout this book I have looked extensively at practitioner enquiry. I have tried to present as clear a picture as I can of what this looks like, the process, the benefits and the issues for consideration. Amongst all of this, I have tried to illustrate each chapter with so many of the big positives and gains that may be experienced by individuals, schools and educational systems. I have also sought to be open and frank about the issues and challenges faced by teachers, schools and systems that come as part of any engagement with the practitioner enquiry approach to professional development.

In this chapter, I want to look at some of the individual pedagogical insights and changes that have resulted for teachers and schools, and that I have seen from my own schools' engagement. In Chapter 8, where I looked at some case studies of schools who have been working with practitioner enquiry, there are illustrations of individual pedagogical changes which have been scaled up from teachers in those schools. As we were engaged with practitioner enquiry for some eight years, I feel it is useful for you to read about some of the pedagogical changes that occurred in the schools I led. This is by no means an exhaustive list, but I hope it gives you a sense of some of the small, and large, changes to pedagogy that the teachers and schools experienced through practitioner enquiry.

When we adopt an approach that is focused on individuals looking systematically, and continuously, at their practice and impact on learning in order to improve learning experiences for all learners, this can only be deemed successful if there are positive changes in that practice as a result, and then that these have positive impacts for learners.

Practitioner enquiry is very much concerned with the development of a disposition or stance that I am advocating teachers to adopt in their practice and their professional development. This is not another 'thing', fad, or trend. It involves a reframing of professional development as part of this ongoing process, which supports a similar reframing of school development. Both should be connected, and each aspect needs to consist of a process in which all elements are connected, in a way which is proportionate and manageable for teachers and for schools. As I have said elsewhere, this is a journey that is career-long, and which has no final destination. There will be points on that journey where you can look back at what you have achieved, and where you have reached, then look forward to what is still to be achieved and experienced. You do this for the benefit of the learners who share that journey with you, for whom you should shape, and measure the impact of your travel.

The teachers I have worked with and spoken to have taken time to consider and speak about the changes they have made to their practice as well as the impacts these changes have made for their learners. I am grateful to them all for their thinking and their willingness to share their insights with colleagues and me. There is a particular culture in Scottish education where we are reluctant to recognise or celebrate what we do well. The psyche seems to like to belittle our achievements, to focus on the things we have not achieved, rather than recognising and celebrating our successes. We can lack confidence at times about our achievements, but I have met enough colleagues from across other education systems who are full of praise for what we have achieved, and continue to achieve. The development of, and thinking about, our practice by teachers – such as I cite here – is an example of what we do really well, and are getting even better at.

You should also understand that, at the outset of our work with practitioner enquiry, both the schools I led and the teachers in them, were already regarded highly and had been praised for the high standards, expectations and achievements for all learners. The key was, we all believed we could still get better. There were various aspects of our performance that disturbed or worried us, both myself as school leader and individual teachers. It was to be through enquiry that we found an approach that allowed us to start addressing these issues in a meaningful and connected way, so that we could get even better.

One of the first, big changes, most of the teachers in the two schools I led, made were as a result of being constantly told by Dr Gillian Robinson of Edinburgh University, 'don't be afraid to teach!' When we first started to work with Gillian, this was a mantra we heard a lot, as she recognised teachers were unsure whether, or when, they needed to intervene in learning experiences, and by how much. Teachers immediately raised the issue of class size in the primary schools which often had 30 or more pupils. When classes are of this size, how do teachers ensure all learners have quality teacher input to support their learning? The common solution to this dilemma faced by teachers every day, is for the teacher to stand at the front of the class, giving instructions and presenting learning, probably unsure about who they are reaching with this, but very sure they are not reaching everyone, especially as they are pitching everything at a general level.

Our teachers were completely frustrated by this scenario, so to support them and point them in a possible direction Gillian provided them with some professional reading on a '*carousel*' or '*learning stations*' approach to consider. On completing the reading, they then came back to discuss this further, led by Gillian. A few were immediately enthusiastic about what they had read, but most could see lots of issues. The main one being around teacher preparation time, in order to ensure that each point on the 'carousel' or 'station' had a meaningful learning activity. Gillian agreed that such an approach would require to be well thought out and planned to ensure all activities were proper learning activities, and not just time-fillers. Her suggestion was that the teacher should lead one of the activities, ensuring that, over the course of a few days or a week, every learner would have had high-level and quality teacher input. With our then current organisation of learning at that time this was not guaranteed, causing frustration for teachers, and a lack of expected progress for some learners.

We proposed that, if they thought this was worth exploring, they could try the approach in one aspect of language teaching, most chose writing, then we would evaluate how it went. This was in our first year, when everyone was focused on the same curricular area, as we were taking our first tentative steps with practitioner enquiry. Some enthusiasts went off to collaborate together and plan how they might use the approach. They gave consideration to how much time they would require to prepare their learners for the new approach, as learners would be required to develop more self-regulation and independent learning practices. The change was trialled by some teachers over a term, supported by input from Gillian. Whilst they found it challenging, they also recognised benefits accruing for all their learners. They reported back that no longer were they frustrated by not being able to work directly with all their learners, as over the course of four days they would have definitely worked with all of them. They were able to shape their teaching and input to where each learner was, and their next steps in learning. Most used mixed-ability groupings, and reported back that this had worked well, as pupils could support each other, especially when not at the station which was teacher-led. When there was classroom support available, this also helped. But, as the learners got more used to and experienced with the change, teachers found they could organise and regulate this on their own. They aimed for usually four 'stations'. Some tried more, but the logistics, and meaningfulness of some of the activities, created more issues for teachers.

It was not all plain sailing, and it did involve more thinking-time and preparation by the teachers. But, as they and the learners got more used to the change, they could see the impacts for teachers and learners.

When teachers shared the outcomes, and issues, with colleagues, they were very enthusiastic about the impacts. As a result, the rest of the teachers tried out the approach in some shape or form, supported by colleagues who had adopted the approach already. Very quickly we were seeing this way of organising teaching happening in classrooms across both schools, not just within the teaching of aspects of language, but as teachers and learners got more enthusiastic. In truth, some went too far and adopted the approach in almost everything. This just didn't work. As teachers gained more experience, and shared developing insights with each other, they came to recognise that this was an approach that supported some areas of learning, but not all. The learning had to be thought about very carefully, then the best way of facilitating this identified. Sometimes, the carousel approach would be appropriate and would support the planned learning, other times a different approach would work better. However, this organisational change, which also impacted on the teacher thinking about their role, is now being used as part of a suite of pedagogical tools by all teachers in both schools, and learning experiences, and classroom organisation has improved as a result.

A key part of the practitioner enquiry approach is the collection of data around a small group of learners, at the outset of any enquiry. This is then repeated, after new interventions or changes have been made for at least a school term. This is so that the teachers carrying out the enquiry have a '*baseline assessment*' of where their focus group are in their learning at the outset of an enquiry, then where they are after a period of teaching and new interventions. In that way, the teacher has quite strong evidence as to the impact of the changes they had made. Often this baseline assessment consisted of a quick exercise to elicit the learner's prior knowledge or understanding. They might be asked about their attitudes to learning and given some form of assessment to test their knowledge or understanding in an area. This would then be reassessed after a period of intervention or change. The teacher could then combine these assessments with any other assessments tools, including teacher observations, in order to identify and quantify impact.

To keep this whole process manageable for teachers, they often gave initial assessment activities to all learners, not just their focus group, then did the same at the end of a block of teaching. What they discovered was that such baseline assessment, when combined with asking learners about what they would like to learn and find out about in an area, provided teachers with very powerful information that would inform their planning for learning. This assessment made visible gaps in understanding and knowledge that teachers could then plan to address in a block of work. In addition, by repeating the exercise at the end of a block of work they could see something of the impact of their teaching, and how learning and understanding had moved on for the learners, or not in some cases.

Through collaboration and discussion, all the teachers in both schools came to the same conclusion. This was that they should carry out such informative baseline assessments at the outset of any block of work, before they completed any planning for future learning in an area. The assessments, before the outset of any new learning experiences, allowed teachers to see exactly what needed to be taught, and gave the 'learner's voice' a meaningful place in the planning process. At the end of a block of work, they now had more evidence and data, if required, to support their professional judgement of where learners were now at in their learning. This also provided powerful information for the planning of future learning or passing on to other teachers. This is not about over-assessing and testing pupils to prove something, or measure teacher performance, but is part of the process of learning, and planning to improve learning, then being able to know its impact, to inform future learning. For all teachers in both schools, this process is now embedded into their practice and their thinking in every area of the curriculum, not just when they are carrying out a focused enquiry.

Because our initial support and input was from Gillian Robinson, and because her area of expertise lay in the teaching of language, some of the most profound pedagogical changes occurred in this area. One of the biggest is that all teachers now better understand the learning required and the teaching required when looking at aspects of genre in writing and reading. Prior to input from Gillian, and the associated professional reading of research from Australia and New Zealand, the teaching of different genres in writing followed a predictable course. We looked at the genres we wanted to cover over a year, or two, then used a variety of resources and activities to teach these over that time. Teaching of genre was very much driven by our programme or our resources. We knew that this did not work for all our learners, but at that time were unsure of what to do about it. In addition, those charged with overseeing such work from outside wanted to see examples of extended pieces of writing in each genre produced on a termly basis! This all meant that we devoted little time to deepening understanding of genres and their characteristics, and gave more time to learners just writing, having been given a topic by us designed to get them to demonstrate a certain genre of writing. No wonder so many of them struggled.

What teachers learned from their engagement with research, with the support of Gillian, was that for learners to deeply understand the aspects and characteristics of different genres, they needed to be immersed in the characteristics of that genre. If you were teaching them about 'reading for information', for example, it was no good just giving them, or letting them pick, a topic then asking them to 'do a mini-project' or write about it. What you need to do is to expose them to lots of different examples of information texts and writing, then to go through and collectively identify all of the different characteristics found in them. Teachers and children need to discuss these and why they are being used, then compare them with other genres they are aware of. When you have engaged in this systematic process of examination and discussion, the learners are in a much better position to begin to use some of these in their own writing, with a better understanding of why they are doing so. By then, they may understand about headings, titles, use of diagrams and pictures, photos, subtitles and headings, spacing, the difference between facts and opinions, the use of colour, different fonts, layout and style, contents and indexes, only then can you ask them to think about how they incorporate some of these into their own writing, designing a poster, producing a pamphlet, or however you decide they will demonstrate their deeper learning. This will be influenced and informed by your baseline assessment.

The process is the same for looking at all genres. Immersion of the learners in the characteristics of each genre is crucial, so that they see and understand these characteristics, and can see differences between them. This is especially important if they do not read much, or are reluctant readers, and have not been exposed to lots of different types of reading and writing. It is the teacher's job to pull out the characteristics of each and to make these visible for their learners. The teachers in both the schools I led understand this better, their teaching has changed as a result. Importantly, the standard of writing, and ability to identify characteristics of different genres, improved significantly amongst our learners. They were not producing as much writing as previously, but because of the support and scaffolding they were now exposed to, their writing had improved in both content and organisation.

Linked to the last point on immersion is another significant change teachers have made in their pedagogy. This is to do with pace. No, they have not got quicker and cover more, they have, in fact, *slowed down the pace of learning* as they are much more interested in depth over coverage.

Whenever I have found teachers who have engaged with enquiry, and where their findings have had embedded impacts, the pace of teaching and learning has generally slowed down, in order to facilitate deeper learning. This is not because teachers are trying to do less, but because they better understand the complexity of learning, recognising that young learners need time and space to deepen and assimilate new learning. In the example above, of learners being immersed in genre, such an approach takes time, with the learners needing that time and space to discuss with their peers and their teachers, to better understand the learning experiences.

In my experience, when you slow down learning, giving it the appropriate time and space, understanding deepens as learners have more opportunities to place and use that learning in different contexts. We are still too fixated on coverage and 'pace of learning' in many systems. The usual interpretation of 'pace' is as an increase of speed. This leads to issues for everyone involved in the learning process, learners, teachers, school and system leaders, then to 'tick-box' approaches to curriculum and learning. This disadvantages learners and does not give them the time they need to assimilate new learning. They need time and space for dialogue amongst themselves and with their teachers. Schools and teachers need to create and protect such time. Teachers also need 'permission' from school leaders for this to happen, for a relaxation of timetabling constraints to support them in deepening learning. We have talked of this for many years, then have proceeded to put in place new systems and structures that work against providing such time and space, which prevents teachers from being able to slow down the learning process for the benefit of learners. As I say, the teachers I have seen engage successfully with practitioner enquiry understand this, and so slow down to support the deeper learning they are looking for. School and system leaders need to recognise this too if we are ever to change some of the practices and cultures that exist in systems which work against deeper learning.

The fact that teachers were also adopting more *dialogical approaches* to developing learning, as result of their reading and enquiries, also contributed to an apparent slowing down of learning. They recognised from their work with Gillian, as well as their reading, that they needed to allow more time in their lessons for learners to talk about and discuss their learning. They identified that this developed deeper shared understandings amongst their learners, but for this to happen the teachers needed to create time for such discussion during learning activities. They started planning for such periods of discussion, but also recognised the power of them happening spontaneously, driven by the questions and curiosities of learners. For some, this meant letting go of the desire to 'control' the learning. For myself, it meant getting used to seeing and hearing a lot more talking and listening, as well as understanding how this was still an important part of the learning process.

The way teachers *plan for learning* will change as a result of engaging with practitioner enquiry. You will have seen above some of the ways this will happen as a result of how they use assessment to support learning. But the changes I have witnessed are much bigger than this. Teachers completely change how they think about plans and planning. The most skilful ones, with the highest levels of adaptive expertise, plan more loosely, as they recognise that any learning plan needs the flexibility to be able to change and be modified as the learners engage with different learning experiences. The best teachers are able to do this during every lesson, in response to the learners' responses and reactions, they are highly skilled in this. It is part of their professional identity, how they function as a professional educator. To an untrained eye, they make it look like a very easy and a seamless part of the learning process. Anyone who is involved in teaching and education, knows how difficult this level of 'flow'[1] in teaching is to achieve. One of the most skilled teachers I have worked with demonstrated such high levels of adaptivity in her practice. She also possessed the ability to be reflecting on the learning happening at any time, beginning to consider where that might lead in the future, and what she may do differently or better. She did all this analysing and synthesising of information almost unaware that she was doing it herself at times. But, whenever I spoke to her after lessons she could articulate exactly what was happening, as well as where she needed to go next for her learners. Sometimes she surprised herself with everything she was thinking about and considering as she interacted with her learners. I saw her deliver some outstanding learning for her class, but she was never completely satisfied and always felt there were things she could have done better or improved.

The first change teachers make then, is to reduce the amount, and type, of planning they do. They narrow their focus onto the learning and success criteria. Not in a mechanistic way, that we have all seen, for example, when formative assessment became a 'must do' for all, and had to be seen to be done. This soon became about written learning outcomes, success criteria, WALTs (We Are Learning To), WILFs (What I Am Looking For), lollipop sticks, traffic lights plus a host of other visible techniques, as it lost much of its original purpose and impact in doing so. The changes teachers make to their planning, when informed by enquiry, are much more to do with learning, and how learners will be able to demonstrate new learning has taken place.

Most of the teachers in my schools stopped putting 'activities' into their plans. They recognised themselves that when they planned previously, they had included all the elements recognised as part of 'good' planning. These included learning intentions and outcomes, success criteria, assessment tasks, evaluations and activities. They spent a lot of time thinking about all of these aspects. What they began to recognise, however, was that once they began a teaching block their attention became fixated on the activities at the expense of the intended learning. So, they made a decision to take out the 'activities' section in their plans, to encourage themselves to be thinking more about the learning they wanted their learners to experience rather than focusing on the activity. When they were clear about the intended learning, they then identified the activity necessary to support and promote that learning. They saw this as the final part in any planning process. Instead of putting these activities in their plans, they decided to recorded them in their daily diary. Often, they would begin blocks of work only having an idea of the activities they wanted their learners to engage with, but they were absolutely clear about the learning their learners would experience. They also made this clearer to their learners. When I or other visitors asked children what they were learning, they were less likely to say 'about the Vikings', and were more likely to say 'I am learning to collect information from different sources through looking at the Vikings.'

Another important change around planning was that the planning teachers undertook was much more *informed by data* and information they held about their learners. Previously, teachers had simply referred to school programmes and curricular frameworks to identify what they needed to plan for next. Now they used a whole raft of data and information to support and direct their planning in order to better meet the needs of their learners. Sometimes, it had been difficult for me, as a school leader, as well as the teachers themselves, to see how a block of learning connected to previous blocks. This now became clearer for all, including parents, making more sense to ourselves, and our learners. Teachers had also developed a range of techniques and strategies they could use to harvest such data, as a part of the learning and teaching process, in a way which kept this proportionate and manageable for them and their learners.

When they changed the way they planned, it was a reflection of how they had changed their thinking about learning and meeting learning needs. The focus of everyone was on the learning, not the activity, they made sure learners understood this too. They made explicit not only what they would be learning, but also how this connected to previous learning. Teachers also became better at sharing with learners the skills and aptitudes they were going to develop in the particular learning context they were engaged in, and importantly how all this connected to real-life contexts. This *increased focus on learning* is another outcome for those engaged in practitioner enquiry. Their thinking and their practice changed as a result, leading to improved outcomes and learning experiences for all learners. When teachers better understand the complexity of learning and how to deconstruct that learning for their learners, as well as how to identify and address gaps in learning and the necessary steps in this process, it impacts not only on their thinking, but also on their pedagogy.

Another big impact I observed in teachers in my own schools, and that I have observed in other teachers from elsewhere, is around their understanding of the *importance of metacognition* to support learning and understanding. Because they better understand this, and have engaged with the research of Black and Wiliam[2] and others, they not only recognise the importance, but also how they may facilitate and promote it in their classroom practice. In our own schools, we looked closely at metacognition as a result of teachers noting how many learners struggled to verbalise or explain how they came up with various answers, or conclusions. They would commonly get answers like, 'I just did it in my head', or 'I used my brain' when they asked learners to explain how they came to a certain answer or conclusion. This told them that our learners were not good at thinking about their thinking, or the strategies they used to solve various problems they came up against. Metacognition, and the ability to think about their thinking, has been shown by Black and Wiliam, Hattie,[3] and others, as having a high impact on learner attainment, so we determined that we should look further into this.

As result, a few teachers decided to enquire into improving metacognitive skills in learners, particularly in relation to the children's ability to work mentally with number. They read around this, being particularly interested by the work of Sherry Parrish in America.[4] She had looked closely at children's ability to work mentally with number in elementary education. Out of this work, she had produced an approach she called '*Number Talks*'. This provided teachers and learners with a systematic approach to developing an increasingly complex range of strategies for working with number mentally. She demonstrated how these could be taught and developed in learners as they progressed through school. The teachers made themselves familiar with this work, as well as the research around it, then began to implement these mental activities as part of their daily maths lessons. What emerged was an improvement for learners, in that they began to develop a range of different strategies they could deploy to solve mental number problems. They were also able to verbalise and explain these, as they had been provided with a model and framework, by the teacher and their peers, for doing this. Teachers found that these abilities in their learners improved and developed over time, as did their confidence in maths.

In this enquiry, metacognition in maths had definitely improved for learners, but there were other benefits too; all the teachers commented on the fact whenever there were discussions of other areas of learning happening in class. More learners were now able and willing to be active participants in these. They were more able to give opinions or reasons for their choices and answers, whilst becoming more reflective about their own thinking. As the teachers saw the benefits across the curriculum, in terms of developing dialogue and discussion about thinking, they began to ensure that they planned and prepared more opportunities for this to happen in all of their teaching. Again, their thinking and their practice had altered for the better, in order to be more able to support the learning happening in their classes. From an initial focus, or enquiry, into one area of the curriculum, improvements and benefits had accrued in another. There had also been pedagogical changes that benefitted learners across their learning.

Linked to this focus on metacognition, came another that focused on feedback, another key aspect of formative assessment strategies which have been demonstrated to have big impacts on pupil learning. We decided as a whole staff that we needed to revisit formative assessment to remind ourselves again of the principles and research that sat behind Black and Wiliam's seminal work, *Inside the Black Box* published in 1998. This had been added to by John Hattie's conclusions in *Visible Learning For Teachers* that giving and providing effective feedback was one of the most impactful practices for improving learner attainment. Like many teachers, the teachers in our schools had struggled for a number of years to make such feedback meaningful with impact for learners. We had been encouraged to use 'three stars and a wish', traffic lights, feedback grids, feedback linked to learning intentions, plus lots of other ways to give and 'show' feedback to learners. We had used all of these, but were still dissatisfied.

When we went back to the original research and writing about the giving of feedback, we began to understand where we might have gone wrong. The key thing about feedback of any sort is what the learner receiving the feedback does with it. We soon established that everyone was giving feedback, but not many teachers were giving their learners any time to do anything with this, or, in some cases, even expecting their learners to do anything with it. When this was recognised, we discussed together what we were going to do about this? At that point, the feedback given was probably aimed at 'others', not at the learners. This was more about teachers being able to prove they had marked a piece of work, had given formative feedback based on the success criteria or learning intentions and were engaged in formative assessment practices. We decided that teachers would create time to allow learners to engage with the written feedback they had been given, then use this to re-edit or improve work. This of course meant more slowing of the learning process, but we all felt it was necessary if we were to be serious about our use of feedback.

This change in practice helped, but didn't end there. There was still the issue of the amount of time teachers were spending marking and giving written feedback, with remaining niggles about the impact of this on learning. We continued to read and discuss. We recognised that actually the most powerful feedback occurs during the learning process and is given orally by the teacher as an active part of that process. Teachers working directly with learners as they engage in learning, giving them immediate advice and feedback directly at the time when they are engaged in learning, so they can do something with it immediately, works well for most learners, in most situations. When we recognised this, it again made teachers think about their current practices and how they could adjust these in the light of the new insights. It also meant I, as a school leader, had to think about what the implications were for me in terms of my monitoring of standards role. It is easy enough to see if teachers are giving written feedback, but not so much if more and more of this is becoming verbal at the point of learning.

As a result, not only did teacher pedagogy change, so did my own. I had always aimed to be in classrooms as much as possible, which meant daily. This was part of how I led and managed the schools, as did other members of our small leadership team. The insights around feedback made it even more important that we did so, but that we focused more on the learning going on, not the teacher. I actually came to believe and understand that the daily and regular informal visits to classrooms, working with teachers on collaborative planning, speaking to learners, gave me far more useful information about where the schools and teachers were, and their impact; much more so than the 'formal' visits set out in our monitoring and observation calendar of activities.

When you develop such insights together, you support pedagogical development of all participants, as well as school-wide growth and development. It is also incumbent on school leaders to ensure that teachers then have the space, time and support to implement the changes that they have identified they wish to make.

Prior to engagement with enquiry, teachers were definitely driven in their teaching by resources and programmes. Following quite quickly on from using practitioner enquiry, because teachers become so much more focused on learning, there was a major shift for all teachers. That was to *focus on learning* and knowing exactly where each learner was in their learning. When individual teachers, or groups of teachers, carried out an enquiry they were very much focused on issues they had identified in learning. That is, difficulties their learners were facing in their learning, or issues to do with a teacher's practice that they felt was not supporting learning as well as it should.

What teachers quickly discovered was often the issues were to do with the way they planned and used resources to drive the learning. All resources are pretty generic and are not shaped to the individual place that learners are in their learning; how could they be? They are of course useful to support learning and to save teachers valuable time when used appropriately. However, if they become the driver for learning, they can be used in very linear and unresponsive ways, that are inappropriate in supporting learning for lots of learners. If, say, you have a maths resource in the form of a progressive programme, which runs from Book 1 to Book 7, then you use it in that way, or in the way laid out in each book, you are not planning learning to meet the needs of learners. You are requiring learners to meet the needs of the resource. If, however, you start from the point of the learning you want your learners to experience, on the next step in their learning journey, you can then select and shape resources or create them if necessary, to provide those learning experiences tailored to their needs.

This is a much more adaptive approach to learning. One that responds to the learners and which can be shaped to meet their needs, as well as those of the curricular experiences it has been agreed they should have at school, local or national level. Teacher pedagogy changes significantly as a result. Instead of using resources, as directed by the supplier of the resources, their use is shaped and decided by the teacher, and their assessment of where learners need to move next in their learning. We had groups of teachers relooking at all our programmes and resources, almost constantly, for two reasons. The first was to ensure we could match the resources we used to our curricular expectations. The second was to ensure our programmes were directed by the progressive learning pathways we had identified as necessary, then it could be left to the teachers to decide on the resource they would use.

We did identify suggested resources, but it was up to teachers to select the resource or activity they felt most appropriate to facilitate the learning experiences they planned for their learners. For some, this was a big pedagogical shift in their practice. Some struggled at times when the crutch of the resource telling them what to do was removed. But, we all became convinced it was the right thing to do for our learners, though it may present a few more challenges for teachers and school leadership.

This change was all connected to how teachers, and ourselves, began to *think more deeply* about everything we did in school. As we increased our experience with practitioner enquiry, such dispositions became our core stance as teachers and leaders. We used the approach to any issue that arose in our practice. When we became aware of issues, we would use the practitioner enquiry model, or an adapted version, to help us resolve the issue. Teachers now had a systematic way of tackling anything they were concerned about, and a systematic way of thinking. This had powerful impacts on everything they did, with positive results for them, their learners and the schools.

Another enquiry by a single teacher, that had impacts for other staff was in the area of problem solving. This teacher wanted to investigate the process of learning when young children were faced by a problem. She started out thinking about this from a mathematical point of view, but the scope of her enquiry soon changed, as she began reading around this, following conversations with and observations of her learners. She was a P1 teacher, so her pupils were around five years old, at the start of their schooling and mostly full of enthusiasm for everything. I remain in awe of very good early years teachers like this one, who are able to support and develop young learners in exciting ways, which tap into their curiosities and enthusiasm, and who start putting in the foundation blocks of all the learning that is to follow. If you have ever taught in an early-years class you will understand the challenges presented. I have always believed that as a school leader you need to situate some of your strongest practitioners in the early years, as they are so vital in developing a love of learning in young children by putting the foundations in place for all future learning.

Speaking to her class, and observing them in different situations, our teacher quickly realised the first problem she faced was that her children didn't understand what a problem actually was. They had lived their short lives so far with all their problems being resolved and sorted for them by the adults around them. This was a powerful insight for the teacher, leading to her having to reframe the issue so that her young learners would better understand. In addition, she had one pupil who was exhibiting severe behavioural problems, who lacked communication skills or strategies to cope when he didn't get his own way. She identified she may be able to support this pupil better, as well as deal with wider problem solving learning, at the same time. She reframed her issue as being around pupils understanding what a problem was, then how when faced by such issues they could be viewed as learning opportunities by her learners. She wanted to find a simple approach that would help all learners 'to feel empowered to solve problems'.

After more reading around the issue she hit upon the idea of explaining a problem to her learners as being like in front of a door that you can't open, for which you lacked the right key (or strategy). Faced by such a problem, you needed to find a key (or strategy) to solve the problem so you can open the door to move on. She had the school janitor show the children all the keys he used and some of the doors they unlocked. She also read to them lots of stories that involved keys and locked doors, and made a 'door' for her classroom wall. She hung some large cardboard keys next to this door.

She explained to the children that when they were 'stuck' with a problem or issue they could lift a key to get help to unlock the door, to help them become 'unstuck'. The teacher used classmates who would then act out the problem then they would suggest possible solutions to the issue their classmate was facing collaboratively. This was quite structured until the pupils better understood how the 'stuck' door worked. When they had a solution, they could act out using the key to open the door.

For the child with the behavioural and coping issues, she used the door, so that when he was not coping or lashing out, or when she saw signs this was about to happen, she could say 'stop, we can solve this problem together'. She and the child would then go to the door to explore different strategies or 'keys' he could use instead of just lashing out or losing his temper.

She found the results of her enquiry and these interventions were that all the children better understood what problems were, more of them understood how they were part of learning that could lead to new learning and opportunities. With the individual child, his behaviour began improving over time as he developed more coping strategies, and he understood what to do when he felt he was not coping. Other staff also noticed changes in his behaviour around the school or in the playground. One commented how he had asked 'can I go to the door?' when he lost his temper in the playground.

When this teacher shared her findings with her colleagues, they were first amazed by her insights and the creative ways she found to address these issues, but second, she made them think more carefully about problem solving and behaviour of children in their own classrooms. There were benefits for their practice in supporting learning for all learners, as well as in developing their thinking around this and behavioural issues. People made changes to their approaches to such issues in their own classrooms as a result of this one teacher's enquiry.

I have supported and observed a number of teachers who have decided they wanted to enquire into the learning and teaching of spelling strategies with young learners. In every single one of them, they have changed their pedagogical practices as a result of their engagement with research and changes they have trialled in their teaching. For many a year the teaching of spelling in primary schools has remained unchanged, with young learners being taught sounds and common letter strings, prefixes, suffixes, etc., building up to longer and more complex words. This was often alongside years of spelling word lists and sentence writing in class and for homework. Some of them got it and became good or fluent spellers. However, many others got so far and then struggled, or struggled right from the start.

A lot of the issues experienced are connected to the complexity of the English language, but I think more of them are to do with how we have traditionally taught spelling and the fact that too many of us have not taught a range of spelling strategies in a systematic and connected way, or which actually takes note of how children learn.

Teachers engaging in enquiries into the learning and teaching of spelling, soon begin to understand what the issues might be, and how they might address these. One of the first changes I saw teachers make was so simple, but very powerful for learners. When learners had been given words to learn, and were then tested on these, teachers, or classmates, 'ticked' every letter that was in the right place in the written word, rather than only those words that were 100% correct. The change this brought about in learner attitude was amazing. Now pupils who misspelled a word, saw they got credit for the letters they had correct. Often there was only one or two letters missing or in the wrong position. Everyone suddenly got more motivated, and could see that they were not that far from getting the spelling correct. They learnt how to spell words they struggled with more easily and quickly as a result of this simple step.

Teachers started employing much more engaging and active strategies to help support learners in spelling activities, as well as to learn how to spell all those difficult words found in English that seem not to follow any of the 'rules' or conventions they have been previously taught. Teachers started using plasticine, shaving foam, sky-writing, mnemonics, pictures, technology, games and a whole host of other techniques, to engage with learners to help them improve their spelling ability and confidence. What went out the door was lots of lists of unconnected words going home, to be put into random and meaningless sentences, or to be 'learnt' then tested on back at school. Some words did go home, but these were thought about carefully and were connected to other learning going on in the classroom. Also they may have been identified by the learners themselves, as ones they wanted, or needed, to learn. In addition, teachers collaborated to look at, and write, a progressive spelling pathway for learners, to sit alongside our language pathway in order to support their reading and writing activities. A systematic and developmental experience for learning to spell ensued, and this was driven by learning, not by a resource.

The pedagogical changes teachers made regarding the teaching of spelling, ensured the learning was more engaging and was tailored to meet the learning of individual pupils. When the teachers, who had enquired into learning in spelling, shared their findings with colleagues, changes occurred in the practice of others, which had positive impacts for them and their learners too. This also meant further development and improvement, all connected to learning and teaching, for both schools as well.

Teachers' ability to *collaborate and support* each other also developed. They recognised that it was more powerful when they planned collaboratively, so that children's learning experiences were more connected and progressive. We went from teachers planning in isolation to teachers naturally getting together to plan and think about learning. They supported the development of each other's practice through *peer observation* and helping with enquiries, as they came to see this as a way of working that supported the learning of everyone, teachers and pupils. Their practice changed through this collaborative approach, the fact that they were thinking more deeply about the learning going on in their classrooms, and how they could develop this for all their learners. They would *read more*, and understood better about how to critically engage with *research and data*, so that they could use this to inform their practice, in order to improve what they did.

I have observed many large and small changes to pedagogy, as a result of teacher enquiry. Perhaps the crucial aspect of these is that teachers came to understand and implement those themselves, not because they were told to do so by someone else. Over the last five or six years of my career as a school leader, I was used to visiting classrooms and seeing and hearing about tweaks and changes teachers had been making to their practice. What I was always impressed by, was the enthusiasm of the teachers as they showed these and talked about the impact for learners. In my last year as a school leader, I was still witnessing more of this, and from teachers who were not just at the start of their careers, but from colleagues at the other end of that spectrum and approaching retirement. As a school leader, if you have staff enthusiastic about developing their practice, displaying their love for teaching and pupils, I am not sure there is anything to beat that to demonstrate some of the influence you have had on that setting. I cannot take all the credit for this, as it was undoubtedly a collaborative achievement, but I am proud of being able to help create conditions that allowed teachers to continually grow and develop their practice, in order to improve the learning experiences for all learners. Many of these are subtle and imperceptible, unless you are experienced and embedded within the culture of a particular school, but their impact can be profound for learners and teachers.

Once we had the vison for what we were wanting to achieve, we were clear about our values, and had established cultures focused on learning, it was the vehicle of practitioner enquiry that allowed staff to get to that point. Fortunately, I am seeing more and more teachers and schools who are discovering some of the same impacts. This gives me great hope for the future of education in Scotland and beyond.

Notes

1   Csikszentmihalyi, M., 1990. *Flow: The Psychology of Optimal Experience*. New York: Harper and Row.

2   Black, P. and Wiliam, D., 1998. *Inside The Black Box*. London: King's College.

3   Hattie, J., 2012. *Visible Learning for Teachers*. London: Routledge.

4   Parish, S., 2010. *Number Talks: Helping Children Build Mental Math and Computation Strategies*. Sausalito, CA: Maths Solutions.

10 Some final thoughts and considerations

We have almost completed this introduction to, and consideration of, practitioner enquiry. By now I hope you understand more about such enquiry, the process, the conditions, the benefits and some of the issues to be found from such an approach. I have given you some case studies to consider and to promote your thinking and conversations around practitioner enquiry, so that you may begin to consider what such an approach may look like in your own setting or context. In this concluding chapter, I would like to add some final thoughts and considerations for your deliberation. As in all the previous chapters, I do this based on my own experiences, and engagement with research, but not in any way am I saying, 'do it this way, and this is what will happen and this is what you will find'. I don't know you and your context, because of this, all I can aim to do is share my experiences and insights in such a way that they may help inform your own thinking and decisions.

This book is very much written by a practitioner, speaking to other practitioners, and I hope you have found it more 'real' and useful because of this. Whilst a school leader, I always aimed to keep everything grounded in reality for the schools I led and the teachers who worked in them. To do this, you need to remain both grounded and authentic in your leadership. I have aimed for the same in this book. It is informed and shaped by my own practice and experience, garnered over eight years of using practitioner enquiry as the main vehicle for professional, school and learner development. Its authenticity lies in the fact that I have 'walked the walk' with practitioner enquiry. Yes, I have embraced the theory and have used this to inform my actions, but I have always sought to engage critically and shape the results of that engagement to the context in which I was working, whilst remaining true to the principles of enquiry. I would advise you to do the same.

Every single teacher, and every single school, is on their own individual journey of development and growth. Models for professional development, and school development, that seek to impose one solution in a generic way are doomed to failure because of this. Those seeking to impose such models fail to understand this basic fact about personal, professional and school development. That is not to say all schools and individuals should be operating in isolation of each other, as Fullan,[1] Harris[2] and most recently Lieberman and colleagues[3] have demonstrated, collaboration and collegiality are key to individual, school and system growth and development. It is absolutely vital that we are informed by research and build on the experiences of others. But, it is just as important that we engage critically with such research and experience, to consider carefully what this means for us and our context. It is with this understanding that I have presented the contents of this book, and hope you will apply the same approach as you engage with the content.

In this chapter, I consider some insights and reflections following my own engagement with practitioner enquiry, in order to support your own reflections and considerations for action.

As I have said consistently throughout the book, culture and ethos are crucially important in school development in order to produce deep embedded change which has positive impacts for all learners. The climate created within a school, as it is within a classroom, decides the success or failure of any change agenda aimed at improvement. I believed this to be true before I engaged with practitioner enquiry. However, I am even more convinced of its truth following my engagement. If time is not spent in ensuring the climate is one that promotes lifelong learning for all, with high levels of trust, agency and collaboration, then it is unlikely that it will support a fully successful engagement with enquiry. Get this wrong and you may well fall at the first hurdle with practitioner enquiry, at best you may get just another 'tick-box' approach with surface-level engagement. If you truly want to deepen and develop your practice so that changes become embedded in your professional and personal identity, then you need a culture, ethos and climate which expects and promotes this, combined with personal commitment.

It is not just me who believes in the impact of school cultures to support professional growth, and to create conditions that give practitioner enquiry the best opportunity to have the greatest impacts. Alma Harris in her book *Distributed Leadership Matters* recommends the use of professional learning communities (PLCs) 'to define a schoolwide culture that is focused upon building and sustaining school improvement'. Michael Fullan identifies six 'secrets of change' and one of these is in developing a culture of improvement in schools and systems. 'This means that learning to improve things must be built into the day-to-day culture of the work.'[4] Tracey Ezard in her book *The Buzz* who has worked with schools and leaders in Australia writes, 'Schools with a thriving professional learning community – with a buzz – were able to collaborate on their strategic work more effectively.'[5] These researchers and writers, as well as many others, point to the importance of creating learning cultures in schools which support school, as well as professional, development.

As you have seen, some schools have also tried to use practitioner enquiry as a vehicle to develop the sort of cultures described above. They have had mixed success. My own view remains that it is worth spending time developing a supportive and collaborative culture before you engage with practitioner enquiry. This gives you the greatest chance for success as an individual and a school. The creation of PLCs (Professional Learning Community) or TLCs (Teacher Learning Community) with a common focus and purpose can be a step towards enquiry. If you combine these with reflective and collaborative enquiry-based approaches, then you are certainly moving towards the development of mindsets and cultures which will fully support practitioner enquiry. Cultures do not change through structures alone, though these can provide useful support. They need individuals to examine their own practice and mindsets, to consider how reflective and collaborative they really are in their daily practice. They need to recognise their individual responsibility for all learners, not just the ones in their class, or their subject. They need to embrace and endorse their professional responsibilities, to develop career-long dispositions to act and think professionally, with a responsibility to keep developing their own practice, whilst supporting the development of others. All of this is done with a focus on improving outcomes for all learners.

School leaders need to develop the same qualities and dispositions. They have responsibility for facilitating and supporting the creation of collaborative cultures which are high on trust and low on threat. They need to be driven by values and a moral imperative to provide the very best learning conditions and practices they can for all their learners. They should aim to support and protect staff, so that they are able to focus on what really makes a difference, and be prepared to defend that position to others in the system, or outside of it, if necessary.

Other leaders in the system, at local and national levels, need to deeply understand the complexities of the development of learning cultures that make a difference in schools. They need to have the same dispositions and understandings of individual teachers and schools, in order to develop a self-improving system with high levels of agency, adaptive expertise, with leadership dispersed, and embraced, at all levels. The formal leaders in systems often seem to use the terminology, many frequently, but can lack any real understanding around practitioner enquiry, or the complexities of deep professional development. This needs to change. I acknowledge their 'busyness', but they should be more wary of a lot of the 'data' they use to demonstrate the impact of all that 'busyness'.

I admit these are lofty aims, that we have some way to go. But, it is my belief that if we truly embraced the thinking and practices, we would dramatically change cultures and systems in ways that would have tremendous positive impacts for all learners.

Practitioner enquiry does open a Pandora's Box in terms of professional development, practice and thinking. It can have large impacts on attitudes as well. Once this particular box is opened, and engaged with deeply, there really is no going back to previous ways of working and behaving. If your professional identity, practice and dispositions, have changed, they are changed forever through practitioner enquiry. Of course, these will continue to develop further in the light of new knowledge and research, not fads and trends. This poses challenges for individual teachers and for school leaders. Teachers are challenged by the changes that have occurred for themselves, not only because of their previous thinking and practice, but also if they find themselves surrounded by colleagues who don't think, or act, in the same way, or when they move on to another setting. Everyone can also be massively challenged if they are located in systems that 'talk the talk' about enquiring dispositions, adaptive expertise or teacher agency, but then don't allow practitioners to 'walk the walk' of this, and all that entails or ensues as a result.

For school leaders, having teachers operating and thinking at deeper levels, with developing expertise and agency, can also present challenges. Such teachers are no longer likely to meekly agree to the constant imposition of poorly thought out or justified change upon them, but will expect to see and understand the research evidence for what they are being asked to do, especially concerning learning and teaching. If you are a school leader who still believes in strict hierarchies in schools, supported by clear command and control structures and practices, and your go-to stance is one of micro-management, you will be forced a long way outside of your comfort zone by practitioner enquiry.

When you embrace the process and dispositions yourself it can also lead you into conflict with those above you in such traditional hierarchies. You are less likely to welcome interventions and changes imposed from outside of the school, which have not been shaped or adjusted taking account of your unique circumstances and context. Through practitioner enquiry, and the development of your own agency as a school leader, you will find that more and more you may come to resist the short-term, often highly disruptive, demands from those who would seek to tell you what to do, as well as how you should be doing it. In such situations, you may fall back on Michael Fullan's suggestion that 'we should learn to exploit policy',[6] which is a polite way of saying school leaders need to find ways of doing what they know is right for their learners and schools in the face of policy and system demands imposed by others. That is, we need to find a way of doing this without losing our jobs!

I have always argued that if your learners are happy, parents are happy, teachers are happy and you can demonstrate high levels of attainment and achievement, then who can challenge the approaches you are taking? A lot of school leaders still fail to recognise the power that resides within their position, and fail to exploit it sufficiently to do what they need to do in the face of opposition from outside. We all need to be more professionally courageous at times. Such courage will come from knowing what you are doing is right, and is making a difference for learners.

My own view is that we need to open this particular Pandora's Box if we are to really change a lot of the ill-informed and ill-considered practice that is still embraced by many teachers and school leaders. That old maxim 'if we keep doing what we have always done, we will still get what we've always got' still holds true for me. We need a radical change in our thinking and our practices if we want to truly embrace the concept of self-improvement for individuals, schools and systems. Practitioner enquiry, and other enquiry approaches, offer us the opportunity to bring about the changes so many of us seek within our systems, equipping us to take more responsibility for tackling the neoliberal agendas that sit around many education systems at the moment.

I would add that much of what I have described above, is what many education systems around the world purport to seek. In the Scottish system politicians and national educational organisations have policies or standards that seek to encourage teacher leadership, teacher agency, adaptive expertise, research-informed practice, high-quality school leaders, who can engage with research and are able to think and act independently, as well as a self-improving system operating at all levels. Looking at policy, structures and systems, it would seem everything that I have described is what is wanted by our political and system leaders. However, when you have all of these qualities and characteristics in place, are these same leaders prepared to accept the consequences?

My experience is that education in Scotland, and elsewhere, is still riven by hierarchies, with leadership that is still not comfortable with teachers and schools having high levels of true agency, able to make informed decisions based on local context, which is informed by research. There are still those at the top who want to tell everyone what they should be doing. Unfortunately, there are also too many in the system who are happy to be told what to do. Such mindsets have to change if we are to really move our system forward. System change will only come about when individuals truly have the dispositions and responsibilities laid out as desirable by national policy and structures.

Looking at other systems around the world, it would appear Scotland's situation is common to many others. But there are examples of some countries and systems being more open and trusting of schools, their leaders and their teachers. Finland is the obvious example, but Canada is another system that is growing and developing in similar ways. Perhaps this is no coincidence, given that many of the world's leading thinkers and academics in the world of education are now to be found working in the Canadian system of education.

The speed of change needs to be considered and sympathetically controlled

Using practitioner enquiry is not about a search for 'silver bullets', 'quick fixes' or finding more things to keep us busy. It is about thinking about and changing our practices in terms of both school development and professional development in those schools. It is about connecting up school development so that we are able to use a narrow focus to bring about connected, meaningful change in every key area that impacts on learning and teaching. Through practitioner enquiry, we understand that small changes can, and will, produce big impacts. This is core business for schools and we really do have to get better at it. It is no longer acceptable to be constantly busy, with little consideration of impact for our learners, or research evidence around which we shape our change agendas. It is about the profession acting more professionally, taking full responsibility for what goes on in our classrooms and our schools, to ensure all our learners are getting the best learning experiences we can deliver.

Practitioner enquiry is about individual teachers, and leaders, looking systematically and continuously at their practice and the impact they are having on learning for their learners. This is professional development shaped by individuals and issues they have identified in their own practice and current context. It is about practitioners being critically informed by evidence and data, in a proportionate and manageable way, so that they can develop themselves as adaptive and self-improving professionals with agency.

To achieve all of this, engagement with practitioner enquiry has to be managed and controlled by individual teachers, supported by school leadership. Not controlled in the sense that school leaders will say what is to be done or when. But controlled in a way that understands the needs of the individual teachers and their schools, protects them from themselves at times, but certainly protects, and defends, them from outside forces and conflicting agendas.

Individuals need to apply measures of control to themselves too. They need to manage their engagement with their enquiry, so that they are not trying to go too quickly or to cover too much. This is a deep and complex engagement, to bring about change and improvements that are equally deep and sustainable. As such, individuals and school leaders need to recognise the need to slow down at times, making sure they have the appropriate headspace to think deeply and collaboratively, in order to develop new professional identities and dispositions. All of this, needs to be understood as part of the whole process of developing 'enquiry as stance.'[7]

To reach the position described above takes time. Individuals and school leaders need to understand the importance of allocating, and protecting, development time and space so that teachers can embrace the process fully. There may well be some 'quick wins' for teachers and school leaders, but generally we are talking about an ongoing professional development process that is relentless, which needs support and understanding that is equally relentless. This is about a different approach to school and professional development, and as such needs to be understood, supported and managed differently by all in the system. Don't always expect to see immediate impacts. Many are very subtle but powerful. Impacts will follow. Those impacts will be felt by learners, teacher, schools and systems. If we lose our nerve, or look to demonstrate dramatic change quickly, we may well fall back to what we have always done in terms of professional and school development. That is top-down directed approaches that seek to impose and mandate 'improvement'. My view is that our learners, and we the profession, deserve better than that.

You will already have an understanding of the challenges of this approach. It is challenging to all participants. It is intellectually challenging, it can also challenge your sense of being as an educationalist and teacher. As such, it is important that participants collaborate and share, and are provided with the necessary support structures to allow this to happen in a non-threatening way. The successful adoption of practitioner enquiry practices and dispositions cannot take place against a backdrop of other busyness or constantly changing agendas. It requires a consistency of climate, so that teachers and school leaders have the opportunity to embrace a different way of being, in order to offer all their learners an improved opportunity to learn deeply and experience success in their learning.

Anyone who has worked in schools and learning, understands what a complex undertaking this is. Indeed, Dylan Wilam has often spoken about teachers being located in one of the few professions who come into work expecting to fail every day. We come in each day understanding that we will fail in some way. This will either be in terms of meeting all our learners' needs, or in our own planning and expectations. It will always be so, I am afraid. Learning is a social activity and, as such, is very complex. The more people involved in any learning situation or context, the more complicated it becomes. It also becomes differently complicated every day, as everyone will be in a different personal space. The teacher has to cope with and accept all of this, adjusting the learning experience they are offering as they go.

Practitioner enquiry recognises and understands the importance of context. The context in which individuals and schools are operating has to shape their engagement and their practice. This is not a 'one-size-fits-all' approach, but one which needs to acknowledge context and be shaped and adjusted in the light of this.

So, learning and teaching presents everyone with challenges. The process and thinking involved in practitioner enquiry also presents challenges to everyone in the system. But, isn't this all part of the allure of teaching and learning? It certainly is for me. Facing those challenges, whilst still being able to make a difference in so many lives has always remained part of the great attraction of teaching. It is also why teaching should never be viewed as a technical delivery system. It is much more than that.

There are no easy solutions for many of the major issues that remain in education, if they were easy they would have been solved by now. Perhaps the biggest challenge faced by education systems across the globe, and over time, is that they have always recognised that they could be working better for more of their learners. To get better at what we do requires change to happen. But such change needs to be well thought out, considered and informed by research evidence. I have always been an advocate of evolution, rather than revolution, with regards to educational change. We need to recognise what we do well, there is so much, then use this as a base from which to continue to build improved systems. To do that we need to use data and research to inform our actions.

Practitioner enquiry provides an opportunity for all in the system to think and act in ways that, as they become reflected and embedded in all levels in the system, can have profound effects for all.

If we are serious about thinking differently and holistically about what we do, we need the dispositions and understandings to allow this to happen. If all we do is keep doing what we are told to do by others, we do a disservice to our profession and every learner in the system.

We really can make a difference and help close gaps. To achieve this, we have to allow teachers to grow their practice and their thinking, so that they push everyone's thinking and practice towards truly delivering the schools and education systems our learners are entitled to.

Notes

1 Fullan, M. and Hargreaves, A., 2008. *What's Worth Fighting for in Headship?*, second edn. Maidenhead: Open University Press.
2 Harris, A., 2014. *Distributed Leadership Matters: Perspectives, Practicalities and Potential*. San Francisco, CA: Corwin.
3 Lieberman, A., Campbell, C. and Yashkina, A., 2017. *Teacher Learning and Leadership: Of, By and For Teachers*. London: Routledge.
4 Fullan, M. and Hargreaves, A., 2008. *What's Worth Fighting for in Headship?*, second edn. Maidenhead: Open University Press.
5 Ezard, T., 2015. *The Buzz: creating a Thriving and Collaborative Learning Culture*. Melbourne: Tracey Ezard, p. 6.
6 Available at: https://michaelfullan.ca/wp-content/uploads/2016/06/00_13_Short-Handout.compressed.pdf, p. 5.
7 Cochran-Smith, M. and Lytle, S., 2009. *Inquiry As Stance*. New York: Teachers College Press.

Appendix
Research posters

What you have in this appendix are some examples of enquiry research posters produced by some of the teachers from the two schools I was leading. I also include one produced by myself and my deputy head teacher (DHT) which aimed to capture where we were in the process, and how our journey had developed over the early years of our engagement. These posters were produced at the end of our third year after introducing practitioner enquiry. There is no way that we could have produced these any earlier in the process, though we did share our findings in different ways at the end of our first two years.

The other health warning I would give is that, no matter how powerful these posters were in recognising and celebrating the level of staff engagement with practitioner enquiry, it was the process of thinking about, then adapting the practice, that sat behind them that was the really significant factor. This should always be the case. The process of enquiry, and associated dispositions, should always be given primacy.

Hopefully, the posters allow you to see the elements of enquiry 'made real' in the teachers' thinking, helping them to improve their practice for the learners they had at that time. The consequences of these enquiries included teachers shifting their identity as professional educators, and considering their impact on learning continually as a disposition.

I should acknowledge the support of Gillian Robinson and Edinburgh University in having these posters made by the reprographics department at the university, and providing us with an A3 copy for each teacher and the school. These became invaluable tools to help us share with colleagues, and to support others on their own journey. I have blurred any photos of children to protect their identity.

An investigation into the acquisition of preschoolers' number skills with a focus on the conservation of number

Parkside Primary School Nursery

Introduction

This enquiry began with my interest in how children become successful in their number skills and what I can do as a Nursery teacher to help them succeed and also to prepare them for their start at primary school. In discussion with Dr. Gill Robinson I decided to include number conservation as this had not previously been included systematically in the nursery maths programme.

I began this enquiry into research into preschool maths and numeracy. I also interviewed an experienced Primary 1 colleague so that we could come into a shared understanding of what children need when they arrive in primary 1.

What the children need for P1

1. To count by rote to at least 10
2. Recognise numerals
3. One to one correspondence
4. Labelling Numicon tiles
5. Ordering Numerals
6. Subtilising - recognising quantity without having to count
7. Number conservation recognising that quantity stays the same when arrangement of objects changes (for some children)

Initial Reading

In my reading there was general agreement as to what children need to learn over the general order of their learning beginning with counting by rote, then recognising numerals and then beginning to apply this. When it came to subtilising and number conservation however, I came across quite different views as to what children can do when.

There are two opposing views as to how children subtilise. The Plagetian view is that small children see small quantities of one, two, and three as a pattern or arrangement and that they see each arrangement as a different arrangement and just happens to be labelled 'three' (Barooly 1987). In this view there is no understanding of number it is just a label for an arrangement. Children are not expected to recognise that arrangements or patterns have both a wholeness which can be labelled with a number and individual elements until they reach the Plagetian stage of operational thinking.

In a different view, counting precedes subtilising. They learn to count how many in small groups before they recognise the general set of 'threes'. This view was put forward by Gelman and Gallistel (1978). They believe that once children are confident with numbers and begin to develop recognition patterns of how many, that is, they see a pattern of 'threeness' (conservation of number) which they respond to immediately.

It is quite possible that children can both recognise a number arrangement and count how many. This would depend upon the experience of counting and recognising number arrangements that they have had, and on the size of the quantity.

Both models regard subtilising as an essential skill in the child's developing understanding of number (Gelman & Gallistel (Barooly 1987) postulated that it is possible that from their ability to subtilise, children may begin to form generalisations about number; for example that sets that have the same number of objects do not need to be in the same arrangement.

(adapted from Mathematics in Nursery Education by A Montague-Smith)

To teach or not to teach?

In addition to the differing views on children's maths learning I also came across opposing views on teaching in nursery. One view is that all learning in nursery should be done through play with the teacher's role being one of facilitating that play and not directly teaching children. Research however, suggests that children engaged in free play very rarely engage in maths activity spontaneously in their play. One study which involved videoing 70 hours of children at play found that children used maths skills just 1.6% of the time (see teaching mathematics 3-5 S. Gifford pg2).

I came to the conclusion that as long as teaching was fun, playful and non threatening then it was appropriate and indeed necessary for children to acquire the necessary skills.

Children should have the opportunity to develop...the expectation that numbers can amuse, delight, illuminate and excite

(New Zealand Ministry of Education 1993:92)

My Research
Step 1

I began my research by choosing 4 children with varying ability and assessing them based on the 7 criteria initially identified (what the children need for P1). The results from most of the initial criteria were much as expected but when it came to subtilising only one of the children appeared to be able to recognise small quantities without counting the objects and this was the child who was generally weak in counting by rote and numeral recognition. This was tested through a cheeky monkey game with some magic stones who rearranged them when the child had their eyes closed. Each of the other children carefully tagged each of the stones and gave the correct quantity.

In reflecting afterwards I considered that the other children may have tagged the stones to count them because of the emphasis placed on one to one correspondence in nursery and the need to be systematic (Mediated Learning approach) rather than necessarily being unable to subtilise.

Step 2

The children were taken individually for a new game involving the cheeky monkey again and the magic stones. It was explained to the children that this was a different game and this time they had to say the number of stones they could see but for this game – they weren't allowed to count any stones. In this game the children were only allowed to look at the stones for a second and they were covered up so as to prevent the children having the opportunity to count. The game was continued until the child was obviously struggling to identify the number of stones.

Conclusion

Contrary to what my initial findings appeared to indicate all of these children were able to subtilise and then conserve the number when the objects were rearranged.

I next decided to move the children on from using concrete objects – the stones and to see how they coped using symbols as this is a necessary progression in maths.

Children taking part in number conservation games

Experimenting with number conservation – the cheeky monkey game and his magic stones to see if children could identify quantities without counting when the arrangement of stones was changed.

Assessing the ability of children to conserve number using a flash card game – counting not allowed and practising "good guessing".

Observation of problem solving activity where the children have to sort cards using their own criteria to see if they choose to use their number conservation skills.

Step 3

For this activity I designed and made a flash card game which included different arrangements of basic shapes and familiar objects. The children were asked to identify the quantities on the card without counting to see if their skills were transferable from concrete objects to symbols.

The children all enjoyed taking part and all achieved some success in correctly identifying the number of objects (subtilising) on the cards. They could identify different arrangements of the same quantity to some extent (number conservation) but appeared to be less accurate than they were using concrete materials. According to theory, this is likely to be a combination of maturity and experience factors. Children need to be given lots of opportunity and playful experience to help them build mental pictures of quantities in their heads to help them build on their skills.

Step 4

For this activity I used the same set of card as step 3 but explained to the children individually that I needed their help to sort out the cards. I then watched them as they sorted them out. 3 of the 4 children decided to sort them out by quantity and were not counting them so were using their subtilising/conservation skills. The other child started sorting by colour, then by object and then by quantity. He was able to correct himself each time he realised his criteria wouldn't work and was able to use his number skills to quickly sort the cards.

Conclusions

As a result of my research and my work with the children there is a clear need to ensure that children are given every opportunity to acquire number skills. This usually begins with learning numbers by rote, numeral recognition and then counting skills and this is done in an embedded approach though nursery activities including songs and rhyme. It should not however stop there and should go on to include subtising and number conservation. These skills can be "taught" in a way that is fun, playful and non threatening and which encourages the children to be excited about number and maths. Each of the children in my study when given the opportunity could subtise and conserve number and apply these skills in the final problem solving activity.

Next Steps

My previous experience of teaching infants and each year finding children being unable to count objects accurately through one to one correspondence in P3 has meant that I have emphasised the need for children to be able to tag and count correctly.

In researching number conservation I have realised that I need to give children the opportunity to do "good guessing" and free them to experiment with estimation. I also need to make sure that children are systematically given opportunities to learn to subtise and conserve number in their preschool year.

As part of my enquiry I also interviewed the parents of the 4 children I had been working with. In each case the parents said they felt the children had been applying what they had been learning in nursery. One child in particular had started wanting to sort things because he had been doing this with his teacher. I feel it is important to keep parents informed of what we are doing in nursery and even making suggestions in our weekly newsletter of possible follow up activities.

Reading

Learning Mathematics in the Nursery Desirable Approaches by Early Childhood Mathematics Group

The little Book of Maths Songs & Games by Sally Featherstone
Practical Maths Activities by Sally Featherstone

Teaching mathematics 3-5 by Sue Gifford

The Little Book of Maths through Stories inspired by Neil Griffiths
Stories can be counted on by Neil Griffiths

Maths through Play by Rose Griffiths

Mathematics in Nursery Education by Ann Montague-Smith

Mathematics through Play by Kate Tucker

Professional enquiry - research into schemas
http://psychology.about.com/od/anitodev/g/def_schema.htm

Poster 1 An investigation into the acquisition of preschoolers' number skills

Poster 1: An investigation into the acquisition of preschoolers' number skills

Poster 1 reflects the enquiry of our nursery teacher at that time. She was working with three- and four-year-olds and was particularly interested in how pre-schoolers developed the concept of number, as well as how she could develop this in a semi-structured playful way. Amongst the significant aspects of this poster is the level of thinking and collaboration that was involved by the teacher. She did a lot of groundwork by talking to colleagues and through professional reading before she narrowed her focus further, then identified interventions and strategies she would try with her young learners. Another powerful aspect are her reflections and identification of 'next steps' for her at the end of this particular part of her process of enquiry.

This is a very detailed poster, with lots of information, as she found it difficult to identify what she could leave out, when sharing her findings. However, she and others realised that posters could be as powerful when they contained less, but more focused, information and insights.

An investigation into the acquisition of preschoolers' number skills with a focus on the conservation of number
Parkside Primary School Nursery

Introduction

This enquiry began with my interest in how children become successful in their number skills and what I can do as a Nursery teacher to help them succeed and also to prepare them for their start at primary school. In discussion with Dr. Gill Robinson I decided to include number conservation as this had not previously been included systematically in the nursery maths programme.

I began this enquiry by research into preschool maths and numeracy. I also interviewed an experienced Primary 1 colleague so that we could come into a shared understanding of what children need when they arrive in primary 1.

What the children need for P1

1   To count by rote to at least 10
2   Recognise numerals
3   One to one correspondence
4   Labelling Numicon tiles
5   Ordering numerals
6   Subitising - recognising quantity without having to count
7   Number conservation recognising that quantity stays the same when arrangement of objects changes (for some children)

Initial reading

In my reading there was general agreement as to what children need to learn and the general order of their learning beginning with counting by rote, then recognising numerals and then beginning to apply this. When it came to subitising and number conservation however, I came across quite different views as to what children can do when.

There are two opposing views as to how children subitise. The Piagetian view is that small children see small quantities of one, two, and three as a pattern or arrangement and that they see each arrangement as a different arrangement that just happens to be labelled 'three' (Baroody, 1987). In this view there is no understanding of number it is just a label for an arrangement. Children are not expected to recognise that arrangements or patterns have both a wholeness which can be labelled with a number and individual elements until they reach the Piagetian stage of operational thinking.

In a different view, counting precedes subitising. They learn to count how many in small groups before they recognise the general set of 'three'. This view was put forward by Beckman in the early 1920's. Through many experiences of counting, it is suggested that children begin to develop recognition patterns of how many, that is, they see a pattern of 'threeness' (conservation of number) which they respond to immediately.

It is quite possible that children can both recognise a number arrangement and count how many. This would depend upon the experiences of counting and recognising number arrangements that they have had, and on the size or the quantity.

Both models regard subitising as an essential skill in the child's developing understanding of number. Glaserfeld (Baroody, 1987) postulated that it is possible that from their ability to subitise, children may begin to form generalisations about number; for example that sets that have the same number of objects do not need to be in the same arrangement.

(adapted from *Mathematics in Nursery Education* by A Montague-Smith)

To teach or not to teach?

In addition to the differing views on children's maths learning, I also came across opposing views on teaching in nursery. One view is that all learning in nursery should be done through play with the teacher's role being one of facilitating that play and not directly teaching children. Research however, suggests that children engaged in free play very rarely engage in maths activity spontaneously in their play. One study which involved videoing 70 hours of children at play found that children used maths skills just 1.6% of the time (see teaching mathematics 3-5, S. Gifford pg. 2).

I came to the conclusion that as long as teaching was fun, playful and non-threatening then it was appropriate and indeed necessary for children to acquire the necessary skills.

> Children should have the opportunity to develop ... the expectation that numbers can amuse, delight, illuminate and excite.

(New Zealand Ministry of Education 1993: 92)

My research

Step 1

I began my research by choosing four children with varying ability and assessing them based on the seven criteria initially identified (what the children need for P1). The results from most of the initial criteria were much as expected, but when it came to subitising only one of the children appeared to be able to recognise small quantities without counting the objects and this was the child who was generally weak in counting by rote and numeral recognition. This was tested through a cheeky monkey game with some magic stones who rearranged them when the child had their eyes closed. Each of the other children carefully tagged each of the stones and gave the correct quantity.

In reflecting afterwards I considered that the other children may have tagged the stones to count them because of the emphasis placed on one-to-one correspondence in nursery and the need to be systematic (Mediated Learning approach) rather than necessarily being unable to subitise.

Step 2

The children were taken individually for a new game involving the cheeky monkey again and the magic stones. It was explained to the children that this was a different game and this time they had to say the number of stones they could see but for this game – they weren't allowed to count but to do "good guessing". The children were only allowed to look at the stones for a moment and they were covered up so as to prevent the children having the opportunity to count. The game was continued until the child was obviously struggling to identify the number of stones.

This time all of the children could identify quantities of stones without counting. Three of the children could identify groups of 2, 3, 4 or 5 stones without counting and when the cheeky monkey came and rearranged the stones could still identify the quantity correctly. One child could identify arrangements of stones up to 6.

Conclusion

Contrary to what my initial findings appeared to indicate all of these children were able to subitise and then conserve the number when the objects were rearranged.

I next decided to move the children on from using concrete objects – the stones and to see how they coped using symbols as this is a necessary progression in maths.

Step 3

For this activity I designed and made a flash card game which included different arrangements of basic shapes and familiar objects. The children were asked to identify the quantity on the card without counting to see if their skills were transferable from concrete objects to symbols.

The children all enjoyed taking part and all achieved some success in correctly identifying the number of objects (subitising) on the cards. They could identify different arrangements of the same quantity to some extent (number conservation) but appeared to be less accurate than they were using concrete materials. According to theory, this is likely to be a combination of maturity and experience factors. Children need to be given lots of opportunity and playful experience to help them build mental pictures of quantities in their heads to help them build on their skills.

Children taking part in number conservation games

Experimenting with number conservation – the cheeky monkey game and his magic stones to see if children could identify quantities without counting when the arrangement of stones was changed.

Assessing the ability of children to conserve number using a flash card game – counting not allowed and practising "good guessing".

Observation of problem solving activity where the children have to sort cards using their own criteria to see if they choose to use their number conservation skills.

Step 4

For this activity I used the same set of cards as Step 3 but explained to the children individually that I needed their help to sort out the cards. I then watched them as they sorted them out. three of the four children decided to sort them out by quantity and were very efficient at sorting cards with four or fewer objects and were not counting them so were using their subitising/conservation skills. The other child started sorting by colour, then by object and then by quantity. He was able to correct himself each time he realised his criteria wouldn't work and was able to use his number skills to quickly sort the cards.

Conclusions

As a result of my research and my work with the children there is a clear need to ensure that children are given every opportunity to acquire number skills. This usually begins with learning numbers by rote, numeral recognition and then counting skills and this is done in an embedded approach through nursery activities including songs and rhyme. It should not however stop there and should go on to include subitising and number conservation. These skills can be "taught" in a way that is fun, playful and non-threatening and which encourages the children to be excited about number and maths. Each of the children in my study when given the opportunity could subitise and conserve number and apply these skills in the final problem solving sorting activity.

Next steps

My previous experience was of teaching infants and each year finding children being unable to count objects accurately through one to one correspondence in P3 has meant that I have emphasised the need for children to be able to tag and count correctly.

In researching number conservation I have realised that I need to give children the opportunity to do "good guessing" and free them to experiment with estimation. I also need to make sure that children are systematically given opportunities to learn to subitise and conserve number in their preschool year.

As part of my enquiry I also interviewed the parents of the four children I had been working with. In each case the parents said they felt the children had been applying what they had been learning in nursery. One child in particular had started wanting to sort things because he had been doing this with his teacher. I feel it is important to keep parents informed of what we are doing in nursery and even making suggestions in our weekly newsletter of possible follow up activities.

Reading

Learning Mathematics in the Nursery: Desirable Approaches by Early Childhood Mathematics Group

The Little Book of Maths Songs & Games by Sally Featherstone

Practical Maths Activities by Sally Featherstone

Teaching Mathematics 3–5 by Sue Gifford

The Little Book of Maths through Stories inspired by Neil Griffiths

Stories Can Be Counted On! by Neil Griffiths

Maths through Play by Rose Griffiths

Mathematics in Nursery Education by Ann Montague-Smith

Mathematics through Play by Kate Tucker

'Professional enquiry – research into schemas' http://psychology.about.com/od/sindex/g/def_schema.htm

Problems as Possibilities   Positive problem solving as an attitude of mind
An enquiry process with Primary One

Our whole school decided to work on aspects of maths problem solving. I went right back to the beginning and thought about how children approach problem solving. I wondered why some children get 'stuck in' to any problem while others don't. I considered a broader view of problem solving for life, not just maths. I felt that children had to take a positive view and believe it was possible to find a solution before they started. I also felt that a problem could be seen as offering possibilities rather than difficulties. **How could I find a simple approach that would help all my pupils feel empowered to solve problems?**

Baseline Assessment
Ongoing, daily observation
'Three children identified who lacked problem solving skills in everyday school life, despite support. Child 1 was passive, Child 2 distressed and Child 3 very disruptive.
'Situations in school identified where this was particularly evident on a daily basis.

Reading and Reflection Journey

At the start I had an intuitive hunch based on teaching, parenting and my own experiences as a learner

I needed more information.

I read quite broadly.

The most useful books about problem solving - Key points for me:

- being able to recognise a problem
- communication skill of getting help
- functional fixedness (only being able to see problems in one way, not seeing options)

The most useful books and the key points I took from them were:

Feel the Fear and Do It Anyway Susan Jeffers
The title says it all!

The Secret of Happy Children Louise Hay
An aggressive, negative child is mirroring how they have been treated. This is the only way they know how to interact.

You Can Heal Your Life Louise Hay
The voices you heard when you were very young impact on how you feel about yourself and the world. Changing what you say can change what you believe.

Making links from theory to practice, as a teacher, I realised that we assume children understand the language and concepts of 'problem' and 'solve' and have the self-belief that they can solve problems.

This seemed so simple!
I couldn't believe it!
I kept reading more!

Siblings Without Rivalry Adele Faber & Elaine Mazlish

' **I think the most useful for teachers:**
' *Problem solve with children: really listen, then summarise how the child is feeling, calmly and simply state what they need to do with no judgement or encourage them to find their own solutions.*

I decided I needed concrete imagery for the abstract 'I'm stuck but there is something I can do.' I also needed a simple script for children to use and hopefully internalise.

I redefined my research question.

Intervention

(Although my focus was on three children I carried out the process with the whole class. This gave opportunities to see the modelling of positive problem solving behaviours.)

- Picture books with a door which needs to be opened
- A school 'key tour' with our Janitor to make sure the children knew about keys.
- A big cardboard door (that the children could open and walk through) as concrete imagery for the abstract concept "I'm stuck".
- Big cardboard keys as imagery for 'there is something I can do'
- Simple script
- Collaborative problem solving to introduce concepts, language and thinking: volunteers acted out the 'problem' I gave them. I said that when you have a problem and feel stuck it is like you are standing in front of a door that you can't open. You need a key to solve the problem and open the door. We used forum theatre to stop and invite suggestions. The volunteer then decided how to solve the problem and acted their solution out. The class were asked to identify what the 'key' was and a big cardboard key was then used to open the cardboard door and walk through. We repeated this for several problems. The children got the idea very quickly.

I was shocked at how well almost all of the children took to the process! They grasped the imagery within minutes, were able to use the language and showed good understanding of the concepts.
After just one session lots of children in the class started using the strategies that had been introduced as keys. I thought it would be much harder! We continued to talk about the problem solving strategies as issues arose in class. Now 'problem' and 'solve' are just part of everyday language in Primary One.

Ongoing focused observation of events whenever they occurred

Before	After – Initially needed some reminders, but now consistently:
Child 1 Passive, stood helplessly eg couldn't pack bag.	Lifts bag onto bench and packs successfully
Child 2 Distressed, found everything an emotional crisis eg too much to carry to cloakroom	Calm. Takes two trips. No longer a big event

I thought I could use the door, keys and script as an intervention for further problems as they arose, but had to put the door away when Child 3 tried to manipulate the situation. I was disappointed but am really surprised to notice that to date a school 'problem' situation hasn't yet arisen when Child 1 has been helplessly passive or Child 2 distressed. They either have a go themselves or ask for help.

For Child 3 I took a different approach and used the door and keys as a positive alternative to very disruptive behaviour. I decided to focus on 'Stop, we can solve this problem together'. I used real keys on a ring and stuck photos of us both working together on them. The keys were:

"I lift up my coat."   "I tidy up."   "I do what grown ups say."

Participant observation during event – how did the strategy work in potentially volatile situations?

	Before	During
Child 3	Screamed, kicked, ran, then had to use the Safe Space to calm down	We were able to stop at the moment just before a kick off and go and get the relevant key, then think about a positive behaviour. This proved a turning point, creating a calm gap. I had to abandon the door and keys after a few weeks when he tried to manipulate the situation
	After	I thought that would be that, however he continues to use the problem solving language and will now carry out these positive behaviours and others with only a couple of firm reminders.

Incident observation from colleague
Accidentally tipped over his lunch and was able to go to an adult, **wait, and then tell them he had a problem.**
We have started to be able to use a time out chair rather than the Safe Space because we have a 'gap', language and concepts to use.
Child 3 has now been on several trips out of school and managed well with some support. I would have considered it unsafe to take him out of school a few months ago.

Next Steps
I am now reading the class stories where problems are solved. The children are able to identify the problem and how it was solved. **Will the children sustain their positive approach to solving everyday problems?**
I plan to find out if the children's understanding of the concept of problem solving will transfer to a maths sorting activity where they have to come up with their own sorting criteria. **I think the approach has lots of possibilities. I will use it with my new class next year and discover where it takes us.**

Parkside Primary School, Jedburgh

Can't carry everything to cloakroom, trail of things dropped

Take two trips

Two children want the same toy

Use the one minute rule

Can't pack bag, things everywhere

Lift bag down onto bench

When you have a problem…it's like you stand in front of a door that you can't open. You need a key to solve the problem and open the door.

I don't know what to do. I'm stuck and I can't get through.

I need a key.

I can.

Child thought

Teacher talk through modelling think aloud strategy

What happens when I identify a problem solving image and script and support the children in using them?

Poster 2 Problems as possibilities

Poster 2: Problems as possibilities

Poster 2 was produced by a very experienced early years teacher, who was teaching a Primary 1 class at that time. She was a teacher who 'naturally' thought deeply about her practice and engaged with professional reading before we started our journey with practitioner enquiry. I have written about her enquiry, which started out with a focus on problem solving in maths, but which soon became wider, though more focused, as she faced different issues and challenges.

I really like how this teacher captures her journey, and that of individuals in her class, using simple graphics, including some of her pupils' drawings. Her poster reflects the thinking and stages involved in the enquiry process, as well as the impacts of changes to her practice. These, like many other insights, were significant not just for her and her learners, but also for her colleagues.

Problems as possibilities

Positive problem solving as an attitude of mind - An enquiry process with Primary One
Parkside Primary School, Jedburgh

Our whole school decided to work on aspects of maths problem solving. I went right back to the beginning and thought about how children approach problem solving. I wondered why some children get 'stuck in' to any problem while others don't. I considered a broader view of problem solving for life, not just maths. I felt that children had to take a positive view and believe it was possible to find a solution before they started. I also felt that a problem could be seen as offering possibilities rather than difficulties. How could I find a simple approach that would help all my pupils feel empowered to solve problems?

Baseline assessment

Ongoing, daily observation

*   Three children identified who lacked problem solving skills in everyday school life, despite support. Child 1 was passive, Child 2 distressed and Child 3 very disruptive.
*   Situations in school identified where this was particularly evident on a daily basis.

Reading and reflection journey

At the start I had an intuitive hunch based on teaching, parenting and my own experiences as a learner
I needed more information.
I read quite broadly.

Psychology papers about problem solving - Key points for me:

*   being able to recognise a problem
*   communication skill of getting help
*   functional fixedness (only being able to see problems in one way, not seeing options)

The most useful books and the key points I took from them were:

The Secret of Happy Children Steve Biddulph

An aggressive, negative child is mirroring how they have been treated. This is the only way they know how to interact.

Feel the Fear and Do It Anyway Susan Jeffers

The title says it all!

You Can Heal Your Life   Louise Hay

The voices you heard when you were very young impact on how you feel about yourself and the world. Changing what you say can change what you believe.

Making links from theory to practice, as a teacher, I realised that we assume children understand the language and concepts of 'problem' and 'solve' and have the self-belief that they can solve problems.

> This seemed so simple!
> I couldn't believe it!.
> I kept reading more!

Siblings Without Rivalry Adele Faber & Elaine Mazlish

I think the most useful for teachers.
Problem solve with children: really listen, then summarise how the child is feeling. Calmly and simply state what they need to do with no judgement or encourage them to find their own solutions.
I decided I needed concrete imagery for the abstract 'I'm stuck but there is something I can do.' I also needed a simple script for children to use and hopefully internalise.
   I redefined my research question:

> What happens when I identify a problem solving image and script and support the children in using them?

Intervention

(Although my focus was on three children I carried out the process with the whole class. This gave opportunities to see the modelling of positive problem solving behaviours.)

*   Picture books with a door which needs to be opened
*   A school 'key tour' with our Janitor to make sure the children knew about keys.
*   A big cardboard door (that the children could open and walk through) as concrete imagery for the abstract concept "I'm stuck".

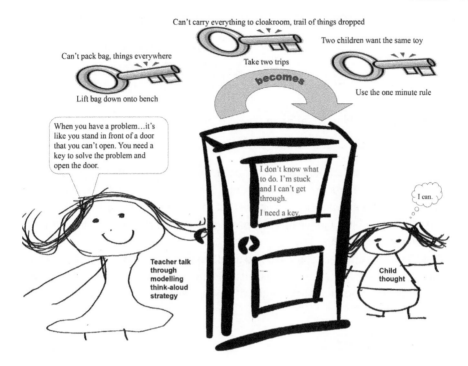

- Big cardboard keys as imagery for 'there is something I can do'.
- Simple script
- Collaborative problem solving to introduce concepts, language and thinking: volunteers acted out the 'problem' I gave them. I said that when you have a problem and feel stuck it's like you are standing in front of a door that you can't open. You need a key to solve the problem and open the door. We used forum theatre to stop and invite suggestions. The volunteer then decided how to solve the problem and acted their solution out. The class were asked to identify what the 'key' was and a big cardboard key was then used to open the cardboard door and walk through. We repeated this for several problems. The children got the idea very quickly.

What happened?

Observation of responses during drama

I was shocked at how well almost all of the children took to the process! They grasped the imagery within minutes, were able to use the language and showed good understanding of the concepts. After *just one session* lots of children in the class started using the strategies that had been introduced as keys. I thought it would be much harder! We continued to talk about the problem solving strategies as issues arose in class. Now 'problem' and 'solve' are just part of everyday language in Primary One.

Ongoing focused observation of events whenever they occurred

Before	After – Initially needed some reminders, but now consistently:
Child 1 Passive, stood helplessly eg couldn't pack bag	Lifts bag onto bench and packs successfully
Child 2 Distressed, found everything an emotional crisis eg too much to carry to cloakroom	Calm. Takes two trips. No longer a big event

I thought I could use the door, keys and script as an intervention for further problems as they arose, but had to put the door away when Child 3 tried to manipulate the situation. I was disappointed but am really surprised to notice that to date a school 'problem' situation hasn't yet arisen when Child 1 has been helplessly passive or Child 2 distressed. They either have a go themselves or ask for help.

For Child 3 I took a different approach and used the door and keys as a positive alternative to very disruptive behaviour. I decided to focus on 'Stop, we can solve this problem together'. I used real keys on a ring and stuck photos of us both working together on them. The keys were:

"I do what grown ups say."

"I tidy up."

"I lift up my coat."

Participant observation during event – how did the strategy work in potentially volatile situations?

Before	During
Child 3 Screamed, kicked, ran, then had to use the Safe Space to calm down	We were able to stop at the moment just before a kick off and go and get the relevant key, then think about a positive behaviour. This proved a turning point, creating a calm gap. I had to abandon the door and keys after a few weeks when he tried to manipulate the situation.

After	I really thought that would be that, however he continues to use the problem solving language and will now carry out these positive behaviours and others with only a couple of firm reminders.
	
	Incident observation from colleague
	Accidentally tipped over his lunch and was able to go to an adult, **wait,** and then **tell them he had a problem**.
	    We have started to be able to use a time-out chair rather than the Safe Space because we have a "gap", language and concepts to use.
	    Child 3 has now been on several trips out of school and managed well with some support. I would have considered it unsafe to take him out of school a few months ago.

Next steps

I am now reading the class stories where problems are solved. The children are able to identify the problem and how it was solved.

Will the children sustain their positive approach to solving everyday problems?

I plan to find out if the childrens' understanding of the concept of problem solving will transfer to a maths sorting activity where they have to come up with their own sorting criteria. I think the approach has lots of possibilities. I will use it with my new class next year and see where it takes us.

What happens when I adopt a systematic approach to teaching and assessing problem solving through play?

Ancrum Primary School, Jedburgh

Research Focus

The teaching of problem solving is an area of the curriculum I personally felt I neglected. It was taught but not in a systematic and concise manner. I began to question my teaching of problem solving and wanted to find out if developing problem solving through play would develop their skills and confidence.

I wanted to find out the children's ability to identify and continue patterns both with shapes and then with numbers. (Primary 1)

Students should be pattern sniffers. We should foster within students a delight in finding hidden patterns. (Habits of Mind: An Organising Principle for Mathematics Curricula-AI Cuoco, E.Paul Goldenberg, June Mark)

Methods used

Patterns with shapes

• Pupil /teacher interaction – "Can you tell me what the next shape in this pattern would be? How do you know that?"

• Observations of pupils building patterns, then more sophisticated patterns, using a variety of variables

• video recordings of pupils making repeated patterns using body shapes

• Visual data- pupils were asked as an assessment, to show a repeated pattern using a variety of 2D shapes

Patterns with numbers

• Acting out situations and devising a strategy (drawing pictures) to help solve problems involving numbers.

• Scaffolding strategies and verbalising thoughts.

Figure 1-building patterns

Picture 1 shows a pupil building a simple repeat pattern. The way he chose to build the pattern was interesting in that he chose to make lots of red and green cubes separately rather than 1 long line of cubes which is how all the other children chose to do it.

Picture 2 shows a more sophisticated pattern and picture 3 is an assessment piece which shows this child in particular understands exactly what is meant by a repeat pattern.

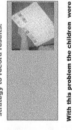
Figure 2-acting out the situation then using a shown strategy to record results.

With this problem the children were told 16 guests were coming to a party. They had to work out how many tables had to be pushed together in a row so that everyone could sit around the table. They were told 4 people could sit around a square table and 6 people could sit around 2 tables pushed together. After having made sure the pupils understood what was being asked of them, they then began to act out the story using Compare Bears.

One child in particular in this group was very good at verbalising and saying what she was discovering.

"Mrs xxxxi All the numbers are even and they're getting bigger each time!"

This was the first time they had been asked to try and record their findings and all children found this tricky. They were then shown how to record this particular problem by colouring in squares.

Figure 3-devising their own strategy.

After having scaffolded a strategy and verbalised my thinking when working on problems with the pupils, I was interested to discover if the children would now be able to devise a strategy of their own to solve a problem.

With this problem, the pupils were told 24 people were waiting for a train. Only 3 people could fit into a carriage and the carriage had to be filled before moving onto the next one. The pupils had to find out which carriage the 24th person would be in. The children acted this out first of all using Compare Bears and all pupils found the answer. They were then asked to devise their own strategy for recording this.

In picture 1, this child showed a very mature way of recording her results. She drew a line of 3's down one side (number of people in each carriage) She then counted in 3's until she reached 12 then continued to add on 3 in her head until she reached 24.

In picture 2, this child drew a carriage then added 3 people, drew a carriage then added 3 people until he had counted 24 in total.

Most pupils were able to devise a strategy to solve the problem.

Discussion of analysis and interpretation

Significant issues from my data -

• To show understanding, pupils need to be encouraged to talk, in their own words, about the problems they have been given.

"Communication is an essential process in learning mathematics. Through communication, students are able to reflect upon and clarify their ideas, their understanding of mathematical relationships, and their mathematical arguments."
Polya's How to Solve It, 1945

• Don't underestimate pupils – some pupils surprised me with how well they devised strategies to solve problems.

• I need to learn to 'take a back seat' and let pupils enjoy discovering for themselves!

Findings

• Pupils were not good *initially* at verbalising and sharing their ideas with each other.

• I talk too much ! I need to give pupils more 'Thinking Time' and time to talk and discover for themselves.

• All pupils could talk about what makes a pattern a repeated pattern.

• *Most* pupils enjoy problem solving.

I like problem solving. Its fun. It's hard to figure it out and you have to use your brain!
Child A

I don't like problem solving, I have to use my brain and I don't like having to use my brain !
Child B

• With number problems, getting pupils to describe it in their own words was a good way of getting them to understand what the problem was asking them.

• Getting pupils to identify key information in the problem was important.

• Acting out problems involving numbers , helped most pupils find a solution.

• After having shown pupils a strategy (eg draw a picture) most pupils were able to devise and use this to solve various problems.

• Some pupils could record a sequence of numbers for a problem

• All pupils found difficulty in identifying patterns in number sequences.

Final thoughts

Having chosen only one strategy to work on in this enquiry has been beneficial to both myself and the pupils. Most pupils have shown that they can now devise a strategy on their own to solve a problem and because I have looked more closely and more in depth at problem solving I feel I have a deeper understanding and will be more confident when approaching it in the future.

Next steps

• Continue to adopt a systematic approach to teaching and assessing problem solving through play.

• Work with colleagues to identify teaching and learning resources.

• Continue to work on appropriate strategies to help pupils identify and record patterns in number sequences.

• Make problem solving fun!

Poster 3 What happens when I adopt a systems approach to teaching and assessing problem solving through play?

Poster 3: What happens when I adopt a systematic approach to teaching and assessing problem solving through play?

Poster 3 was produced by another very experienced teacher, who was teaching a composite class of Primary 1, 2 and 3 at that time. She too was wanting to look at developing her young learners' ability to problem solve, particularly in mathematics. She wanted to develop such learning by taking a 'play-based' approach. She is a fantastic practitioner, who thinks deeply about how she engages all her learners, but can lack a little confidence in herself. She didn't find the production of her poster as easy as some others, but, as with everything, she was prepared to have a go, and I think the results demonstrate a lot of the qualities she brings to her role.

Again she demonstrates all the significant aspects of the enquiry process, as she explains her focus and the outcomes and insights she achieved.

I should add that Gillian Robinson had provided us with electronic frameworks for our posters. This meant we could use these, and adapt them as we went, without having to worry about creating the layout and graphics, or letting this worry get in the way of the process and our engagement.

What happens when I adopt a systematic approach to teaching and assessing problem solving through play?
Ancrum Primary School, Jedburgh

Research focus

The teaching of problem solving is an area of the curriculum I personally felt I neglected. It was taught but not in a systematic and concise manner. I began to question my teaching of problem solving and wanted to find out if developing problem solving through play would develop their skills and confidence.

I wanted to find out the children's ability to identify and continue patterns both with shapes and then with numbers. (Primary 1)

> Students should be pattern sniffers. We should foster within students a delight in finding hidden patterns.
>
> *(Habits of Mind: An Organising Principle for Mathematics Curricula*
> *- Al Cuoco, E.Paul Goldenberg, June Mark)*

Methods used

Patterns with shapes

- Pupil/teacher interaction - "Can you tell me what the next shape in this pattern would be? How do you know that?"
- Observations of pupils building patterns, then more sophisticated patterns, using a variety of variables
- Video recordings of pupils making repeated patterns using body shapes
- Visual data - pupils were asked as an assessment, to show a repeated pattern using a variety of 2D shapes

• Questioning the pupils about missing pieces in patterns- "How do you know which piece might fit in here? Why?" **"The pattern should be red, green, black, red, green, black and there's no red here and there's no black there."**

Figure 1 Building patterns

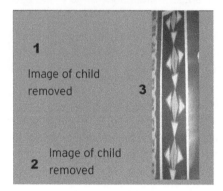

Picture 1 shows a pupil building a simple repeat pattern. The way he chose to build the pattern was interesting in that he chose to make lots of red and green cubes separately rather than one long line of cubes which is how all the other children chose to do it. **Picture 2** shows a more sophisticated pattern and **picture 3** is an assessment piece which shows this child in particular understands exactly what is meant by a repeat pattern.

Figure 2 Acting out the situation then using a shown strategy to record results

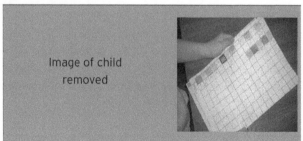

With this problem the children were told 16 guests were coming to a party. They had to work out how many tables had to be pushed together in a row so that everyone could sit around the table. They were told 4 people could sit around a square table and 6 people could sit around 2 tables pushed together. After having made sure the pupils understood what was being asked of them, they then began to act out the story using Compare Bears.

One child in particular in this group was very good at verbalising and saying what she was discovering.

"Mrs xxxx! All the numbers are even and they're getting bigger each time!"

This was the first time they had been asked to try and record their findings and all children found this tricky. They were then shown how to record this particular problem by colouring in squares.

Figure 3 Devising their own strategy

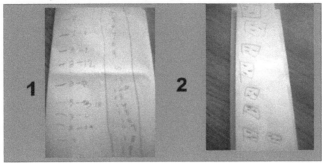

After having scaffolded a strategy and verbalised my thinking when working on problems with the pupils, I was interested to discover if the children would now be able to devise a strategy of their own to solve a problem.

With this problem, the pupils were told 24 people were waiting for a train. Only 3 people could fit into a carriage and the carriage had to be filled before moving onto the next one. The pupils had to find out which carriage the 24th person would be in. The children acted this out first of all using Compare Bears and all pupils found the answer. They were then asked to devise their own strategy for recording this.

In picture 1, this child showed a very mature way of recording her results. She drew a line of 3's down one side (number of people in each carriage) She then counted in 3's until she reached 12 then continued to add on 3 in her head until she reached 24.

In picture 2, this child drew a carriage then added 3 people, drew a carriage then added 3 people until he had counted 24 in total. Most pupils were able to devise a strategy to solve the problem.

Patterns with numbers

- Acting out situations and devising a strategy (drawing pictures) to help solve problems involving numbers.
- Scaffolding strategies and verbalising thoughts.

Findings

- Pupils were not good *initially* at verbalising and sharing their ideas with each other.
- I talk too much ! I need to give pupils more 'Thinking Time' and time to talk and discover for themselves.
- All pupils could talk about what makes a pattern a repeated pattern.
- *Most* pupils enjoy problem solving.

- With number problems, getting pupils to describe it in their own words was a good way of getting them to understand what the problem was asking them.
- Getting pupils to identify key information in the problem was important.
- Acting out problems involving numbers, helped most pupils find a solution.
- After having shown pupils a strategy (eg draw a picture) most pupils were able to devise and use this to solve various problems.
- Some pupils could record a sequence of numbers for a problem.
- All pupils found difficulty in identifying patterns in number sequences.

Discussion of analysis and interpretation

Significant issues from my data:

- To show understanding, pupils need to be encouraged to talk, in their own words, about the problems they have been given.

  Communication is an essential process in learning mathematics. Through communication, students are able to reflect upon and clarify their ideas, their understanding of mathematical relationships, and their mathematical arguments.

  Polya's How to Solve It, 1945

- Don't underestimate pupils – some pupils surprised me with how well they devised strategies to solve problems.
- I need to learn to 'take a back seat' and let pupils enjoy discovering for themselves!

Final thoughts

Having chosen only one strategy to work on in this enquiry has been beneficial to both myself and the pupils. Most pupils have shown that they can now devise a strategy on their own to solve a problem and because I have looked more closely and more in depth at problem solving I feel I have a deeper understanding and will be more confident when approaching it in the future.

Next steps

- Continue to adopt a systematic approach to teaching and assessing problem solving through play.
- Work with colleagues to identify teaching and learning resources.
- Continue to work on appropriate strategies to help pupils identify and record patterns in number sequences.
- Make problem solving fun!

Research Focus

Having worked with Primary and Secondary colleagues, I was aware that children were still finding the retention of their times tables a challenge. This made me consider aspects of my own teaching in the Upper Primary and what I might need to do to improve the pupils retention and understanding of their times tables. The focus of this research was therefore to explore:

'What happens when I adopt a systematic approach to planning, teaching and assessing times tables?'

In particular I am interested in ways I can promote children's instant recall and understanding of the times table facts.

Methods used

Pre-assessment: I timed the pupils on their instant recall of facts for the 2, 5 & 10 times tables in a random order, plus any other tables they felt they were confident with. I recorded the times and noted down any significant strategies I could see they were using.

Thought Shower: This was done at the start of the research project. The pupils were asked to work individually to produce their own maps (text and/or pictures) to explore what they felt they already knew about multiplication and the times tables as well as what they did not know and/or needed to develop.

Audio-taped Learning Conversations: I chose this method as studying their children's 'Thought Showers' would give a one-dimensional view. I felt giving the children an opportunity to talk about their learning and feelings about maths, plus their views on learning in maths. I could then revisit the recording as often as required to establish children's perceptions of their engagement, enjoyment and confidence in Multiplication work.

Record of ongoing assessment & evaluation: Continual use of mini-whiteboards to focus on facts within the discussion. The children's formal written work were monitored. The pupils also self-evaluated themselves by updating their 'Thought Showers' at regular intervals throughout the enquiry.

Learning Journal/Observations: This journal was kept up-to-date throughout the Enquiry process. It enabled me to note down anything significant from everyday classroom observations and conversations.

I used the data to look at:

1. Strategies children currently have/use to multiply:
 - Conceptual understanding
 - What strategies have been taught/retained
 - Rapid mental recall of facts
 - Body language (engagement, motivation & thinking)

2. Pupils' perceptions of their learning
 - Explanations of how they learn
 - Their interaction with others
 - How they could apply what they learned to their life beyond the classroom

3. Pupils' engagement, enjoyment & confidence:
 - Responses
 - Tone of voice
 - Quality of their responses

Outline of project - approach/ intervention

Children being literate and numerate when they leave school is what is expected by parents, teachers and the Education body of the Scottish Government. As an Upper Primary School teacher I found that some children still did not know/ understand the times tables. My concern was my teaching of the times tables, as children were appearing to find it difficult to grasp them securely and had poor instant recall.

Mike Askew stated that he felt 'learning multiplication and division facts need not be a long and laborious task. Armed with a toolkit of mental strategies, children can figure out all manner of what we understand and can associate with things that we already know (Jones, 2003). Finding patterns or an effective cognitive strategy (Stewart, 2010). I decided to trial a more systematic approach to planning, teaching and assessing times tables to establish if this would improve their conceptual understanding and recall of facts.

Findings/presentation of data

Children's Thought Showers

I examined the children's 'Thought Showers' and from studying their initial thoughts it was apparent that they could be developed. It was also apparent that few children could identify or explain 'how' they actually learned the tables. At the mid-way point of my enquiry I asked the pupils to update their sheets in a second colour to illustrate where their thinking was and repeated this again at the end of my enquiry, using a third colour.

Figure 1. Example of pupils' 'Thought Showers' showing initial thoughts and updated self-assessments throughout the enquiry.

These examples show how learning progressed throughout the enquiry. Pupils also became aware of strategies that helped them learn and recognised that regular revision is also good practice. This was a useful visual tool for pupils to refer to throughout their learning.

Figure 2. Audio Recorded Learning Conversations:

Below are examples of pupil comments made about their learning during the discussion.

'Daunting to begin with as I think there is a hundred facts to learn.'

'Once we've learned a few times tables then you know other sums in other tables.'

'Tricks and patterns help in the 9 times table.'

'Flashcards made it easier and making it competitive makes you try harder.'

'Using songs makes it more fun and exciting.'

'Also playing computer games make it fun.'

'Times tables is my favourite thing because it's fun and helps me with division.'

'Dad gives me random times table questions at home. It helps me keep it in my head.'

'At home I say the tables in my head. It's become a habit.'

I listened in to a recorded discussion between a group of my pupils and a colleague about learning their multiplication tables. The responses made were of a very upbeat nature. The pupils were animated, confident and enthusiastic about their Maths, which was conveyed through their positive tone of voice and detailed comments about their learning.

Figure 3. Assessment Table

Pupil	3x	3x	6x	6x	9x	9x
A	36 sec	26 sec	32 sec	20 sec	61 sec	37 sec
B	59 sec	49 sec	75 sec	51 sec	65 sec	15 sec
C	72 sec	23 sec	84 sec	62 sec	59 sec	38 sec
D	27 sec	19 sec	86 sec	68 sec	117 sec	29 sec
E	91 sec	54 sec	102 sec	58 sec	123 sec	70 sec

Pre-Assessment Final Assessment

The results in the table show how learning had progressed throughout the enquiry by pupils' recalling their times tables quicker. Pupils also became more confident in applying strategies they had learned throughout the enquiry and less reliant on using their fingers to tag the facts.

Discussion of analysis and interpretation

A summary of points emerged from my data:

1. The pre-assessment highlighted the pupils' strengths but more significantly, where there were gaps in their learning.

2. The systematic approach to planning, teaching & assessing, in conjunction with a greater variety of activities, helped to develop the pupils conceptual understanding of their times tables.

3. This approach has developed pupils' metacognitive awareness of how they learn their times tables, beyond simply learning the facts by rote.

4. Pupils now seem to be fully engaged in Maths lessons, conveying their enjoyment through animated discussions.

Having analysed the pre-assessment it showed that the pupils' strengths were in recalling the facts for the 2, 5 and 10 times tables. This led me to question how I could teach the other tables in a more systematic and meaningful way. I divided the class into 2 groups based upon the pre-assessment and 'thought shower'. Introducing more active learning activities for the group working independently enabled me to teach a specific concept more successfully to the other group, and vice versa. The activities included flashcards, pair work, ICT games and times tables songs. Whilst the focus group had the opportunity to develop their understanding of the tables through higher order discussions facilitated by myself. After implementing this approach over a term the pupils' ability to explain their thought processes on the whiteboards significantly improved. The number of positive comments pupils could relay about how they learned and retained their tables has given them strategies and confidence that they can apply in future learning.

Final thoughts/next steps

Having carried out this enquiry, the data gathered along with personal reflection, has convinced me to continue using a systematic approach to planning, teaching and assessing the times tables.

The strategies and practice I would continue to use and develop are:

- Use of pre-assessment to establish where individuals are

- The order in which I teach the tables - 10x, 5x, 2x, 4x, 8x, 3x, 6x, 9x and 7x - to support the children in making links and develop their conceptual understanding e.g. 4 x 3 is double 2 x3

- Teaching & Learning practice of flashcards; timed challenges; pair/group work; ICT games and times tables songs

- Discussion with pupils before, during and after learning and encouraging them to explain their thought processes

- Begin to develop applying their knowledge and understanding of the times tables beyond the classroom setting

In addition, my school has been developing new Numeracy planning formats in line with implementing CfE. My research can enhance the content of these plans and subsequently be circulated across sectors within our learning community.

References

Askew, M. (2009) 'On the Double', BEAM Education, pp 4-5.

Francis, E. (2010) Tricks to the Multiplication Tables, [Online] Available at: http://www.teachitmath.com/wordpress/?category_name=tricks-for-teaching-the-times-tables [23 Apr 2013]

Jones, S. (2003) Times Tables Practice, [Online] Available at: http://www.resourceroom.net/math/Timestables.asp [16 May 2013]

Poster 4 I want to find out what happens when I adopt a systematic approach to planning, teaching and assessing times tables?

Poster 4: I want to find out what happens when I adopt a systematic approach to planning, teaching and assessing times tables?

In Poster 4, the young teacher demonstrates the process and outcomes from her enquiry into the teaching of the times tables in maths. I particularly like how she illustrates the various methods she employed to gather information about her enquiry, including her learners, in a Primary 6 class. She is also able to show some 'hard' data about improvement in her learners knowledge of their tables, as a result of the new strategies she was trying out.

This particular teacher thinks carefully about her practice and impact on learning, this being reflected in her analysis and the identification of her next steps. She was someone who really grew her practice and her understandings as a result of her engagement with the enquiry process, but especially from her collaboration with her colleagues as they all supported each other.

"I want to find out what happens when I adopt a systematic approach to planning, teaching and assessing times tables?"

Research focus

Having worked with Primary and Secondary colleagues, I was aware that children were still finding the retention of their times tables a challenge. This made me consider aspects of my own teaching in the Upper Primary and what I might need to do to improve the pupils retention and understanding of their times tables. The focus of this research was therefore to explore:

'What happens when I adopt a systematic approach to planning, teaching and assessing times tables?'

In particular I am interested in ways I can promote children's instant recall and understanding of the times table facts.

Methods used

Pre-assessment:
I timed the pupils on their instant recall of facts for the 2, 5 & 10 times tables in a random order, plus any other tables they felt they were confident with. I recorded the times and noted down any significant strategies I could see they were using.

Thought shower:
This was done at the start of the research project. The pupils were asked to work individually to produce mind maps (text and/or pictures) to explore what they felt they already knew about multiplication and the times tables as well as what they did not know and/or needed to develop.

Audio-taped learning conversations:
I chose this method as it would enable me to focus on facilitating the discussion about pupils' engagement and learning in maths. I could then revisit the recording as often as required to establish children's perceptions of their engagement, enjoyment and confidence in Multiplication work.

Record of ongoing assessment & evaluation:

Continual use of formative assessment, evidence on whiteboards and in children's formal written work were monitored. The pupils also self-evaluated themselves by updating their 'Thought Showers' at regular intervals throughout the enquiry.

Learning journal/observations:
This journal was kept up-to-date throughout the Enquiry process. It enabled me to note down anything significant from everyday classroom observations and conversations.

I used the data to look at:

1   Strategies children currently have/use to multiply:
   • Conceptual understanding
   • What strategies have been taught/retained
   • Rapid mental recall of facts
   • Body language (engagement, motivation & thinking)
2   Pupils' perceptions of their learning
   • Explanations of how they learn
   • Their interaction with others
   • How they could apply what they learned to their life beyond the classroom
3   Pupils' engagement, enjoyment & confidence:
   • Responses
   • Tone of voice
   • Quality of their responses

Outline of project - approach/intervention

Children being literate and numerate when they leave school is what is expected by parents, teachers and the Education body of the Scottish Government. As an Upper Primary School teacher I found that some children still did not know/understand the times tables. My concern was my teaching of the times tables, as children were appearing to find it difficult to grasp them securely and had poor instant recall.

Mike Askew stated that he felt 'learning multiplication and division facts need not be a long and laborious task. Armed with a toolkit of mental strategies, children can figure out all manner of calculations'. It is also considered that it is easier to remember what we understand and can associate with things that we already know (Jones, 2003). Finding patterns is also an effective cognitive strategy (Stewart, 2010).

Based upon this theory and my personal experience, I decided to trial a more systematic approach to planning, teaching and assessing times tables to establish if this would improve their conceptual understanding and recall of facts.

Figure 1 Example of pupils' 'Thought Showers' showing initial thoughts and updated self-assessments throughout the enquiry.

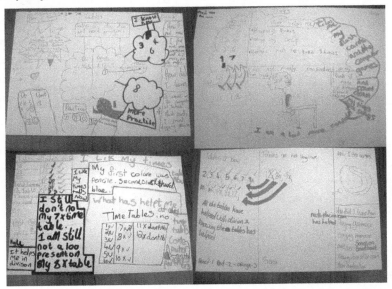

These examples show how learning progressed throughout the enquiry. Pupils became aware of strategies that helped them learn and recognised that regular revision is also good practice. This was a useful visual tracking tool for pupils to refer to throughout their learning.

Figure 2 Audio recorded learning conversations:

Below are examples of pupil comments made about their learning during the discussion.

'Daunting to begin with as I think there is a hundred facts to learn.'

'Once we've learned a few times tables then you know other sums in other tables.'

'Tricks and patterns help in the 9 times table.'

'Flashcards made it easier and making it competitive makes you try harder.'

'Using songs makes it more fun and exciting.'

'Also playing computer games make it fun.'

'Times tables is my favourite thing because it's fun and helps me with division.'

'Dad gives me random times table questions at home. It helps me keep it in my head.'

'At home I say the tables in my head. It's become a habit.'

Figure 3 Assessment table

Pupil	3x	**3x**	6x	**6x**	9x	**9x**
A	36 sec	**26 sec**	32 sec	**20 sec**	61 sec	**37 sec**
B	59 sec	**49 sec**	75 sec	**51 sec**	65 sec	**15 sec**
C	72 sec	**23 sec**	84 secs	**62 sec**	59 sec	**38 sec**
D	27 sec	**19 sec**	86 sec	**68 sec**	117 sec	**29 sec**
E	91 sec	**54 sec**	102 sec	**58 sec**	123 sec	**70 sec**

Pre-Assessment   **Final Assessment**

The results in the table show how learning had progressed throughout the enquiry by pupils' recalling their times tables quicker. Pupils also became more confident in applying strategies they had learned throughout the enquiry and less reliant on using their fingers to tag the facts.

Findings/presentation of data

Children's thought showers

I examined the children's 'Thought Showers' and from studying their initial thoughts it was apparent that they could self-assess what tables they knew and which ones needed to be developed. It was also evident however, that few children could identify or explain 'how' they actually learned the tables. At the mid-way point of my enquiry I asked the pupils to update their sheets in a second colour to illustrate where their thinking was and repeated this again at the end of my enquiry, using a third colour.

I listened in to a recorded discussion between a group of my pupils and a colleague about the pupils views on learning their multiplication tables. The responses made were of a very upbeat nature. The pupils were animated, confident and enthusiastic about their Maths, which was conveyed through their positive tone of voice and detailed comments about their learning.

Discussion of analysis and interpretation

A summary of points emerged from my data:

1   The pre-assessment highlighted the pupils' strengths but more significantly, where there were gaps in their learning.
2   The systematic approach to planning, teaching & assessing, in conjunction with a greater variety of activities, helped to develop the pupils' conceptual understanding of their times tables.
3   This approach has developed pupils' metacognitive awareness of how they learn their times tables, beyond simply learning the facts by rote.
4   Pupils now seem to be fully engaged in Maths lessons, conveying their enjoyment through animated discussions.

Having analysed the pre-assessment it showed that the pupils' strengths were in recalling the facts for the 2, 5 and 10 times tables. This led me to question how I could teach the other tables in a more systematic and meaningful way. I divided the class into 2 groups based upon the pre-assessment and 'thought shower'. Introducing more active learning activities for the group working independently enabled me to teach a specific concept more successfully to the other group, and vice versa. The activities included flashcards, pair work, ICT games and times tables songs. Whilst the focus group had the opportunity to develop their understanding of the tables through higher order discussions facilitated by myself. After implementing this approach over a term the pupils' ability to explain their thought processes on the whiteboards significantly improved. The number of positive comments pupils could relay about how they learned and retained their tables has given them strategies and confidence that they can apply in future learning.

Final thoughts/next steps

Having carried out this enquiry, the data gathered along with personal reflection, has convinced me to continue using a systematic approach to planning, teaching and assessing the times tables.

The strategies and practice I would continue to use and develop are:

- Use of pre-assessment to establish where individuals are
- The order in which I teach the tables – 10x, 5x, 2x, 4x, 8x, 3x, 6x, 9x and 7x – to support the children in making links and develop their conceptual understanding e.g. 4 x 3 is double 2 x3
- Teaching & Learning practice of: flashcards; timed challenges; pair/group work; ICT games and times tables songs
- Discussion with pupils before, during and after learning and encouraging them to explain their thought processes
- Begin to develop applying their knowledge and understanding of the times tables beyond the classroom setting

In addition, my school has been developing new Numeracy planning formats in line with implementing CfE. My research can enhance the content of these plans and subsequently be circulated across sectors within our learning community.

References

Askew, M. (2009) *On the Double*, BEAM Education, pp 4–5.

Francis, E. (2010) 'Tricks to the Multiplication Tables', [Online] Available at: http://www.teachildmath.com/wordpress/?category_name=tips-for-teaching-the-times-tables [23 Apr 2013]

Jones, S. (2003) 'Times Tables Practice', [Online] Available at: http://www.resourceroom.net/math/1timestables.asp [15 May 2013]

Poster 5: Leadership to learning: enquiry, involvement and impact

Poster 5: Leadership for learning: enquiry, involvement and impact

Poster 5 was produced by me and my DHT. Our aims were twofold. First, we wanted to demonstrate our own commitment to the enquiry process, showing staff that we were not expecting them to do anything we were not prepared to do ourselves. Second, we thought this was a great way to capture and demonstrate our own journey and thinking with practitioner enquiry.

A lot of what you will see in the poster is illustrated further in the text of the book, and I think reflects accurately where we were after those first three years. As I have said elsewhere, this whole book is actually a reflection of my enquiry into practitioner enquiry and its impacts. I am not sure if I could encapsulate my position, after eight years, into another poster, so this book will have to suffice.

Leadership for learning: enquiry, involvement and impact

Critical reflections on a 3 year journey focused firmly on capacity building through teacher learning

George Gilchrist, Headteacher and Alison Monteith, DHT Parkside and Ancrum Primary Schools, Jedburgh.

Context-setting

We are part of the senior management team for two partnership primary schools in the Scottish Borders. Parkside is a town school with a role of 260 pupils from nursery to P7. Ancrum is a village school with a role of 42 pupils.

> Leadership for learning means putting learners and learning at the centre of the agenda
> (Harris & Mujiis, 2004, HMIE, 2007)

We worked with all 15 teaching staff across both settings (including a mix of experience from NQTs to staff with 15 or more years experience) Promoting and supporting teachers' learning so that it might have identifiable impact on the pupils they teach was our key aim.

Our own self evaluation activities had told us that staff were lacking confidence in the teaching of aspects of Language. They said they would like to undertake professional learning that would help address this.

As senior managers, we had been dissatisfied with the impact for pupils of previous 'continuing professional development' (CPD) events staff had attended. Our quest became for CPD that would lead to changes in understanding, pedagogy and practice that could become deeply embedded as a way of being and doing for staff

> The biggest effects on student learning occur when teachers become learners of their own teaching
> (Hattie, 2012)

Adopting a critically informed approach to school improvement, we decided that taking a practitioner enquiry stance could help us develop the practice and understanding of individual teachers. We believed it would also promote whole-school development, which was focused on improving outcomes and impact for our pupils in a managed, connected and meaningful way.

Year one

- All staff agreed focus, use of collegiate time and CPD funds
- Focus: aspects of teaching of reading and writing in both schools
- Individuals/ pairs looked really closely at one aspect
- Professional reading around focus
- Discussion and sharing around reading and findings
- HMIe inspection positive impact for learners identified and reported

Year two

- More input around language and aspects of genre
- Input on data gathering and meaningful analysis
- Staff identified aspect of their language teaching to examine closely and carried out enquiry
- GTCS conducted evaluation of impact

Year three

- Decided to refocus on aspects of Maths
- Input from Primary Maths specialist, Susan McLarty, around teaching of maths and problem solving
- Teachers carried out enquiry into teaching of maths. Most chose problem solving
- Teachers produced posters to document their enquiries
- Posters and enquiry results shared with colleagues and whole staff discussion of learning and teaching

Practitioner Enquiry is an evidence rich approach to critically informed thinking and practice

(GTCS, 2012)

It is a lot of work but...it was great. I've kept my own learning journal since September. You know, this is like a kind of timeline of what we've been doing and how I have progressed from there as well. And it is a lot a' work but it's, for me this, the whole enquiry thing was getting inside their [the pupils'] brains. That was the biggest thing for me, that's what I'm really interested in: what and how they're thinking. Their behaviours; what they're thinking and how I can use that knowledge to better my teaching to help them. And I think that's, well I know that is what has definitely happened. And, and I am getting the results, you know. And I'm getting the results from it.

(Teacher speaking in focus group)

Last year [session 2012-13] made me really recognise the gaps in my understanding, and changes I could make to my practice, in the teaching of maths.

(Extract from very experienced teacher's conversation at PRD)

Change is best evaluated against impact and outcomes

(MacBeath, 2009)

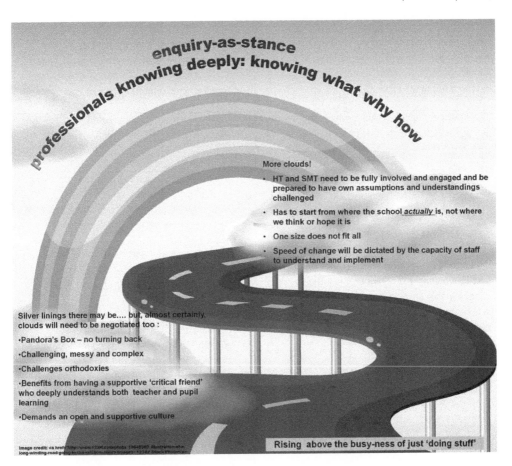

Impact	Evidence
Pupil attainment and achievement improved	• School tracking and monitoring records • Pupil sampling conducted by SMT • Pupils' assessment evidence: collected, collated and analysed by teachers throughout enquiry process • Teachers Learning discussions with pupils about their learning progress • Audio-recorded and written records
Teachers make explicit connections across practice, theory and research, drawing on a range of relevant literature	• Teachers' enquiry posters • Audio-recordings of professional dialogue within scheduled consultations between teachers, SMT and university staff
SMT and teachers, themselves, report they have markedly expanded and deepened, their understanding of: • learning (across curricular areas) • individual pupils and their learning needs • how to assess, design teaching and learning for progression (as opposed to activity-led planning, teaching and assessment) • how to gather and analyse data that they believe meaningfully informs their teaching	• Audio-recorded semi-structured interviews with individual staff • Audio-recorded focus group interviews • Teachers' learning journals
Evidence of critically informed teaching in most teachers' planning and professional dialogue, where connections across practice, theory and research are made explicit	• SMT reports of their formal planning for learning consultations with staff • School self-evaluation and quality assurance mechanisms related to School Improvement and Action Planning
Teachers' confidence in their own ability to meet the needs of the pupils they teach has increased as a direct result of engagement with enquiry and related CPD	• HMIe inspection feedback and report • Reports from PRD procedures
Teacher leadership has been promoted and adopted as regular practice	• Audio-recorded semi-structured interviews with individual teachers • Audio-recorded focus group interviews with groups of teachers • Audio-recorded semi-structured interviews with members of SMT • Teachers' enquiry posters
SMT and teachers perceive that significant change in the learning culture within both schools has improved for both teachers and pupils	• Audio-recorded focus group interviews with groups of teachers • Audio-recorded semi-structured interviews with members of SMT • Quality assurance mechanisms related to School Improvement and Action Planning
Teachers' professional identity has changed	• Audio-recorded focus group interviews with groups of teachers • Audio-recorded semi-structured interviews with members of SMT • Reports from PRD procedures

What is learned with great engagement becomes more nuanced and possesses better chance of being remembered and applied ... The concept of transformative learning comprises all learning that implies change in the identity of the learner.

(Illeris, 2013)

Both of these I would endorse as a result of the practitioner enquiry approach we have taken. The key is a level of engagement that requires the individual to adjust their concept of self-identity and their practice and actions as a result.

(George Gilchrist, Headteacher)

References

GTCS (2012) 'What is Practitioner Enquiry' www.gtcs.org.uk/professional-development/practitioner-enquiry/what-is-practitioner-enquiry.aspx

Harris, A. and Muijs, D. (2005) *Improving School Through Teacher Leadership* Maidenhead: Open University Press

Hattie, J. (2012) *Visible Learning*. Oxon: Routledge

Illeris, K. (2013) *Transformative Learning and Identity*. Oxon: Routledge.

MacBeath, J. (2009) *Connecting Leadership and Learning*. Oxon: Routledge

* * *

What I am sure of is that our engagement with practitioner enquiry has produced significant impacts for all the individuals involved, as well as the schools. Hopefully, these posters reflect a lot of the impacts of the early engagements we were involved in, and I leave them with you to consider and discuss in relation to your own journey.

My suggestion would be that you begin your journey before you share these with colleagues and staff. You are then in a better position to illustrate the 'health warnings' I have given through our own experiences.

Index

accountability 42, 47, 63

achievability 38, 72

action research 10, 13-14

active involvement 46

adaptive expertise 2-3, 7, 12, 17, 50, 58, 67, 121

adaptive practice 25-6, 93, 125, 134

agency 5, 7, 11, 25, 51, 58, 68, 72, 78-9, 131-4

appreciative enquiry 16-17

assessment 34-6, 49, 56, 70, 85, 90, 119; baseline 118; formative 56, 77, 93, 121, 123-4

Australia 1-2, 8, 29, 55, 60, 119, 131; Australian Institute for Teaching and School Leadership (AITSL) 1-2, 8, 37, 67

authenticity 59, 81, 130

autonomy 12

benchmarks 71

bias 34

Black, P. 56, 77, 123-4

Black-Hawkins, K. 19

Blanchard, K. 75

Blansford, J. 12

Boyd, B. 56

Boyle, A. 42, 53

busyness 46-7, 132

Canada 9, 134

carousel approach 117

case studies 12; primary schools 101-5, 110-15; rural schools 97-101; secondary school 105-9; whole school approach 83-95

challenge agendas 48

China 95

Cochran-Smith, M. 11-12, 17, 30, 66, 71, 80, 94, 103

collaboration 3, 20, 22-3, 39, 50-1, 53, 74-6, 130-2, 134; collaborative professional enquiry 15-16, 106, 131; enquiry across contexts 98-9, 105; focused 74; pedagogical changes 119, 128; role of the teacher 58-60; school leaders 50-1, 53; whole-school approach 84, 89; why practitioner enquiry? 10-11, 14-15

collective vision 21

collegiate activity time (CAT) 87-9, 92, 94, 99-100, 102-3, 107, 111-12

communities of practice 9

compliance 45

conditions for success 19-26

confidence 33, 78-9, 93, 113-14

conservatism 10

continual improvement 53, 65

core business 46

counter-flow 53

creativity 53

credibility 38, 111

critical friends 25

cultures 19, 23, 48, 75, 97, 101, 131; learning culture 5, 22, 58-9, 74, 76, 98, 107, 131; school culture 78, 85, 96, 104

curricula 10, 50, 56, 70, 73, 87, 90, 93, 118-19, 123; Curriculum for Excellence 69-70, 85-6, 89; curriculum support teachers (CSTs) 111; development 10, 16, 85; frameworks 122

Darling-Hammond, L. 12

data 11, 48-9, 62, 68, 70, 81, 90, 122, 132, 135;
analysis 39; collection 32-6, 38, 72, 87, 113;
driven 49
de-privatisation 53
de-professionalisation 56, 66, 78
deconstruction 31
deficit models 16, 29, 78
demographics 84
depth 70-2, 81, 91, 107, 120, 125, 132
deputy headteacher (DHT) *see* school leaders
development 16-17, 44, 69, 79, 84, 86, 121, 130;
capacity 53, 98; cognitive 51; frameworks
67; leadership 11; pedagogical 124; personal
17; professional 17; self-development 12-13;
teacher 12, 19, 55, 71, 133 *see also* professional
development (PD); school development
developmental psychology 103
Dewey, J. 74
dialogue 14-15, 21-3, 39-40, 71, 96, 119; critical
debate 22; dialogical approaches 102, 121;
professional 44, 58, 71, 77, 99
Dimmock, C. 42, 53, 75
discourse 75; professional 22
dispositions 12, 19, 25, 56-8, 109, 115-16, 132-3;
benefits of enquiry 68, 79-81; school leaders
42-3, 48, 51, 53
Donaldson, G. 67
Drew, V. 106
Dudley, P. 14
Dweck, C. 4, 57, 77

echo chambers 50
economic factors 67
Edison, T. 106
efficacy 10, 74
embeddedness 21, 24, 31, 60, 66-7, 131, 136; enquiry across contexts 99-101, 105, 108; pedagogical changes 119-20, 128; school leaders
45, 47, 51, 53; whole-school approach 86, 91,
93-4; why practitioner enquiry? 7, 9, 15
emotional awareness 58
empiricism 42
enabling 55
engagement 58, 72, 77-8, 83, 93, 121, 125, 131, 134;
critical 36-7, 131; disengagement 10; enquiry
across contexts 101-3, 111-12, 114
England 8-9, 60, 95; Department for Education

8; General Teaching Council for England 56
enquiring professionals 8, 67
ethics 33, 131
evidence 3, 51, 62, 70, 73-4, 81, 90, 113, 134-5
Ezard, T. 56, 131

facilitation 55
fads 3, 7, 36, 46, 67, 77-8, 80, 116, 132
feedback 8, 21, 39, 107-8, 111, 123-4; peer 21
Feuerstein, R. 52
Finland 60, 134
flexibility 59
Flexible Route to Headship (FRH) 106
focus groups 34, 118
Fullan, M. 3, 9, 11, 15, 23, 42-3, 46, 50, 53, 74, 130-1,
133
funding 45, 88

gamification 49
gate-keeping 46-7
General Education Reform Movement (GERM) 47
General Teaching Council Scotland (GTCS) 1, 8-9,
30, 47, 60, 67, 76; enquiry across contexts 98,
106, 112; whole-school approach 92-3, 95
Germany 95
Goleman, D. 58
Google Scholar 39
governments 8, 47

Hargreaves, A. 3, 9, 11, 23, 36, 42, 49-50, 53, 74
Harris, A. 3, 11, 15, 23, 42, 49-51, 53, 59, 75, 130-1
Hattie, J. 11, 28, 42, 46, 55, 77, 81, 123-4
head teachers *see* school leaders
Her Majesty's Inspectorate of Education (HMIE)
47, 76, 90
hierarchies 10, 23, 50, 52, 66, 74, 85, 132-3
Hill, R. 76

ideology 51
Illeris, K. 40, 62
impact 33, 42, 72, 80, 99, 106, 108, 111, 113-14, 126,
135
India 95
individualism 11, 16, 30, 71
initial teacher education (ITE) 78
initiativitis 46
inquiry as a stance 12, 17, 80, 94, 103, 134

inquisitiveness 60
International Congress for School Effectiveness
    and Improvement (ICSEI) 73
interventions 38-9, 58, 119, 127, 133

Japan 14

knowledge base 14, 40
Koshy, V. 13

leadership 5, 23, 25, 44, 56, 62, 64; development
    11; dispersed 74-6; distributed 11, 75; instruc-
    tional 53; situational 75; system 5, 7, 12, 40,
    51, 53, 61, 63, 75-7; teacher 25, 74-6 *see also*
    school leaders
learning capacities 68
learning culture 5, 22, 58-9, 74, 76, 98, 107, 131
learning experiences 28, 70
learning journeys 76
learning needs 4, 8, 41, 68, 78, 80, 114, 122
learning stations 117-18
lesson study 14
Lieberman, A. 130
lifelong learning 40, 52, 57, 62, 131
linearity 29-30
literature review 19
local authorities 23, 26, 40-1, 47, 99-100, 103;
    benefits of enquiry 69-70, 75-6; whole-school
    approach 84-6, 89-90, 92, 94
Lytle, S. 11-12, 71, 80, 94, 103

McClarty, S. 92
McIntyre, D. 19
McLaughlin, C. 19
manageability 44, 72-3, 77, 80, 91, 98
meta-analysis 42
meta-enquiry 4
metacognition 123
micro-management 23, 48, 79
mindset 19, 22, 57-8, 103, 105; growth-mindset 4,
    130
monitoring 49, 63

National College for School Leadership 76
National Council of Teachers of English (NCTE) 15
New Zealand 68, 119
newly qualified teachers (NQTs) 75, 78, 94, 102-3,
111-12

observation 50, 124, 126; peer 128
OECD 49, 55
organisational behaviour 16
ownership 23, 102

parents/guardians 20-1, 32, 76, 78, 133
Parrish, S. 123
partnership working 84-5
pedagogical changes 116, 119, 122, 134
pedagogy 7, 12, 33, 68, 70, 78, 85, 90, 99, 107;
    change 56, 116-28
performativity 42
personal growth 61
policy 25-6, 56, 62, 98; exploiting 43, 133
positive models 29
pressures 24, 87
Priestley, M. 16, 106
principals *see* school leaders
process of enquiry 31-3, 35, 37-8
Process Model 10
professional courage 47
professional development (PD) 1-4, 52, 95, 116, 130,
    132, 134; benefits of enquiry 66, 69; continu-
    ous professional development (CPD) 1, 45, 50,
    88, 93; creating conditions for enquiry 21, 23,
    26; dissatisfaction 21; enquiry across contexts
    97, 107, 109, 111, 115; practices/dispositions
    79-80; process of enquiry 29, 37, 40; re-profes-
    sionalisation 17; role of the teacher 55, 61, 63,
    65; why practitioner enquiry? 9, 11
professional identity 61-2, 71, 80-1
professional judgement 34
professional learning communities (PLCs) 9, 14-15,
    59, 106-8, 131
professional learning networks (PLNs) 38
professional practice 2, 11, 37
professional reading 32, 34, 36-8, 62, 71, 88, 102,
    117, 119
professional responsibility 73
professional review and development (PRD) 81,
    88, 100
professional standards 1-2, 8
professionalism 11, 55, 63-4, 68, 108
Programme for International Student Assessment
    (PISA) 55

proportionality 31-2, 37-8, 73, 80, 116
pupil learning 28

re-professionalisation 5, 17
reflective practice 11-12, 25, 60-1
research 51, 62-3, 73-4, 81, 101, 130-1, 133-5; class-room 10, 33
research base 10-13, 17
research posters 92, 94, 102; leadership for learn-ing 163-7; positive problem solving 144-9; preschoolers' number skills 138-43; systematic approach to planning/teaching/assessment 156-61; teaching/problem solving through play 150-5
Robinson, G. 25, 34, 43-5, 50, 52, 69-70, 86-9, 91-5, 101, 117-19
role of the teacher 57, 59, 62
rural settings 97-101

Sagor, R. 13
Sahlberg, P. 47
sampling 32-3
Schleicher, A. 49, 55
school culture 78, 85, 96, 104
school development 11, 13, 19, 95, 111-12, 116, 130, 134; benefits of enquiry 70, 78; school leaders 42, 44-5, 47, 51
School Improvement Plan (SIP) 26, 44, 50, 87-90, 102, 112-13
school leaders 3, 5, 42-53, 78, 81, 130, 132-4; creat-ing conditions for enquiry 19, 21-4, 26; enquiry across contexts 97-101, 104-12; pedagogical changes 120, 124, 128; process of enquiry 28-9, 41; role of the teacher 58, 61; senior manage-ment team (SMT) 44; whole-school approach 83-6, 94; why practitioner enquiry? 7, 11-12, 17
Scotland 1-2, 7-9, 25, 47, 56, 60, 66, 83-97, 105, 110, 117, 128, 133; Education Scotland 41, 47, 111; Scottish College for Educational Leadership (SCEL) 26, 30, 75, 98 *see also* General Teaching Council Scotland (GTCS)
self-awareness 20-1
self-discovery 40
self-evaluation 20-2, 28, 47, 60, 70

self-improvement 12-13, 17, 46, 70, 75, 79, 133-4; self-improving schools 9, 46, 51, 91, 101; system 51
self-regulation 68
silos 11, 15; of practice 74
Smith, A. 106
social media 57
speed of change 134-6
stances 12, 116
standardisation 52
standardised testing 34, 49, 68
Stenhouse, L. 10-11, 13, 74
strategic planning 70
stress 24, 31
structures 19, 25, 51, 56
support 24, 28, 48, 59, 70, 99, 112, 128; mutual 25, 97-101; structures 48, 58, 98, 135; support staff 29; supportive culture 15-16
sustainability 5, 7, 15, 24, 69, 96, 101, 115, 134; ben-efits of enquiry 79-81; school leaders 43, 45-7; self-sustainability 93
system performance 63
systematic approach 40, 59, 126, 134

teacher learning communities (TLCs) 14-15, 23, 131
Teacher as Researcher 10
teacher training 51-2
Teachers College Press 12
Timperley, H. 2-3, 11, 23, 29, 37, 46, 67-8, 72-4
tracking 49
transformative learning 40, 62
trust 22, 47, 59, 75, 131-2, 134

United Kingdom 8
USA 11, 95, 123

validity 9, 33
values 22, 47, 59-60, 132
vision statements 21-2

Wales 95
ways of being 37
whole-school approach 44, 68; case study 83-95
Wiliam, D. 11, 56, 73, 77, 123-4, 135